LOST AND FOUND

CHRISTIAN VOCATION IN CONTEXT

A Series from the D. James Kennedy Institute of Reformed Leadership

"Christian Vocation in Context," a *D. James Kennedy Institute of Reformed Leadership Series* with Wipf and Stock Publishers, is edited by Michael A. Milton, Ph.D., and offers comprehensive guidance for Christian evangelists, teachers, and shepherds in the Secular Age. This series includes major releases that are designed to support the Christian shepherd in navigating the treacherous narrows of a post-Christian West. Each book offers biblical and scholarly insights for personal study, small groups, college and seminary courses, as well as for teachers, counselors, and thoughtful Christians in various vocations.

LOST AND FOUND

PUBLIC THEOLOGY IN THE SECULAR AGE

CHRISTIAN VOCATION IN CONTEXT: THE D. JAMES KENNEDY INSTITUTE OF REFORMED LEADERSHIP SERIES

BOOK ONE

SENIOR EDITOR
MICHAEL A MILTON

WIPF & STOCK · Eugene, Oregon

LOST AND FOUND
Public Theology in the Secular Age

Christian Vocation in Context: The D. James Kennedy Institute of Reformed Leadership Series

Copyright © 2024 Michael A. Milton. All rights reserved. Except for brief quotations in critical publications or reviews, no part of this book may be reproduced in any manner without prior written permission from the publisher. Write: Permissions, Wipf and Stock Publishers, 199 W. 8th Ave., Suite 3, Eugene, OR 97401.

Wipf & Stock
An Imprint of Wipf and Stock Publishers
199 W. 8th Ave., Suite 3
Eugene, OR 97401

www.wipfandstock.com

PAPERBACK ISBN: 979-8-3852-1136-4
HARDCOVER ISBN: 979-8-3852-1137-1
EBOOK ISBN: 979-8-3852-1138-8

In Memory of the Reverend Dr. Harry Reeder, a true Shepherd in Israel, who was taken to be with the Lord before he could finish his contribution to this volume.

———

His lord said unto him, Well done, thou good and faithful servant: thou hast been faithful over a few things, I will make thee ruler over many things: enter thou into the joy of thy lord.— Matthew 25:21

———

The present age is demented. It is possessed by a sense of dislocation, a loss of personal identity, an alternating sentimentality, and rage which, in an individual patient, could be characterized as dementia.

Walker Percy (*1916-1990*)
Signposts in a Strange Land 1991

All occasions invite his mercies, and all times are his seasons.

John Donne (1572–1631)
A Sermon at St. Paul's London Christmas Day 1624

Cry aloud, spare not, lift up thy voice like a trumpet.
These things I have spoken unto you, that in me ye might have peace.

In the world ye shall have tribulation: but be of good cheer; I have overcome the world.

Isaiah 58:1a; John 16:33 KJV

Contents

Contributors	xi
Introduction Michael A. Milton	xv
Preface Michael A. Milton	xix
Part I	xxvii
1. CRY ALOUD AND SPARE NOT *The Meaning of Public Theology and the Secular Age* Michael A. Milton	1
2. FOR THE LOVE OF GOD *Nurturing a Christian Intellectual Life* Michael A. Milton	17
3. FRAGMENTS OF NATURE'S LORE *On the Rejection of First Principles* Michael A. Milton	21
Part II	27
4. THE FAMILY IN THE SECULAR AGE *A Christian Response to Marxism* John M. Frame	28
5. WHAT THE BIBLE SAYS ABOUT TRANSGENDERISM *And How to Avoid Personal and Societal Destruction* Michael A. Milton	38
6. TRUE OIKONOMIA *A Christian Mind for Economics* John Panagiotou	49
Part III	61
7. OPEN BORDERS OR OPEN HEARTS? *Are Boundaries Morally Good?* Peter A. Lillback	62

8. THE THANATOS SYNDROME · · · · · · · · · · · · · · · · · 83
   What the Bible Says about Euthanasia
   Michael A. Milton

9. THE COURSE OF NATIONS · · · · · · · · · · · · · · · · · · 98
   Is the Decline and Fall of Nations Inevitable?
   Michael A. Milton

   Part IV · 107

10. REPAVING THE PATHWAY TO POVERTY · · · · · · · 108
    An Urgent Warning Against The New Socialism
    Michael A. Milton

11. LOVING GOD, LOVING OTHERS · · · · · · · · · · · · · 125
    The Evil of Hatred by Accidental Differences in Humankind
    Michael A. Milton

12. THE FINAL HOPE · 139
    On Spiritual Awakening
    Michael A. Milton

    Part V · 153

13. BETWEEN BETHEL AND AI · · · · · · · · · · · · · · · · · 154
    Isaac Watts and Oswald Chambers and a Christian Worldview
    George Grant

14. ENSLAVEMENT BY CATEGORY · · · · · · · · · · · · · · 162
    The Wisdom of Dorothy Sayers
    Michael A. Milton

15. FIELD NOTES FROM BABYLON · · · · · · · · · · · · · · 169
    Faithful Gospel Witness in the Secular Age
    Michael A. Milton

    Notes · 181
    Bibliography · 197
    Acknowledgments · 207
    About the D. James Kennedy Institute · · · · · · · · · 209
    Vision and Mission · 211

Contributors

George Grant

The Reverend Dr. George Grant is one of the nation's most prolific pastor-scholars. He holds multiple degrees, including a PhD, DLitt, MA from Whitefield Theological Seminary, a D.Hum. from Belhaven College, and a BA from the University of Houston. He currently serves as the Pastor Emeritus of Parish Presbyterian Church, Director of the King's Meadow Study Center, Founder of Franklin Classical School and Bannockburn College, and Coordinator of the Chalmers Fund. Dr. Grant is an accomplished author of numerous books covering a wide range of subjects such as history, biography, politics, literature, and social criticism. He has also written hundreds of essays, articles, and columns, and is a regular contributor to World Radio. Dr. Grant's work on Christian justice and mercy, *The Micah Mandate: "What Does the Lord Require of You? to Act Justly and to Love Mercy and to Walk Humbly With Your God,"* remains the standard on the subject.

John Frame

The Reverend Dr. John M. Frame has been called one of the great living Christian philosophers. Dr. Frame holds a Doctor of Divinity degree from Belhaven College, a Bachelor of Divinity from Westminster Theological Seminary, and a Master of Arts and Master of Philosophy from Yale University. He previously served as a professor of theology and apologetics at Westminster Theological Seminary in Philadelphia and Westminster Seminary in California. Currently, he is the J. D. Trimble Professor of Systematic Theology and Philosophy Emeritus at Reformed Theological Seminary in Orlando. Dr. Frame is the author of numerous books, including the four-volume series, *Theology of Lordship*.

Peter A. Lillback

The Reverend Dr. Peter Lillback is one of the leading theologians in the world today. Dr. Lillback holds a PhD from Westminster Theological Seminary, a ThM from Dallas Theological Seminary, and a BA from Cedarville College. He is currently the President and Professor of Historical Theology at Westminster Theological Seminary in Philadelphia. Dr. Lillback has over thirty years of experience in pastoral ministry and has authored several books and numerous articles on the Reformation and post-Reformation era. His most notable work is the best-selling biography *George Washington's Sacred Fire*, which is based on primary-source research and scholarship about the life of George Washington.

Michael A. Milton

The Reverend Dr. Michael A. Milton is a Presbyterian (PCA) minister, educator, and author with over four decades of service. He holds a PhD from the University of Wales, a DMin from Erskine Theological Seminary, an MPA from UNC Chapel Hill, an MDiv from Knox Theological Seminary, and a BA from MidAmerican Nazarene University. Dr. Milton served as the fourth President-Chancellor/CEO of Reformed

Theological Seminary, retiring due to a disease contracted in ministry in South Africa. He is a retired US Army Chaplain (Colonel) and currently serves as the Distinguished Professor of Missions and Evangelism at Erskine Seminary. Dr. Milton has authored over thirty-five books and numerous articles and is a board-certified pastoral counselor.

John G. Panagiotou

Dr. Panagiotou is an experienced theologian and scholar with a long career that has included pastoral ministry as an Orthodox Christian presbyter, denominational administration, teaching at the university and seminary levels, preaching, and business. He has spent nearly three decades researching and teaching early Christianity and Christian stewardship. Currently, he is a professor of New Testament, Biblical Greek, and Patristics at Cummins Memorial Theological Seminary, where he also serves as Liason Officer to the Seminary President.

Introduction
Michael A. Milton

Well, so that is that. — W. H. Auden[1]

———

Some argue *the case* from anecdotal evidence and others from social research. Some point to the ebbs and tides of history. Others to the predictable forces observed in anthropology. All, however, come to the same conclusion: *Western Civilization, as we know it, has reached a tipping point.* And then some.

From a loss of meaning after two world wars, the advent of the atomic and nuclear age with its apocalyptic storm clouds permanently hovering over the ancient, verdant fields of Scandinavia and the war-ravaged urban cities of East Africa alike, casting shadows that many of us prefer to ignore; the Balkanization of peoples within heretofore stable and unified Western nation-states; and a denial of perspicuity in favor of "the theater of the absurd;" the West was becoming a tinderbox for conflagration.[2] It may be that the global pandemic (2020-21) became the accidental spark to ignite the brush pile of the Great Books of Western Civilization. The populist movements within Britain (*viz.*, Brexit) and the United States (American First), with growing dissatisfaction among remaining member nations over the failed dream of the EU, may have been unmistakable signs of coming change, a change for the worse. Reacting to a sense of government overreach, corruption, and a dramatic break between an elite in the centers of influence (Hunter, 2010), and those on the outer rings, nationalism and populism are predictable outcomes of a failure to steward democracy and representative government.

Deconstructionism's pestilence essentially felled a sufficient number of tall oaks of Western ideals to create a dried-debris forest floor of yesterday's ideas—ideas planted in the nutrient-rich soil of Greco-Roman democratic ideals, Pauline teaching of Jesus Christ, Reformation, John Locke (1632-1973), Samuel Rutherford (1600-1661), Jonathan Edwards (1703-1758), Jefferson (1743-1826), Madison (1751-1836), Adams (1735-1826), and Edmund Burke (1729-1797)—ideas that were quietly deconstructed as we slept, worked, and played (Hollis, 1990). Rather than a dramatic new and lasting social experiment, many perceived postmodernism as a dangerous prelude to a more complex multi-layered cake, a cake laced with arsenic, a confection created out of the old yeast of atheism.

There was much work done in defense of the ancient walls. Christian voices from T.S. Eliot (1888-1965) and Karl Barth (1886-1968) sought to strengthen the foundations. Later twentieth-century voices such as Walker Percy (1916-1990) and Thomas Sowell (1930) labored with *ethos, pathos,* and *logos* to identify the enemy breaching the walls (Sowell, 2002). Prodigious voices from literature and academia, the plumbing trades for societal influence, assessed, diagnosed, and treated the signs of pathology with the lights of the Reformation and the American founding—religious liberty and the divine rights of the governed —. However, in hindsight, one could justifiably argue that the more dystopian ideals of the French Revolution and Enlightenment, in the end, proved more appealing than the Magna Carta, more enchanting than the Reformation, and less intellectually demanding than the American founding. Post-structuralists like the Irish playwright Samuel Beckett (1906-1989) and French social philosopher Michael Foucault (1926-1984) continue to influence disciples in the arts and letters, higher education, government and administration, and even religion

(Poster, 1984). The Nietzsche-Derrida-Foucault devotees see the ancient walls of decency and social order as mere bricks to be dismantled. Like an efficient but malevolent wrecking crew, the deconstructionists did their dismantling work in the relatively unseen shadows of the darkness, unnoticed by those entering the freeway in the morning. Yet, day by day, year by year, the project began showing evidence of completion. Their values are despised, though their efficiency is admired, but this is as one admires the unifying efficiency of Stalin by mass murder. Western narratives written in history, taught in nursery rhymes, law schools, and seminaries were re-written with nonsensical assertions, Orwellian word scramble, and revisionist histories. Post-American heroes and heroines were needed to depict the secular age envisioned. Thus, American schoolchildren were introduced to the invention icons of revolution. These tribal figures of history were born of Socialist commitments and usually worked for a veritable Balkanization of America based on group and sub-group identities rather than unity around the Constitution.

It would have been 24 August 410 A.D. Had you been hunting or fishing that day, perhaps, at the very northern edges of the Empire, you would have been distracted by an ominous vibration beneath your feet. An earthquake? You put your ear to the ground. No. it is not an earthquake. This is herd movement, a massive stampede across the northern hinterlands like you have never sensed before or after. How did W.H. Auden (1907-1973) conclude his brilliant poem (1951), *The Fall of Rome*?

> Altogether elsewhere, vast Herds of reindeer move across Miles and miles of golden moss Silently and very fast. (Nicolet, 1972).

Suppose we put our ears to the ground. Would we, too, sense a vast movement of reindeer across the primordial plateaus of Europe, buffalo across the plains of North America, and deer moving across the midlands of England? Australia and New Zealand would surely not be exempt from the startled herds, for they are the West in law, language, customs, and media connectedness. Why do they move so "silently and fast?" In 410 A.D., the massive movement of the reindeer preceded the allied armies of Alaric: the unified Goths and Vandals. The mighty

Roman Empire had passed the tipping point. King Alaric's powerful armies, more brutal than Rome, more determined, and more unified, defeated the Eternal City and rendered it finite.

The example of Alaric and the Gothic-Vandal sack of Rome is, perhaps, an overused historical illustration of decline and fall. However, some things that seem trite are told and re-told because they carry ageless wisdom and warning.

If we in the West have reached the tipping point, the point of no return on the downward slide of the bald rock, how will we live, move, and pursue happiness in a new age now arrived? To put it another way, how shall disciples of Jesus Christ live out their faith with Biblical and doctrinal integrity in an unknown Babylon? The Secular Age (Taylor, 2009)and the possibility of a post-secularism (Habermas, 2010)—the character of both representing likely obstacles to the faithful expression of the Christian faith, if not outright oppression, isolation, and exclusion —represents the intellectual classifications of the times in which we live in the early years of the twenty-first century. Voices such as Miroslav Volf (1956) of Yale (Volf, 2011) and James Davison Hunter (1955) of the University of Virginia have wrestled with this question and provided well-considered responses (Hunter, 2010).

This book aims to assess, diagnose, and respond to the challenges of Christian living in *A Secular Age* (Taylor, 2009), an all-encompassing phrase borrowed from Charles Taylor (1931) by discipline or, if you prefer, by areas of common life. How does the Secular Age affect healthcare? What does that mean for believers? What might we anticipate? How do we respond? What are the salient features of healthcare in the new Babylon should concern us? How shall we respond?

Reputed Christian scholars and practitioners from various disciplines and backgrounds come together to conduct theology in the service of the Church—to support Christians in our rapidly changing milieu in the West, to pose questions, consider the issues, and provide responses. This book is an anthology of essays that seeks to be a "signpost in a strange land" (Percy, 2000) a torch, a guide, and a trusted shepherd for a flock embarking on, likely, a most treacherous journey.

Preface
Michael A. Milton

> The Faithful, to whom [God] has given eyes, see sparks of His glory, as it were, glittering in every created thing. The world was no doubt made that it might be the theatre of divine glory.—John Calvin[1]

The content of *Lost and Found: Public Theology in the Secular Age* is presented with a primary concern for the glory of God and the good of His creation. Specifically, we have sought to shine the light of God's Word on the ideas and activities that bring hurt to human beings. "Human flourishing," a phrase at times employed for humanistic views of Man, is nevertheless an aptly stated goal for the book you are reading. We hold that true human flourishing is realized when people embrace their divinely planted purpose for life: "To glorify God and to enjoy Him forever."[2] In this sense, we present the work as a pastoral counselor might conduct ministry: assessing, diagnosing, and guiding.

Assessing

Public theology exists at the nexus of faith and life. At that luminal point in time, the Christian shepherd, viz., a pastor, speaks for the sake of the Gospel and the benefit of God's creation. Public theology is not political but instead an expression of the cure of souls. The vicar is not at the council meeting to oppose or propose a new highway. He is present because a highway can affect people. Like John Donne, he is involved with mankind. A highway can become a pavement for evangelism or can disrupt the peacefulness of life and affect the spiritual lives of the community (Thus, "I exhort therefore, that, first of all, supplications, prayers, intercessions, and giving of thanks, be made for all men; For kings, and for all that are in authority; that we may lead a quiet and peaceable life in all godliness and honesty" 1 Timothy 2:1-2). *Public theology is the pastoral work of engaging the presenting issues of life for the glory of God and the good of God's creation.*

In this book, we seek to evaluate significant presenting issues in this new secular era. The list of cases to assess is admittedly selective and limited. Other issues deserve careful, pastoral-scholarly attention. Other Christian shepherds (pastor-scholars) should join us in this work. We welcome the wise and thoughtful voices of Christian shepherds on additional matters facing the Church. If you, the reader would like the Institute to address specific matters from a Biblical and Reformed commitment, you may write us at info@djkinstitute.org. When you, as a pastor or teacher, address these in books, articles, blogs, or other media, do let us know. We will direct others to your work. For all: we welcome your thoughts and suggestions.

Diagnosing

Assessing means locating, isolating, examining, and naming. We render a spiritual diagnosis by gathering the variables and applying critical thinking and theological reflection. To do so allows us to recognize the origins of the bad ideas or actions as being from the devil, the flesh, or the world. We can pose questions about the sinful condition. Then, we desire to apply critical thinking and theological reflection to evaluate the presenting issues from a Christian worldview (Creation, Fall, Covenantal Promises, Redemption, and Consummation).

Guiding

Out of our diagnoses, we offer a biblical response. One does not need to be a "subject matter expert" in a respective field to be a pastor to those in that field. Our attention is on human beings. The powers, systems, and organizations engaged with the human spirit vary. Human beings, in the image of God, are consistent in many complex variables that are part of one's person. Christian shepherds do not have to be experts in political theory to say that someone is mistreated or someone else is profiting off of another's misery. I am not a medical doctor. Yet, I know from God's Word that abortion is wrong, deadly wrong. And that the victims of abortion include the mother whose baby was killed, the abortioner who performed the procedure, and quite possibly a father, the mother's other children, or future children. I speak about that issue because God has called me to announce His Word. His Word can save, redeem, forgive, restore, and, in short, transform the brokenness of humanity. It is in this authority, the authority of God's Word, that we speak—no other.

The Book

The presenting issues are in five parts:

- Ideas: Philosophical and Theological forces.
- Daily Life: Matters that are closer to home.
- National Life: Issues of broader impact.
- Triggers: Sometimes called "hot topics," these are issues that are combustible and which are so because of their importance to human life.
- Faith: Living the Christian life in the secular age.

Our "faculty" of pastor-scholars for this mission includes some of the most outstanding voices in contemporary evangelical and Reformed

Christian service. I am honored to have them join me in this undertaking. We pray that these responses will support God's people (and anyone reading this volume). We always recall that any believer at any age has access to God and His wisdom in Christ as the Holy Spirit prompts us to pray and study the inherent and infallible Word of the Lord (James 1:5). Thus, we make this verse our prayer:

> "O our God, wilt thou not judge them? for we have no might against this great company that cometh against us; neither know we what to do: but our eyes are upon thee" (2 Chronicles 20:12 KJV).

On behalf of the D. James Kennedy Institute of Reformed Leadership, I pray that the Lord of Life blesses this book to His glory and your good.

M. A. Milton
The Twenty-fourth Sunday after Pentecost, 2023

Part I
IDEAS

Cry Aloud and Spare Not
The Meaning of Public Theology and the Secular Age

Michael A. Milton

> The earth stands still: and earthly Men may be content to do so: but he whose conversation is in heaven is as the heavens are in continual progress . . . A Christian is always in a proficiency, or deficiency: If he goes not forward, he goes backward.
>
> —John Donne, Sermon at Lincoln Inn[1]

The Lord instructed Isaiah to cry aloud and spare not: the truth of God applied to the presenting issues in the most public form possible. But to whom? To warn an oppressor of coming judgment? There are places in scripture where such urgent warnings are given. But not here. To alert a regent and his government to sins that are hurting humanity? John the Baptist did so. Even Jesus said of Herod, "Go tell that fox . . ."[2] But not this time. The divine demand in this instance is this: Isaiah is to cry aloud and spare not to a People going through an oppression of their own making. There is a grace, a most severe grace, in announcing, "You are killing yourselves." Thus, we begin this book by hearing God speak to His own.³ And we go from there.

Isaiah 58

Cry aloud; do not hold back;
    lift up your voice like a trumpet;
    declare to my people their transgression,
    to the house of Jacob their sins.
² Yet they seek me daily
and delight to know my ways,
    as if they were a nation that did righteousness
    and did not forsake the judgment of their God;
they ask of me righteous judgments;
they delight to draw near to God.
³ 'Why have we fasted, and you see it not?
Why have we humbled ourselves, and you take no knowledge of it?'
Behold, in the day of your fast you seek your own pleasure,
and oppress all your workers.
⁴ Behold, you fast only to quarrel and to fight
and to hit with a wicked fist.
Fasting like yours this day
will not make your voice to be heard on high.
⁵ Is such the fast that I choose,
a day for a person to humble himself?
Is it to bow down his head like a reed,
    and to spread sackcloth and ashes under him?
Will you call this a fast,
    and a day acceptable to the Lord?
⁶ "Is not this the fast that I choose:
to loose the bonds of wickedness,
to undo the straps of the yoke,
to let the oppressed go free,
and to break every yoke?
⁷ Is it not to share your bread with the hungry
and bring the homeless poor into your house;

when you see the naked, to cover him,
and not to hide yourself from your own flesh?
[8] Then shall your light break forth like the dawn,
and your healing shall spring up speedily;
your righteousness shall go before you;
the glory of the Lord shall be your rear guard.
[9] Then you shall call, and the Lord will answer;
you shall cry, and he will say, 'Here I am.'
If you take away the yoke from your midst,
the pointing of the finger, and speaking wickedness,
[10] if you pour yourself out for the hungry
and satisfy the desire of the afflicted,
then shall your light rise in the darkness
and your gloom be as the noonday.
[11] And the Lord will guide you continually
and satisfy your desire in scorched places
and make your bones strong;
and you shall be like a watered garden,
like a spring of water,
whose waters do not fail.
[12] And your ancient ruins shall be rebuilt;
you shall raise up the foundations of many generations;
you shall be called the repairer of the breach,
the restorer of streets to dwell in.
[13] "If you turn back your foot from the Sabbath,
from doing your pleasure on my holy day,
and call the Sabbath a delight
and the holy day of the Lord honorable;
if you honor it, not going your own ways,
or seeking your own pleasure, or talking idly;
[14] then you shall take delight in the Lord,
and I will make you ride on the heights of the earth;
I will feed you with the heritage of Jacob your father,
for the mouth of the Lord has spoken."[4]

This book is about theology according to the Old and New Testament scriptures applied to the lives of believers living in a strange land, viz., *in a state of captivity*. Thus, Jeremiah speaks theological truth applied to people living in Babylon, that peculiar habitat for God's people:

> And seek the peace of the city where I have caused you to be carried away captive, and pray to the LORD for it; for in its peace you will have peace (Jeremiah 29:7 NKJV).

In a sense, all of life is a strange land. However, strange lands are, for wandering exiles, always strangely familiar. We have lived in such a state since the Fall in the Garden of Eden. Yet, there are particularly harsh times that distinguish their epoch by an accentuated evil, a more noticeable wrong, and a more intensely felt suffering. There is a spring when the times are recalled for the warm rays of favor. This is the season of anointing leaders, expanding the kingdom, and building temples. There are also long summer seasons when we forget the dedications made in the previous season. Playfulness with the cute baby adders is a dangerous excitement. Sometimes Autumn comes, and we begin to see a different kind of harvest, once infected with the weeds we failed to remove during otherwise sunny days (and mature vipers coiled in the sheaves). Then comes winter. Babylonian captivities happen in such times. These stark Baltic seasons may be triggered by Nebuchadnezzar, Nero, Communists, or COVID-19. However, they arrive to borrow the image from Revelation: winter seasons are beastly times.

Nevertheless, captivity seems to always begin at home. We are bound and led captive by an "unraveling" of our own doing. Of course, God is sovereign. He never leaves us nor forsakes us. God is in control in our springtime and in our winter. *He changeth not.* Such theology is a prickly mercy. For the enigma of captivity, when evil is in ascendancy, while God is sovereign, seems as harsh as the icy winds that rip across the bleak midwinter landscape. But that is winter for you.

This book is about biblical-scholarly insight, pastoral guidance, and spiritual formation during the wintertime of our lives.

Walker Percy wrote a collection of essays on life and faith in the postmodern world. The editors called it *Signposts in a Strange Land*. Percy is the kind of author who is helpful as we navigate winter roads. The highways are icy. The piles of snow are tricky. What looks pretty and pure can form a covering over a bottomless crevasse. Writers like Percy and O'Connor and Lewis and Eliot put warning signs before such traps. Likewise, preachers, professors, and pastors serve us well when they speak wisdom from God that establishes signposts in the strange land. "Bridge out ahead" is just the kind of fire and brimstone I like when the sky snows so heavily that I cannot see. These are not the kitschy electric signs many rural churches in the U.S. and Canada purchased and set out in front of the church facility in the 70s and 80s. *These* signs are not cute. "Cry aloud and spare not" is a stark truth delivered urgently in life-or-death situations. That, too, is what this book is about.

So, when we say "public theology in the secular age," what do we mean? Let's start with the former.

What is Public Theology, and is it Biblical?

One cannot read the Bible without coming into contact with what we now call public theology. If public theology is the proclamation of theological truth—viz., truth revealed about God and Man and his world—then it is as good for the believer as the unbeliever. But public theology is not just truth spoken, but saving truth spoken aptly, wisely, and compassionately proclaimed at just the right time. Dietrich Bonhoeffer was, thus, a public theologian. The great Lutheran seminary professor and pastor studied the Bible, isolated truth to apply to the lives of believers in embattled times. Bonhoeffer preached for the glory of God and in the service of Christ's sheep during days of intense evil. He was the spiritual guide for those who would listen in the harshest days of winter in Germany in the 1930s through 1945. He was a signpost in a strange land. But let's not get ahead of ourselves. Let's go back to the Bible.

God gave the prophets a mandate to conduct what has become known as public theology. These men spoke God's Word to a particular people at just the right time. Their messages were aimed at individuals, but individuals living in community with each other and, often, in difficult times. This is public theology: *Text in context made plain for the good of those who hear and obey.* Such work is *public theology.* Of course, that phrase was not popular until 1974 (when Dr. Martin Marty, a Lutheran church historian, wrote about the public theological work of H. Richard Niebuhr, the author of the essential book on public theology, *Christ and Culture*). The phrase is new, but the concept is as old as Moses.[5] Sebastian Kim states, "Public theology is Christians engaging in dialogue with those outside church circles on various issues of common interest. It involves urging Christians to take the opportunity to participate in the public domain in modern secular democracies and to converse with other citizens on issues wider than religious matters."[6] E. Harold Breitenberg Jr. wrote about public theology in his work honoring the significant contributions of a public theologian, Max Stackhouse. For Breitenberg, public theology is "theologically informed discourse that seeks to be understandable both to those within its own religious tradition and to those outside it."[7] Breitenberg rightly divides books about public theology into those works about public theologians, those describing the meaning of public theology, and public theology as a practical, ethical construct to be used in the public square. There is a word of caution necessary.

Public theology is often used in a framework of understanding that is, in our opinion, out of step with the Word of God. For instance, Liberation Theology, a Roman Catholic movement that arose in Latin America, uses the phrase public theology in a way that is radically different than, say, the way that Dietrich Bonhoeffer practiced public theology. Liberation Theology is a Marxist-Leninist framework of oppressors and oppressed nailed together with words, stories, and concepts from the Gospel. So, public theology uses Marxist ideology baptized with familiar Christian themes to "speak truth to power." But it is not the truth. And the power may or may not be sinister, just an authority they want to overthrow. Such public theology has nothing to do with the preaching of Jesus Christ. To cite Jesus' rebuke of those who were misusing authority to hurt human beings to promote your Communist ideology is not only poor exegesis but lousy theology. And wrong.

We are indebted to Matthew Kaemingk's critical analysis of public theology from a Reformed commitment. Kaemingk cited nine features of public theology, in general, and nine distinctive and observable traits of what he calls "public habits of the Reformed heart."[8] He confirms what we all know is true of any assertion about Reformed theology or theologians: "To be clear, these marks are not universally held by Reformed Christians around the world." The summary of public theologians in general and those from the Reformed faith is a helpful contribution. However, my impressions are that the insights in the respective chapters follow a pattern of global ecumenical messaging, if not a more specific concern arising from Dutch theology in South Africa. The book is a fine example of public theology at work, and I commend the book to anyone interested in how such commitments are expressed. Yet, it is not our focus in these chapters.

Kathryn Tanner commented on the work of contemporary public theologians,

> As these theologians hope to show, Christian symbols and doctrines have a public dimension to them; the religious outlook that these symbols and doctrines inform is a religious outlook on life as a whole, with ramifications, therefore, not simply for a narrowly conceived religious sphere, but for all dimensions of life.[9]

Neither are we seeking to inform a religious outlook on life as a whole, although Dr. Tanner's concerns are getting closer.

When we speak of public theology, we recognize and use a reasonable phrase to describe the ethical implications of God's Word for all mankind. In short, we believe God's Word applies in every area of life. As ministers of the Gospel, we seek to speak the Gospel publicly so that people will be warned, turn to Christ, and be saved. We speak against those practices that limit or hurt human beings. Our concerns are not political. Our interests are not merely academic. When we pray for public officials as we are commanded to do in public worship services, we do so that it may go well for the governed to fulfill the great mandates of God in the world, viz., the creation mandate, to steward the earth, the great commandment, to love one another, and the great commission, to go and baptize, teaching whatsoever things Jesus taught. Our interest lies in God's Kingdom. Yet, God's Kingdom, not of this world, has come into the minds and hearts of those who live in this world. Thus, like John Donne, we are interested in all mankind because God has created us, sustains us, and desires that men everywhere be saved.

Thus, our understanding of "public theology" is that public theology is a pastoral act in obedience to the Lord as revealed in His Word. This pastoral office is prophetic in the sense that one is proclaiming a message from God, according to Holy Scripture, with community concerns, implications, and promises. Public theology engages Biblical Critical Thinking, which seeks to isolate presenting issues, categorize them according to Scripture, and conduct theological reflection on presenting issues that lead to diagnosis and treatment by preaching the Gospel of Jesus Christ. This is so whether the presenting issue is immigration (as Dr. Peter Lillback addresses in this volume), philosophical threats to the stability of the community, or the family (as Dr. John Frame writes about).

Looking at Isiah 58, in synoptic view with the rest of Scripture, we can assert essentials for the faithful preaching of the Gospel in the public square.

Isaiah 58 has a general rather than specific context, which guides us. Indeed, Gary Smith commented, "The setting of chaps. 58–59 is left unidentified and thus is the subject of a good deal of speculation."[10] Given that, Smith adds,

> This message appears to be communicating a series of general principles that everyone should avoid (actions that do not please God) because God is just (58:2) and is against injustice (58:6). In the end God will break forth his light (58:8); he will unfold his righteous deeds of salvation (59:15b, 16b–17) to the redeemed. In the distant future God will establish justice (59:21) through his own work of salvation, and the redeemed will come to Zion to enjoy his wonderful kingdom forever (59:20–21).[11]

From this context and divine revelation, we assert the following standards for preaching in the public square:

Speak out of God's revealed burden for His work, not yours.

Isaiah chapter 58 records the proclamation of God to sin in the believing community. Authentic public theology is, therefore, a response to God's original call to men and their community (the public expression of truth lived out in common life together). We must speak out of God's burden and not our own. If it is God's burden based on his revealed will, then the vision – the promises of redemption of the broken things —will more likely be a faithful representation of God's will.

Speak what you know, not what you don't.

God's range of concerns for Israel and the world is all-consuming. Expositing the entire covenantal scheme, across the salvific spectrum from Genesis to Revelation, we see that God speaks to kings and queens (higher history) as well as to anonymous servants but to God (lower history); e.g., the indispensability of those like Rahab, Esther, and Ruth to the fulfillment of the Abrahamic covenant to all people). We who bear the mantle of a call to preach must do so for the glory and honor of God and in the service of His people and all of those who will believe on His name. 1 Corinthians 14:9 says, "So with yourselves, if with your tongue you utter speech that is not intelligible, how will anyone know what is said? For you will be speaking into the air." Because one may be a farmer and a minister of the Gospel, your opinion on fertilizer treatment plans is helpful—yet, only to the degree that it is employed, pastorally, in support of the mission of God in the word.

Speak plainly so that all may understand the message.

Those of us who write and speak in the context of the academy must be especially careful. You have nothing to say if you must resort to academia's contingent, conditional, deliberative syntax. In a similar way, a pastor (or military chaplain) must be careful to use language that reaches the minds of the people with as few insider words as possible. On the other hand, we must do so without sacrificing the theologically rich expressions, metaphors, and stories that call for the hearer's attention. If there are questions about "the blood of Christ" or "the atonement" then all the better. This is precisely what we want people to think about. If public theology is an exercise in doctrinal collective bargaining to secure the common good at the price of conviction of biblical truth, then we must have nothing of it. If we speak God's Word into the public square with as much confidence as the Mars Hill philosophers assert their positions, we will see the blessings of such public proclamation: some will hear us again on these matters.

Speak specifically.

The one who is called to speak God's truth publicly to a troubled community—whether Jonah to Nineveh, Amos to the Northern Kingdom, or Jonathan Edwards to the Calvinistic Congregational church at Northampton, Massachusetts (until his dismissal in 1750)—must follow God's revealed pattern.[12] Name the presenting issue that is or will bring about pain and judgment. In Isaiah 58 (vv. 2-5), there is religious hypocrisy that leads to an absence of self-awareness:

> Yet they seek me daily and delight to know my ways, as if they were a nation that did righteousness and did not forsake the judgment of their God; they ask of me righteous judgments; they delight to draw near to God.'
>
> Why have we fasted, and you see it not? Why have we humbled ourselves, and you take no knowledge of it?' Behold, in the day of your fast you seek your own pleasure, and oppress all your workers. Behold,

you fast only to quarrel and to fight and to hit with a wicked fist. Fasting like yours this day will not make your voice to be heard on high.

Is such the fast that I choose, a day for a person to humble himself? Is it to bow down his head like a reed, and to spread sackcloth and ashes under him? Will you call this a fast, and a day acceptable to the LORD?

The Lord gives both an assessment of the sin and a diagnosis. The presenting issue assessed is fasting while oppressing laborers. The diagnosis is pride. This is a recurring theme with God's people and one that persists today in the New Covenant.

Of course, we recognize that the text of Isaiah 58 is the Lord speaking. We can only "prophesy" with such reflected righteous indignation and boldness when we are sure we have God's Word. Thus, we exposit the Holy Scriptures, a "word made more sure" (2 Peter 1:19).

Speak redemptively

The Lord does not leave us without hope. Even in the ruin and rubble of judgment, Jeremiah reminded the conquered Jews, "It is of the Lord's mercies that we are not consumed, because his compassions fail not. They are new every morning: great is thy faithfulness" (Lamentations 3:22-23 KJV). Thus, we read how the Lord God makes the turn from assessment, diagnosis, to divine remedy:

> Is it such a fast that I have chosen? a day for a man to afflict his soul? is it to bow down his head as a bulrush, and to spread sackcloth and ashes under him? wilt thou call this a fast, and an acceptable day to the Lord?
>
> Is not this the fast that I have chosen? to loose the bands of wickedness, to undo the heavy burdens, and to let the oppressed go free, and that ye break every yoke?
>
> Is it not to deal thy bread to the hungry, and that thou bring the poor that are cast out to thy house? when thou seest the naked, that thou cover him; and that thou hide not thyself from thine own flesh?
>
> Then shall thy light break forth as the morning, and thine health shall spring forth speedily: and thy righteousness shall go before thee; the glory of the Lord shall be thy reward.

Then shalt thou call, and the Lord shall answer; thou shalt cry, and he shall say, Here I am. If thou take away from the midst of thee the yoke, the putting forth of the finger, and speaking vanity;

And if thou draw out thy soul to the hungry, and satisfy the afflicted soul; then shall thy light rise in obscurity, and thy darkness be as the noon day:

And the Lord shall guide thee continually, and satisfy thy soul in drought, and make fat thy bones: and thou shalt be like a watered garden, and like a spring of water, whose waters fail not.

And they that shall be of thee shall build the old waste places: thou shalt raise up the foundations of many generations; and thou shalt be called, The repairer of the breach, The restorer of paths to dwell in.

If thou turn away thy foot from the sabbath, from doing thy pleasure on my holy day; and call the sabbath a delight, the holy of the Lord, honourable; and shalt honour him, not doing thine own ways, nor finding thine own pleasure, nor speaking thine own words:

Then shalt thou delight thyself in the Lord; and I will cause thee to ride upon the high places of the earth, and feed thee with the heritage of Jacob thy father: for the mouth of the Lord hath spoken it (Isaiah 58:6-14 KJV).

Christian shepherds must cry aloud and spare not. Yet we cry aloud with the pleadings of Christ Jesus, the resurrected and reigning Savior in whom there is redemption.

What is the Secular Age, and is it Real?

For sociologist Neil Howe, "The Fourth Turning is Here."[13] Howe's thesis posits that history (Anglo-American history in particular) unfolds in cyclical patterns, which he describes as "Turnings." Each turning spans a generation and culminates in a societal-defining moment or crisis. According to Howe, the "Fourth Turning" is a time of upheaval and redefinition of values and institutions. While there is nothing new under the sun, and human behavior is predictive, Howe's reliance on a secular-cyclical model of history (an assumed "uniformitarianism") potentially underestimates or disavows the sovereignty of

God.[14] We recall Peter's warning concerning secular theories of history:

> Knowing this first of all, that scoffers will come in the last days with scoffing, following their own sinful desires. They will say, 'Where is the promise of his coming? For ever since the fathers fell asleep, all things are continuing as they were from the beginning of creation.' For they deliberately overlook this fact, that the heavens existed long ago, and the earth was formed out of water and through water by the word of God, and that by means of these, the world that then existed was deluged with water and perished. But by the same word the heavens and earth that now exist are stored up for fire, being kept until the day of judgment and destruction of the ungodly (2 Peter 3:3-7 ESV).

Yet, we see that even secular sociological theories recognize that we have entered a new season, a wintry season. In my book, "From Flanders Fields to the Moviegoer," I sought to trace the rise of postmodernity from the collapse of the great empires from 1898-1965.[15] The milieu of modernity in the early twentieth century had created an almost utopian philosophy of humanity and its world, profoundly influencing Western thought. Nihilism, rejecting absolutes and foundational assumptions of what is true, was mostly limited to the German-speaking higher education institutions from whence it emerged (e.g., Universität Basel). However, the horrors of World War I, which lasted from 1914 to 1918, shattered this modernist idealism. The subsequent years after the Great War witnessed a rising skepticism towards modernity's claims, signaling a crisis of meaning. A patron at Café de Flore, where artists and writers sipped "un café" in the spring of 1925, the "Années Folles" ("The Crazy Years") following WWI, would have opined,"Nous étions naïfs à propos de nous-mêmes. Nous sommes toujours aussi barbares" ("We were naive about ourselves. We are as barbaric as ever."). In England, T.S. Eliot (1888–1965) became a literary powerhouse as he reflected on the agony of "the wasteland" of the liminal days of the post-war world.[16]

In contrast, figures like the Irish playwright Samuel Beckett (1906–1989) championed a nihilistic response through works such as "Waiting for Godot" and the Theatre of the Absurd movement in Paris.[17]

Although Beckett dismissed the idea that he was affirming or critiquing any philosophy, the applauding French audiences and bewildered Anglo-American theater-goers justifiably held that Beckett was trying to say something. It is hard to see or read Godot and believe that Becket was just an enigma whose genius could not be understood (except for Left Bank radicals). The Theater of the Absurd was a perspective was deeply rooted in the despair and "God is dead" ideology of Friedrich Nietzsche (1844–1900), presenting a bleaker view of existence. However, during and after World War II, voices like C.S. Lewis (1898–1963) in England, and later Flannery O'Connor (1925–1964) and Walker Percy (1916–1990) in the United States during the fifties and seventies, offered narratives supporting a return to Christian assumptions.

Meanwhile, figures such as Michel Foucault (1926–1984) popularized the nihilism spreading across the continent. By the 1990s, the ascendancy of postmodernity was evident. In 2005, Canadian author Charles Taylor (born 1931) published a significant work, "A Secular Age," demonstrating and lamenting the dominance of postmodern assumptions in Western daily life.[18] Scholars like Tom Holland (born 1968) have since argued that Christianity has not been eclipsed; to discuss a "secular" society is to acknowledge the enduring, albeit challenged, Christian tradition. Likewise, philosophers like Roger Scruton (1944–2020) have argued that the "Soul of the World" remains one that believes in God and cannot escape the unprecedented influence of Christianity. German philosopher Jürgen Habermas (born 1929) and Pope Benedict XVI (b. 1927, papacy 2005–2013) have presented a compelling argument suggesting that the Secular Age is unsustainable, considering the innate spiritual nature of humanity.[19] They propose that a post-secular era is emerging, representing a synthesis between faith and reason. This perspective acknowledges the inherent limitations of a purely secular worldview and anticipates a future where spiritual and rational dimensions of human existence are more harmoniously integrated. Ironically, the swirling debates over the crisis of our humanity seem, at present, to be no more settled than the first "Guns of August" in 1914.[20]

As I pen these words, the philosophical ivy, more like Kudzu, swirls fiercely around the once-sturdy pillars of our institutions. A time there was, not so far removed in the rearview of our collective experience when such tumults would have jolted us from our complacency, but now, in these weary times, nothing holds the power to startle our senses. We stand together, a congregation of souls, bracing against the invisible winds of change, almost in a twisted anticipation for the foreboding event that looms on the horizon. You can practically taste it. There is an electric tension in the air that precedes the storm, a palpable prelude to the chaos that whispers its approach. Auden's startled deer are stilled as troops move on the tundra north of Rome.

In authoring this book, our aim has been pastoral. Our intent is akin to shepherds guiding their flock, offering counsel and direction to the Christian community amidst these unsettling times. While our narrative might resonate with scholars, and we gladly welcome their insights, our primary audience is the Christian "everyman" seeking to make sense of God's grace in a strange new world. We believe that the truth of God's Word will guide us through this uncertain period. The stars shine brightest in the darkest night.

Stay broken at the foot of the cross. Love one another. Keep proclaiming the Gospel to others. Remember His love for you. Sacred memory, practiced often, will give you the strength born of gratitude to turn from the encroaching evil. Remain faithful to the Word of the Lord, that lamp from heaven illuminating the path to the verdant pastures that lie just after the treacherous ledges we must traverse. Rest assured in one unshakeable truth: God is ever with us. His Word, a beacon of propositional truth, and the presence of Jesus Christ provide a divine assurance that we will find our way home. As Donne reminded us, we are not standing still. We were born again in the heavens, and to the New Heaven and the New Earth, we march onward. Yet, like St. David in the Welsh Christian stories of old, who planted a church wherever he went, we hope that wherever we pass, we leave behind a community of people and their posterity transformed by the Gospel of Jesus Christ.

Questions for Discussion and Reflection

Individual | Class | Small Group

1. Do you agree with the concept of public theology presented in the text? What would you add or take away from the definition? Why?

2. How can we ensure that our public theology is based on biblical truth and not influenced by worldly ideologies?

3. The text discusses how we can apply the principles of public theology to address current societal issues from a biblical perspective. In your view, what are some practical ways to do this?

4. The text explores the role of the pastoral office in public theology. What dangers are present? How does one "cry aloud and spare not" in the context of the secular age and in light of biblical mandates for shepherds?

5. The text's interpretation of Isaiah 58 sheds light on our understanding of public theology. What is your take on this?

6. The text highlights the potential dangers of misusing public theology. What do you think are some of these dangers?

For the Love of God
Nurturing a Christian Intellectual Life

Michael A. Milton

> Work creates its instrument for itself. Like the blacksmith who tempers his tools, it forms our character and gives us solidity and therefore confidence.
>
> — A. G. Sertillanges, O.P., *The Intellectual Life*[1]

My professor at the Defense Language Institute in Monterey, California, taught me how to nurture a Christian intellectual life. Dr. Zef Nekaij discerned my need for a structured approach to reading, retention, interaction, and truth extraction from significant works. He introduced me to the methodologies articulated in *The Intellectual Life* (1928) by A.G.. Sertillanges, O.P. (1863-1948).[2] Reflecting on my academic journey, I contemplated the guidance to offer someone eager to delve deeper into the Word of God. I share my insights, hopeful that they may aid others in their spiritual growth in Christ Jesus, our Lord.

"Every hierarchy sees to the policing of its own domain."[3] This principle also applies to the study of God's Word. Its message embodies a single-mindedness, demanding a similar focus in its reading. We seek God's will through prayerful reading, fortifying our hearts, minds, and spirits for His divine purposes. But *how* should we read?

No scriptures were studied in isolation. It represents God's progressively revealed truth, shepherded by the Holy Spirit and verified by Jesus Christ, who died, resurrected, and ascended to heaven. The teachings of our living Savior in the Scriptures are manifestations of Logos. The Holy Spirit acknowledges his influence on the Word, harmonizing his divine intentions with ours. Thus, engaging with scriptures is a sacred gift—a bridge between supernatural and tangible realms.

A poignant memory surfaces when I ponder my interactions with the scriptures. I queried Dr. Laird Harris on the spiritual merit of the Apocrypha compared to the canonical 66 books. His reply, reminiscent of Jesus' pedagogy, was an assignment to read the Gospel of John and two Apocryphal selections. The distinction became clear post-reading: the Gospel of John resonated with the Holy Spirit's presence, while the Apocrypha provided enlightenment about the Spirit. The Gospel of John embodies the Spirit-infused Word of God, while other illuminative writings lack the Holy Spirit's signature. This revelation mirrors Jesus' words: "The wind blows where it wishes," and emphasizes the anointing that we possess:

> But the anointing which you have received from Him abides in you, and you do not need that anyone teach you; but as the same anointing teaches you concerning all things, and is true, and is not a lie, and just as it has taught you, you will abide in Him (1 John 2:27 NKJV).

For instance, the Apostles and Church Fathers interpreted Genesis 1 through the lenses of Matthew 1 and John 3. The omnipotent creativity of God, which crafted the cosmos, also steered the genealogy leading to Jesus Christ, legally adopted by His earthly father, Joseph. This divine craftsmanship resonates with our spiritual rebirth through repentance and faith in Christ.

> Always seek connections, understand the preconditions; let coordinated understanding, not fragments, anchor in your memory.[4]

A profound observation posits that every domain harbors pivotal ideas illuminating the whole. Some of these ideas also guide life, and their reverence lights the inner sanctum of our hearts.

At the core of these insights lies a divine thread woven by God even before the foundation of the world: His sacred promise to accomplish for us what we cannot do ourselves. God's love serves as the divine dynamic that conjoins Scripture with Scripture, life with life, and grace with truth. As Hans Urs Von Balthazar wrote, *Love Alone is Credible*.[5] This sentiment rings true for hermeneutics, evangelism, and preaching, bridging the Scriptures to life and the sacred intellect to God's intent for us as His people.

Questions for Discussion and Reflection

Individual | Class | Small Group

1. How does the principle of "Every hierarchy sees to the policing of its own domain" apply to the study of God's Word?

2. What is the significance of studying scriptures in context rather than in isolation?

3. How did the author's interaction with the Apocrypha and the Gospel of John shape his understanding of the Holy Spirit's presence in the Word of God?

4. In what way do the Apostles and Church Fathers' interpretation of Genesis 1 through the lenses of Matthew 1 and John 3 reflect the divine craftsmanship of God?

5. How does the idea of "Always seek connections, understand the preconditions" apply to our understanding and interpretation of the Bible?

6. In what way does God's love serve as the divine dynamic that connects Scripture with Scripture, life with life, and grace with truth?

———

Fragments of Nature's Lore
On the Rejection of First Principles
Michael A. Milton

> What distinguishes Judaeo-Christianity in general from other world religions is its emphasis on the value of the individual person, its view of man as a creature in trouble, seeking to get out of it, and accordingly on the move.
>
> — Walker Percy, "Morality and Religion," *Signposts in a Strange Land.*[1]

The corruption or absence of controlling first principles leads to suicidal chaos.

If the first principles of our solar system—namely, gravity, inertia, and relativity—were suspended, then it would take a very short order to inaugurate cosmic annihilation. In desiring so-called freedom and independence from first principles, what person would move the moon only several degrees? Or if he were able, growing weary of the perceived tyranny of first principles, tilt the Earth an additional five degrees to port or starboard, forward or aft? Any such undertaking would prove the insanity of rebellion against the "tyrant" (and if one insists that true freedom is impossible while there are first principles, let us at least admit that a first principle, like gravity, is a most benevolent "tyrant"). Too late, the discontented cosmic traveler would realize that first principles are not dictators but guardians. Freedom is only possible because of the immovable nature of those stalwart headers. Mercifully, that most extraordinary but dangerous creature called Man has no power over the first principles of the universe. He might stomp and scream like a spoiled child who demands that he be allowed to play jump rope on a freeway, but the nanny quietly refuses. As juvenile as such insistence may be, it demonstrates how God has endowed humanity with freedom and self-determination without diminishing His sovereignty. Therefore, while Man cannot disturb the first principles of the cosmos, he can choose to suspend them or ignore them in his own life. The stars will fall, and the orbiting celestial bodies will spin out of control to scale, but he can inaugurate such a suicidal course of action. Others can join our philosophical rebel and form a coalition of deniers (or, to borrow from the title of John Kennedy Toole's novel, *A Confederacy of Dunces*). At any scale of human existence, such a foolish move is unthinkable. And yet self-destruction is a state that humans have almost perfected in the way that a Jackson Pollock devotee becomes more adept at slinging primary colors of house paint against a canvas and calling such random chaos a masterpiece. We are, of course, no more righteous nor malevolent than Adam and Eve and are, therefore, prone to the same consequences. Conversely, we are free moral *agents* — even if our *wills*, the controlling navigator of thought and action, are in bondage —and can choose the wiser path. This is, of course, our predicament and our possibility.

A. G. Sertillanges, O. P., wrote in *The Intellectual Life*:

> Order among objects or disciplines of any kind is only established when principles, arranged in hierarchical importance up to the first principle, play their part as principles, as heads —as in an army, a well-ordered house, or a nation. Nowadays we have repudiated first principles, and knowledge is in a rout. We have mere fragments of nature's lore, shining tinsel ornaments and no garments, splendid chapters, and no finished book, no Bible.[2]

"Fragments of nature's lore" refers to the scattered remnants of a civilization: vestiges of greatness void of truth. These fragments are like Jesus' judgment of the scribes and Pharisees: "white-washed tombs" (Matthew 23:27-28). These artifacts of bygone days of wisdom are but a museum. In forsaking the first principles, those who retain their husks show disdain for them, as if they could strip away the spiritual reality that gave life while holding on to the shell. The power that animated the fragments of nature's lore is the essential knowledge and wisdom given by God. These are the first principles present to either judge or offer renewal.

The first of the first principles of knowledge is the knowledge of God. From such a necessary theological source flows philosophy (i.e., "critical thinking," if you prefer), in which we deploy intellect and activate our native senses in the service of ideals to observe, classify, and arrange phenomena. Philosophy begets action. So, we initiate a considered strategy: that is, we plan, we build, and we manage. In doing so, we review the fruit of our labors. We observe our creative processes and inspect their art, making corrections, adjustments, and refinements to improve. Then, we either repeat the well-ordered process to amend our work or, if satisfied that the product is sufficiently representative of the first principle, move on to another phenomenological concern. We pass along the first principles to the next generation so that, across time, in aggregate, we build civilization. Remove and replace the first principles (you cannot choose to live without first principles; you may exchange them with "first things" that are untrue, but you cannot alter the equation of "source, philosophy, action") with alternative governing ideas. You will change the rest of the process. Since God is the single grandest idea of all—for one cannot necessarily conceive of a power greater than the Eternal, the First Mover, and the Great First Cause of all that is seen and unseen—removal of that first principle renders the process either too weak or too wicked to run the factory of invention. Thus, not only do you cease to build an ordered civilization, but you produce mutations that diminish it. This is where we are. No one has stated the case of first principles more concisely or accurately than the Apostle Paul in his epistle to the Christians in Rome (Romans 1:19–23):

> For what can be known about God is plain to them, because God has shown it to them. For his invisible attributes, namely, his eternal power and divine nature, have been clearly perceived, ever since the creation of the world, in the things that have been made. So they are without excuse. For although they knew God, they did not honor him as God or give thanks to him, but they became futile in their thinking, and their foolish hearts were darkened. Claiming to be wise, they became fools and exchanged the glory of the immortal God for images resembling mortal man and birds and animals and creeping things.

Thus, we assess that the actual first principles of a functioning civilization are vital to its philosophy, output, and, by process, human flourishing. The first principle is there is a God, and He has revealed Himself to Man. His revelation is *general* (Creation's witness) and *special* (Holy Scripture). The revelation is to stir the suppressed memories of the Fall. Back to the Percy quotation, "We are in trouble," and on the run. But God . . . The glorious interruption of defiant fugitives from divinity. God came to us while we were running. His Word became incarnate and lived among us. The Word made flesh is our Lord and Savior Jesus Christ. Love God and love others out of the love you have received through the Savior. To know that love is to repent (turn) from your trusting in self (or illusions of salvation in other people or things or activities) and trust in Jesus Christ alone as the One who lived the life you could not live and died the death that should have been yours. This is the Gospel: you are justified by His life (righteousness required) and His death (atonement for sin against God), and by faith in Him, receive eternal life. In Christ, we are made new.

Begin there. Then, go and live. Marry. Rear children. Work. Explore. Research. Teach. Heal. Paint. Sculpt. Compose. Laugh. Weep. Lament. Rejoice. Build. Sell. Invest. Labor. Rest.

Be.

Questions for Discussion and Reflection

Individual | Class | Small Group

1. How does Judaeo-Christianity's emphasis on individual value compare to other religions or secular philosophies?

2. In what ways does Percy's description of humanity align with Christian beliefs about sin, redemption, and salvation?

3. What is the role of first principles in maintaining societal order and preventing chaos?

4. How does the idea of divine knowledge align or conflict with modern philosophical and scientific perspectives?

5. How does adherence to or rejection of first principles impact human flourishing?

6. How does the Gospel represent the ultimate first principle for Christians, and how does it influence everyday decisions, relationships, and societal engagement?

———

Part II
Daily Life

The Family in the Secular Age
A Christian Response to Marxism
John M. Frame

> Eternal God, our Creator, You set us to live in families. We commend to Your Care all the homes where Your people live.—"Prayer for Families,"
>
> — *Presbyterian Book of Common Worship*[1]

The chief contemporary movements of secular thought and politics have announced their hostility toward the "nuclear family," i.e. the family with two parents of opposite sexes and their children. The best-known expression of this hostility was that of Karl Marx, in the *Communist Manifesto* of 1848. Marx saw the abolition of the family as necessary for the abolition of capitalism as an economic system. In the traditional family, he observed, the adults accumulate wealth and put it in their name, so they can support themselves and in time pass the wealth on to their children. So if the nuclear family is society's main institution for perpetuating the race and raising children, that society will see wealth as family property. That is capitalism. To Marx, determined to end the capitalistic system, that is unacceptable.

In his view, society should not permit people to accumulate wealth for themselves, for that leads to inequality, and inequality must be remedied by the state. For Marx the state should be the ultimate owner of all property, and the state, not the family, must determine who is allowed to make use of it.

More recently, the organization Black Lives Matter, admittedly influenced by Marxism, has also called for the abolishing of the nuclear family. While Marx was concerned mainly with economic inequality, Black Lives Matter focuses on racial inequality. They notice that nuclear families tend each to be of one race, and they inculcate values such as hard work, education, and punctuality, that black activists reject as distinctively white behavior. BLM, like Marx, prefers the state as the ultimate guardian of children, as a way of turning children away from the values of nuclear families and toward Marxian socialism.

In this paper I do not plan to criticize Marxist economics at length. History shows us that when Marxian socialism becomes the ruling ideology in a nation it does little to increase the wealth of the poor. It does decrease the wealth of the upper classes, and much of the increase goes to government. To maintain its power, the government typically becomes totalitarian, persecuting anyone (particularly religious people) who don't agree with its ideology. This reduces the population to slavery, a status far different from the utopia advertised by Marxist theory. This is in effect Marxism's substitute for the nuclear family: a nation ruled by an all-powerful state, which stamps out all opposition.

But in this paper I want to explore more deeply the secular (especially Marxian) alternative to the nuclear family. Is Marxian socialism the best way to raise our young? There are empirical as well as biblical reasons for thinking otherwise. When the nuclear family is weakened by divorce, for example, the children are typically harmed in various ways. Wayne Parker notes examples of physical harm:

> . . . research shows that adolescents whose parents have divorced are more likely to experience injury, accidents, and illness than children whose parents have remained married.[2]

A 2011 study found that teens living with both biological parents tended to be more physically healthy than teens from homes without both biological parents present. The study relied on reports from both teens and their parents and it's important to note that their responses were varied. However, researchers still found a stronger correlation between adolescent well-being and family structure than among parents or caregivers.[3]

Children of broken homes also experience emotional and psychological problems. Parker continues,

> For instance, a 2017 study found that children living in intact, nuclear families are about half as likely as children in step, blended, or one-parent families to have a mental disorder or need psychological help.[4]

In fact, studies show that the psychological effects and emotional strain of divorce even linger into adulthood. For instance, researchers at the University of Toronto found that men from families that divorced during their childhood were more than three times as likely to consider suicide than men whose parents never divorced.

Likewise, adult children of divorce may also be vulnerable to drug and alcohol use in adolescence, have fears about commitment and divorce, and have negative memories of the legal system that forced custody and visitation.

Children with divorced parents also disproportionately experience academic problems, as Parker points out:

> Research has consistently demonstrated that children in situations where their parents have been divorced may earn lower grades than their peers.[5] Over the years, statistics on the educational effects of divorce support these findings.

Parker points out that these bad effects can be mitigated in various ways. Caretakers should be aware of potential problems and guard against them, and such precautions do help. He even affirms that some kinds of divorce are better for children than the homes in which they lived before divorce. Ironically, divorce sometimes prevents worse evils. But far better, indeed, is a family not broken by divorce.

Certainly, the remedy here is not total control by the government, but rather improvement in the quality of family life within a free society.

But the family is essential, not just as an alternative to Marxism, and not just as a utilitarian way to minimize children's physical, mental, and academic problems. It is an ordinance of God. Indeed, it is the central ordinance by which God carries out his purposes for the human race. In the beginning, there was one family: a man, Adam, a woman, Eve, and later their children, Cain and Abel. From that time on, there were children and children's children. The Bible is a book of genealogies. Noah, Shem, Ham, Japheth; Abraham, Isaac, Jacob. Later, the genealogies of Moses and David, and in the New Testament, the genealogies (two of them: Matthew 1:1-17 and Luke 3:23-37) of Jesus the Christ. When, after Jesus' Resurrection, in obedience to his Great Commission, the Gospel goes throughout the world, the apostles bring people to Christ by households, as in Acts 16:29-34.

Scripture does not, of course, present the family as a conflict-free zone. At its best, the family is a place of love and nurture. But after sin enters the world, the worst of sin infects it. The first older brother, Cain, kills the first younger brother, Abel. As history continues, there is rebellion, betrayal, estrangement, hatred, bitter rivalry, adultery, and incest. Yet the family continues to be God's chosen place of human reproduction and the place where godly parents teach their children the ways of the Lord (Deuteronomy 6:4-9, Prov. 1:8-9). The family is the place from which human beings go forth to "fill the earth and subdue it" (Gen. 1:28).

That God persists in blessing the family through terrible evil points to something still deeper about this institution: it is not easily dispensable. There is a wonderful glory in the family beyond all the difficulties. Indeed, it is a place holy to God, a divinely appointed image of a great mystery, the marriage of Christ and the church:

> Husbands, love your wives, as Christ loved the church and gave himself up for her, that he might sanctify her, having cleansed her by the washing of water with the word, so that he might present the church to himself in splendor, without spot or wrinkle or any such thing, that she might be holy and without blemish. In the same way husbands should

love their wives as their own bodies. He who loves his wife loves himself. For no one ever hated his own flesh, but nourishes and cherishes it, just as Christ does the church, because we are members of his body. "Therefore a man shall leave his father and mother and hold fast to his wife, and the two shall become one flesh." This mystery is profound, and I am saying that it refers to Christ and the church (Ephesians 5:25-32 ESV).

It is from this wonderfully holy redemptive relationship that children are born and nurtured. Having described that marriage relationship, Paul describes the life of children in such a household:

Children, obey your parents in the Lord, for this is right. "Honor your father and mother"—which is the first commandment with a promise — "so that it may go well with you and that you may enjoy long life on the earth."Fathers, do not exasperate your children; instead, bring them up in the training and instruction of the Lord (Ephesians 6:1-4).

This is the way that every child joins the genealogy: Abraham, Isaac, Jacob, David, Jesus, Willie, and Susan. There is a temple of God, a temple of holy love, in the marriage of their parents. And as the wife is to be subject to her husband and her husband is, like Jesus, to love her unto death, so the children are to obey their parents and thereby inherit the covenant blessing of God's people.

The Christian should never imagine that children could be raised as well in any other environment. Every child should grow up knowing parents who love one another as Christ loves his people. We dare not imagine that we can throw away this profoundly sacred model of marriage and replace it with some man-made scheme.

So, the first thing we should know about the family in the secular age is that the secular age has no idea how sublimely beautiful is this biblical vision of the family. When secularists dismiss it as a mere tradition or a relic of ancient barbarism, the Christian's first responsibility is to show them how transcendently magnificent it is. The secularist must come to understand that setting aside God's creation of the family is not just replacing one scheme of sociological organization with another. It is more like replacing a great work of art with a cave drawing.

It is the source of this institution in God's wisdom and providence that underlies its practical value. As we have seen, Wayne Parker cites studies that show the superiority of the intact family for meeting children's needs: physically, emotionally, and academically. But these studies pose the question, why? Why is it that children do better in intact nuclear families? The Christian answer is that what God ordains is good for his people (Deuteronomy 10:13). The nuclear family is part of God's overall arrangement of generations upon generations. It reflects his vast wisdom and providence. We have seen, to be sure, as with Can and Abel, that this system, good as it is, is corrupted by human sin. But even such corruption cannot prevent God from accomplishing his purposes through the human family over thousands of generations.

The secular alternative to the biblical family is, I suppose, a school, run by a Marxian state, in which children learn facts and values with no reference to God. Recently a video appeared in which a schoolteacher explained his intent to turn his students into revolutionaries in a year of study. To achieve this goal, the teachers must stand against the values of conservative and Christian parents. Typically, this is done, not by reasoned argument against the parents' worldview, but by "cancelation" —that is, *ad hominem* attacks on views that the radicals don't like: ridicule, name-calling, personal disparagement, or even grade penalties for students who question the teacher's secular ideology. In this brainwashing process, there is no limitation of subject matter. In the past, for example, it was thought that sexual matters, beyond the basics, should be taught in the home, rather than in the school. But today secular educators want children to be confronted with homosexuality and transgenderism, and to understand these with secular values, even in kindergarten. The intent of secular educators to prepare a generation of radicals has so far been remarkably successful. One survey says that 51% of young people are more positive toward socialism than toward capitalism.

So secularists are militant in promoting their view of the family. What can Christians do about this? We need to pray and take a stand: *ora et labora*. In my view, Christians should be as militant as the secularists, or more so, in defense of their biblical view and their critique of secularism.

Their critique should reflect the character of Christ, his gentleness and graciousness, and his love of his enemies. Unlike the Marxists, our goal is not a government dictatorship, but a society in which the gospel goes forth freely and offers to all a life of love.

But the Christian critique of secularism should also reflect his wisdom and truth. As we have seen, there are good arguments to show that children fare better in intact nuclear families than in families of divorce or, presumably, in arrangements of a very different kind. Christians need to draw more attention to those arguments. And at the same time, they should maintain a loving and happy life within their families so that they do not fall prey to the evil of divorce.

And Christians need to make more use of the lawful methods of bringing change within a democratic society. It is possible now to educate children outside the public school system, by Christian schools and home schools, so that children may more thoroughly appropriate the values of their families, rather than the secular values of those who would undermine the family. It is also often possible for parents to attend school board meetings to contest ideologies such as Marxism and Critical Race Theory. Remember that Christian citizens can attend school board meetings even if their children do not attend public schools; our taxes have bought for them this privilege. And Christians ought to be promoting voucher plans, by which those taxes can be used for schools other than the secularized public schools. Voucher plans facilitate school choice, and school choice benefits people including Christians against whom the secular schools discriminate. Christians should support plans to give school tax money to parents rather than to schools. Many public schools are educationally deficient even though they have received huge amounts of money. For such schools, as for businesses, competition would enhance quality, and it would also promote a greater focus on education itself and a lesser focus on leftist ideology.

Christians should use their important asset, citizenship, to promote freedom of speech, as they proclaim the gospel in society. And they should oppose attempts to suppress the family, as through wealth taxes and suppression of parental rights.

And Christians need to be advertising the grand vision of the family we saw earlier in Scripture. The mouths of critics will be stopped, when they see that the family is God's way of life for human beings, even more when they see that the family is a revelation of God himself. The family is, again, not just a useful means of organizing society, but a place where we can see Christ's love for the church passed on to obedient children. So the family is gospel as well as law. In the family we see the good news of what God has planned for us to be. When Scripture calls us to trust Jesus as Lord and savior, it invites us into God's family, the family of Abraham, Isaac, and Jacob, a vast multitude in which all are brothers and sisters and fathers and mothers. When Jesus teaches in Matt. 23:30 that in the kingdom there will be no more marrying or giving in marriage, some readers fear that the kingdom will be devoid of the most intimate love. I think, rather, that the new heavens and new earth will be filled with an exponential increase of love. That love will reflect earthly marriage as the wheat reflects the seed. It will be a family love, under our heavenly Father, and with a vast assembly of brothers, sisters, and mothers. It is to this family that God summons us in the Gospel of his grace.

So when we proclaim the benefits of the Christian family in modern secular society, we should present these as a foreshadowing of its fulfillment. It is wonderfully good news that the Son of God gave his life on the cross to secure his children (Hebrews 2:13-14), both for now and for eternity. In our contemporary conflict, we are not fighting only for the freedom to teach as we will, though that is important; we are fighting for the eternal family of God and calling people to join us as members of that precious body of Christ.

Questions for Discussion and Reflection

Individual | Class | Small Group

1. Marxism vs. Biblical Family Structure: In the context of Marxist ideology's view of the nuclear family as an extension of capitalistic systems, how does this stance starkly contrast with the biblical portrayal of the family as an institution ordained by God? Discuss the broader societal and individual implications of these divergent perspectives.

2. Family's Role in Gospel Witness: Based on Frame's comprehensive analysis, how does he perceive the role of the family in effectively witnessing the Gospel in a secular age? Reflect on the interplay between family dynamics and evangelism in today's society.

3. Impact of Family Structure on Child Development: Consider the empirical evidence from Wayne Parker and others on the ramifications of family disintegration on children's physical, emotional, and academic health. How does this information corroborate or challenge the Christian conviction regarding the nuclear family's significance?

4. Rearing Children Amidst Secular Opposition: In a society where institutions may regard core Christian teachings, such as those in Ephesians 5, as outdated or harmful, how should believers navigate the upbringing of their children? Discuss strategies and challenges in maintaining Christian values in child rearing against secular ideologies.

5. Government vs. Family in Child Rearing: Analyze the proposition of the state playing a primary role in raising children, as advocated by Marxist and other secular philosophies. Assess the potential advantages

and pitfalls of this approach, especially considering the biblical teachings on family and parental duties.

6. Christian Response to Secular Family Models: Reflect on the Christian community's responsibility to advocate for the biblical family model in a secular era. What concrete actions can Christians undertake to preserve and promote the sanctity of the family within their circles and in wider societal discourse?

What the Bible Says about Transgenderism
And How to Avoid Personal and Societal Destruction

Michael A. Milton

> The real pathology is not so much a moral decline, which is a symptom, not a primary phenomenon, but rather an ontological impoverishment; that is, a severe limitation or crippling of the very life of 20th-century man. — Walker Percy, "Science, Language, Literature," *Signposts in a Strange Land*[1]

Humankind's potential for self-destruction through the lusts of the flesh appears to be limitless. While there is nothing new in the sensual sins and wanton debauchery that we witness in our culture, technology has undoubtedly advanced its influence. And one such sin is being promoted in a fanatical fashion: transgenderism.

What Is Transgenderism?

The subject of transgenderism includes, specifically, "Trans-sexuality, cross-dressing," and seeking "gender identity development," i.e., physical identity through radical surgeries and hormone treatment; and, more broadly, "gender atypicality" that includes "myriad subcultural expressions of self-selecting gender," and "intersectionality" with other "interdependence" movements, i.e., feminism, homosexuality.1 The idea of transgenderism has its roots in the primordial rebellion of humankind to the creation order of God.

Ancient pagan rituals would have included some aspects of transgender practice. More currently, social anarchists such as the otherwise brilliant French social critic, Michael Foucault, argued that Christianity, in particular, has leveraged its cultural "powers" (a recurring them with Foucault) to repress human sexual expression. Foucault taught that gender is a social construct, not a biological fact. The absurdity of such thinking was largely unchallenged in the 1960s and 70s when Foucault and others were teaching such dogma in prestigious universities in Canada, France, and the United States.

Perhaps, we felt that it was too ludicrous to engage. Recently, in 2019, when a former United States Vice-President was asked how many genders there were, he responded, "At least three." Such a frighteningly fallacious response by a person of influence constitutes an unmitigated endorsement of Foucault's radical deconstruction of reality. For someone to affirm, with a straight face, in serious dialogue, "There are at least three genders" is an Orwellian case study in, "doublethink," "newspeak," and the "thought police" writ large. To speak seriously about a gender other than male and female is surely the untenable subordinating to the inconceivable.

The Medical Truth about Gender Dysphoria

At one time it would have been unnecessary, but it, now, has to be said: The American College of Pediatricians should be awarded a courage award for stating the obvious:

> "Human sexuality is an objective biological binary trait: "XY" and "XX" are genetic markers of male and female, respectively – not genetic markers of a disorder. The norm for human design is to be conceived either male or female. Human sexuality is binary by design with the

obvious purpose being the reproduction and flourishing of our species. This principle is self-evident."

To those who suffer from "gender dysphoria" (the new diagnostic language in DSM-5 replacing "Gender Identity Disorder" in DSM-IV-TR), feeling trapped in a person of the opposite sex, the prestigious association responds with merciful scientific clarity:

> "No one is born with an awareness of themselves as male or female; this awareness develops over time and, like all developmental processes, may be derailed by a child's subjective perceptions, relationships, and adverse experiences from infancy forward. People who identify as "feeling like the opposite sex" or "somewhere in between" do not comprise a third sex. They remain biological men or biological women."

Then, how do otherwise smart people fall for the newspeak of Michael Foucault and Kimberlé Crenshaw, and, increasingly, advocate for public school textbooks that endorse transgenderism? How is it that parents in Long Beach, California, who oppose transvestite "drag queens" (invited by former First Lady, Michelle Obama) reading to their kindergartners, are considered "haters?" And that leads us to the Scripture that describes this incredible cultural transformation.

The Biblical Truth about Gender

Sexual sins, including transgenderism, were among the most heinous practices of the people living in Canaan. The lessons of their judgment because of deviant sexual practices remain as ominous warning signs to us today. When we prefer unbelief to faith in God, in order to advance the lusts of our flesh, we inevitably, and often irretrievably, destine ourselves for judgment. In the cases before us, the people groups living in Canaan digressed from what is clearly shown in creation and in God's Word—that we are born as either male or female, and that our God-given human sexuality is divinely sanctioned, and most beautifully expressed as complimentary (man and woman), and within the covenanted bonds of matrimony (husband and wife)—led to a veritable infestation of the land, which "vomited" the people from the land, and led to judicial hardening of their hearts, and their ultimate destruction.

1. Male and Female He Created Them

God has not left us without His Word and, thus, His will concerning sexuality. Firstly, humankind is binary. There is no third or fourth category of a human being. Nature attests to what Scripture reveals. Human beings are made in God's image and created either male or female.

> "Male and female he created them, and he blessed them and named them Man when they were created" (Genesis 5:2).

Our Savior, Christ Jesus, by whom the world was created and through whom it is sustained, appealed to His own Word in Genesis to affirm the divinely created order, and the sanctity of marriage (Colossians 1:16).

> "He answered, 'Have you not read that he who created them from the beginning made them male and female, and said, Therefore a man shall leave his father and his mother and hold fast to his wife, and the two shall become one flesh? So they are no longer two but one flesh. What therefore God has joined together, let not man separate" (Matthew 19:4-6).

The Scriptures not only provide creation background for what we see plainly in biology, but the texts also show us that God's creation was —and is— good. Male and female are perfectly complementary in biology, physiology, emotion, and spirit. Humanity finds its fullest expression in the unity of people being made one in marriage, a sacred and inviolable covenant instituted by Almighty God. Thus, it is not enough for us to merely point out the evil and, therefore, the consequent tragedy of sexual sin. We must also be diligent to lift up the beauty and blessings that flow from the created order of a loving God.

2. Sexual Sin as Abomination

Secondly, although the text I would cite is concerned with God's command forbidding same-sex relationships, one could deploy the transgender movement's "intersectionality" instrument to include the passage in our study. Nevertheless, the prohibition against same-sex relations is indicative of God's abhorrence of such wickedness: "You shall not lie with a male as with a woman; it is an abomination" (Leviticus 18:22).

3. Cross-Dressing Forbidden

Transgenderism is explicitly addressed in the Bible. This fact reminds us that the phenomenon of trans-sexual expression is not new. The practice is a deviant display of witness rebellion against the created order of God. For those, like Foucault, who saw gender as merely social constructs, enforced by puritanical power structures and subject to deconstruction, the voice of God in the Bible still speaks:

> "A woman shall not wear a man's garment, nor shall a man put on a woman's cloak, for whoever does these things is an abomination to the Lord your God" (Deuteronomy 22:5).

4. Living in the Land of Unbelief

Thirdly, believers should walk carefully in this present, evil "Secular Age," as the imminent Canadian philosopher, Dr. Charles Taylor, has described our post-Christian culture. What did the Lord say to Cain?

> "If you do well, will you not be accepted? And if you do not do well, sin is crouching at the door. Its desire is for you, but you must rule over it" (Genesis 4:7).

Every believer must be alert to the dangerous presence of anti-Christian powers, and demonic spirits of this world, using unrepentant sinners who are beating at the door of our consciences to demand that we accept and approve of what God forbids. God called Israel to be conscious of the seducing powers of the Canaanites, whose wickedness in sexual sins led to divine judgment:

> "For everyone who does any of these abominations, the persons who do them shall be cut off from among their people. So keep my charge never to practice any of these abominable customs that were practiced before you, and never to make yourselves unclean by them: I am the Lord your God" (Leviticus 18:29-30).

Male prostitutes were marked out by God as those whose wickedness brought judgment: "And there were also male cult prostitutes in the land. They did according to all the abominations of the nations that the Lord drove out before the people of Israel" (1 Kings 14:24).

We would do well to mark the comments of the old pastor-scholar John Gill (1697-1771) instructing Christians who live in "this present evil age" (Galatians 1:4):

> "Now Christ gave himself a sacrifice for the sins of his people, that as in consequence of this they might be delivered and saved from the damning power, so from the governing power and influence of all that is evil in this present world; as from Satan, the god of it, who has usurped a power over it; from the lusts that are predominant in it; from the vain conversation of the men of it; from the general conflagration of it at the last day, and from the perdition of ungodly men, and their eternal destruction in hell."[2]

Romans 1 and Transgenderism

It is difficult to imagine a contemporary social movement that is more dangerously consistent with the downward spiral of Romans chapter one than transgenderism. Read these words from St. Paul and ask yourself if we are not living in the times that he describes:

> "For the wrath of God is revealed from heaven against all ungodliness and unrighteousness of men, who by their unrighteousness suppress

the truth. For what can be known about God is plain to them, because God has shown it to them. For his invisible attributes, namely, his eternal power and divine nature, have been clearly perceived, ever since the creation of the world, in the things that have been made. So they are without excuse. For although they knew God, they did not honor him as God or give thanks to him, but they became futile in their thinking, and their foolish hearts were darkened. Claiming to be wise, they became fools" (Romans 1:18-22);

"For this reason God gave them up to dishonorable passions. For their women exchanged natural relations for those that are contrary to nature; and the men likewise gave up natural relations with women and were consumed with passion for one another, men committing shameless acts with men and receiving in themselves the due penalty for their error. And since they did not see fit to acknowledge God, God gave them up to a debased mind to do what ought not to be done" (26-28).

"Though they know God's righteous decree that those who practice such things deserve to die, they not only do them but give approval to those who practice them" (Romans 1:32).

In Romans 1:18-32, the Apostle Paul describes unbelieving man's descent into a hell of his own making. Unbelief in the presence of the undeniable coupled with intellectual and spiritual anarchy devolves into not only the normalization of the irredeemable but the codification of the indefensible. Reading Romans Chapter One is like living through the last twenty years. For as Dr. D. James Kennedy once said, "When your code cracks, your creed crumbles." One is only amazed at the rapid rate of decline.

What's the Big Deal about Sexual Sin?

The truth is undeniable: God abhors sexual sins because it strikes at the image of God in Man. Sexual sin, including transgenderism, explicit and exemplarily condemned in the Word of God, degrades human beings. Our women and children will always suffer the most if we allow such corruption to continue without divine intervention. So, the Lord speaks to us today:

> "Flee from sexual immorality. Every other sin a person commits is outside the body, but the sexually immoral person sins against his own body. Or do you not know that your body is a temple of the Holy Spirit within you, whom you have from God? You are not your own, for you were bought with a price. So glorify God in your body" (1 Corinthians 6:18-20).

The gospel is a perennial word of hope. We do not have to fall into these sins. Paul wrote,

> "I appeal to you therefore, brothers, by the mercies of God, to present your bodies as a living sacrifice, holy and acceptable to God, which is your spiritual worship. Do not be conformed to this world, but be transformed by the renewal of your mind, that by testing you may discern what is the will of God, what is good and acceptable and perfect" (Romans 12:1-2).

Transgenderism is a sad symptom of a soul in torment. The sin is an especially virulent pathology of the human soul. And the disease is spread by normalizing the forbidden, trivializing its lethality to the soul and to the community; and by naïvely promoting its supposed gaiety. Behind the laughing drag queen, however, is always a tragic and dying soul in need of Jesus Christ's love.

If, in fact, you or your loved ones have been infected by the strong spirit-killing viruses of this agent of our present evil age, then, you must know: you can be healed. Life and love may be pure and holy before God. You can be fully human. Gospel transformation is not just available but is inevitable when one confesses his sin, turns to the Lord Jesus Christ to receive His mercy, grace, and receives His cleansing power of the cross: His life lived will cover yours. His death offered as a substitute for the punishment of our sins brings you redemption from the devices of the devil and the fetters of the flesh. St. Paul wrote to the Corinthians, a notoriously noxious group of sinners, who had been caught in every vile trick of the devil, especially in sexual sin. Paul's words are most instructive for our study:

> "Do you not know that the unrighteous will not inherit the kingdom of God? Do not be deceived. Neither fornicators, nor idolaters, nor adulterers, nor homosexuals, nor sodomites, nor thieves, nor covetous, nor drunkards, nor revilers, nor extortioners will inherit the kingdom of God. And such were some of you. But you were washed, but you were sanctified, but you were justified in the name of the Lord Jesus and by the Spirit of our God" (1 Corinthians 6:9-11).

Did you read that? "And such were some of you" (emphasis added). Our Lord welcomes you into the company of the redeemed. The sin that so easily besets you today will become the chains lying on the floor of that old cell where you used to exist. But, praise God, you are not what you were. You are not what you will be. You are who you are: a sinner saved by grace, a child of God, loved by Him, redeemed by Him and destined for a life you only imagined.

Questions for Discussion and Reflection
Individual | Class | Small Group

1. Ontological Impoverishment and Moral Decline: Reflect on Walker Percy's assertion that the core issue of modern man is not moral decline, but an "ontological impoverishment." How does this concept challenge or reinforce your understanding of the spiritual state of contemporary society, especially in the context of rampant transgenderism and other sensual sins?

2. Transgenderism and Theological Anthropology: In light of the chapter's discussion on transgenderism, how should Christians understand and respond to this phenomenon from a theological anthropology perspective, considering it as a manifestation of the primordial rebellion against God's creation order?

3. Scriptural Response to Gender Dysphoria: With the growing societal acceptance of transgenderism, how can Christians faithfully interpret and apply scriptural teachings on gender and sexuality to provide a compassionate, yet truthful response to those experiencing gender dysphoria?

4. Sexual Sins in Biblical Perspective: Analyze the biblical portrayal of sexual sins, including transgenderism, as abominations and their consequences for individuals and societies. How does this perspective inform our response to these issues in pastoral care and gospel witness?

5. Christian Living in a Secular Age: Considering Charles Taylor's concept of the "Secular Age," how should believers navigate their faith

and daily living amidst societal pressures that often oppose Christian values, especially regarding sexual ethics and gender identity?

6. Gospel Hope for Sexual Brokenness: Discuss the transformative power of the gospel in addressing the deep-seated issues of sexual sin and identity crises, as illustrated in the chapter. How can the church effectively minister to individuals struggling with these issues, offering both truth and grace?

True Oikonomia
A Christian Mind for Economics
John Panagiotou

> Some Christians may be tempted to assume that economics is a discipline autonomous from theology. —William T Cavanaugh, *Being Consumed: Economics and Christian Desire* (2008), vii.

True oikonomia (stewardship) in its essential meaning, has nothing to do with money. It has everything to do with one's disposition and phronema (mindset). It is expressed in prayer, worship, and sacrificial giving of time, talents, and financial resources.

I can remember when, after I first left full-time active pastoral ministry to pursue a career in the wealth management business, one of my former parishioners, who is a university computer science professor, said to me, "Why do you want to be involved with the world of finance because it is so tawdry? You should go and teach." The latter part of his teaching advice is near and dear to my heart. Yet, the former part of his reaction to the "tawdry business" of economics led me to realize even more how greatly misunderstood the concept of money is in the contemporary Church.

"For where your treasure is, there your heart will be also" (Matthew 6:21). Jesus' words are simple yet profound. The Scriptures have no less than 2,350 verses concerning money and wealth management. Jesus speaks more about money and its use than any other topic, including heaven, hell, salvation, etc. The topic is crucial for the Christian life. In an often-misquoted verse, St. Paul the Apostle writes, "The love of money is a root of all kinds of evils" (1 Timothy 6:10). St. Paul teaches that our Lord realizes that we have needs to meet so that we can live and carry out His work. God is, however, a jealous God and demands our total commitment, with nothing else taking precedence over His Lordship in our lives. That is why the Apostle Paul warns his first-century Greek congregation that the love of money in and of itself is evil.[1]

With this Biblical basis established, we are left with the more specific question: what particular theology resonates with the Christian today in this time in history that has seen the realm of economics being co-opted by the secular world almost entirely? How does that manifest and shape the Christian's everyday life? This brief essay will tackle these questions and offer a cogent approach.

To help us better understand where we are today, I will summarize the origins of how we got here.

The Biblical and Patristic Beginnings of a Theology of Economics

In the Old Testament, we find a centuries-old developed complex system of tithing which evolved into something very formal and legalistic by the time of Jesus. As I have written on the topic in my book on Christian stewardship:

> From the Scriptures and the ancient history of Judaism, it is commonly understood that the theological purpose, development, and meaning of the tithe were basically three-fold.[2]
>
> First, it is an acknowledgment of the fact that everything belongs to God. It is only by Divine gifting that mankind is given the opportunity

to be stewards of His creation. This can be found in the Psalms where we read, "the earth is the Lord's and the fullness thereof" (24:1) and "for every beast of the forest is mine, the cattle on a thousand hills" (50:10). Second, with this acknowledgment of Divine ownership of all things, God's people are called to give thanks for all that He has given us. Hence, the tithe is an expression of thanksgiving (Genesis 29:20-22). Finally, as we have seen in the references to Josephus, it serves a practical purpose in the subsidization and maintenance of the Levitical priesthood and the cultic life of ancient Judaism.[3]

As I mentioned earlier in this essay, the management of money and material things was a topic that Jesus spoke directly about on many occasions. The Apostle Paul also spoke directly to the topic, particularly to giving for the good of fellow believers. As I have researched the matter, I have come to the following conclusions about what the Biblical texts have to say about economic theology:

> In comparison, the New Testament believer gives out of the same motivation that the Old Testament Israelite did with the understanding that we are ultimately in the Hands of God and that all things belong to Him. We are just stewards of these things. In contrast, the Old Testament came to develop the requisite one-tenth tithe of one's annual income to give towards sacerdotal and cultic purposes. Thus, in the New Testament we are called to be joyous and thankful in our giving to God. This is done without a compulsory specified percentage amount. It is totally a free will offering motivated out of one's love, gratitude, and loyalty to God.[4]

Writing in the fourth century, St. John Chrysostom's central theme throughout his book, *On Wealth and Poverty*, is that a Christian owns nothing because God owns everything.[5] That is exactly the starting point that we should have today when confronted by the secularists in the world and even in the Church. Without this basic understanding, the danger of idolatry is always present in the absence of a phronema of oikonomia. Jesus and the Apostle Paul are very clear about these things in the Scriptures. For them, there is no dichotomy between the sacred and the secular.

The two are integrated into an essential fabric of identity and being in the life of the believer. This is precisely what Jesus was saying in one of His condemnations of the Jewish religious professionals of His day, the priests and the Pharisees, with the hypocrisy of their religious lives and how they lived in their everyday lives. As Arthur McKay points out, "Too many of us suppose that stewardship is primarily, even exclusively, concerned with the giving and spending of money or other material possessions."[6] Stewardship is not only about money, it is about lifestyle. True stewardship knows no disconnect between what we do on Sunday morning in worship and who we are on Monday morning at home, workplace, or school. As a result, no theology of economics can be approached in our age or any age without the context being one of stewardship.

With this Biblical basis of the mindset of stewardship as our compass, a further study of the evolution of the understanding of economics within the Christian world and how it impacts today's worldview in both the secular and the sacred of Western culture can be found in the early modern period in the life and work of the influential Reformer John Calvin.

Calvin's Views on Economic Theory

In the fifteen hundred years from the time of Pentecost to the Reformation, many Christian thinkers and writers have contemplated the words of Jesus. Beginning with the Apostles themselves and their successors such as Ignatius of Antioch, Polycarp of Smyrna, Clement of Rome, Irenaeus of Lyons, Justin Martyr the Philosopher, John Chrysostom, Basil the Great, Gregory the Theologian, Gregory of Nyssa, and the list goes on. Most if not all of these ancient Christian saints, have in one way or another addressed the matter of economics and the Christian by saying the former is not to dominate or be the obsession of the latter. Indicative of the spirit and mindset of Christian temperance in not letting money and possessions dominate one's life and its use it in promoting love for one's neighbor, St. Basil the Great would write:

If you would stop seeking earthly status, you should then find the true resplendent kind that would conduct you into the Kingdom of Heaven. But what you love is simply to possess wealth, even if you derive no help from it. Now everyone knows that an obsession for useless things is mindless. Just so, what I am going to say should seem to you no greater paradox; and it is utterly, absolutely true. When wealth is dispersed, in the way the Lord advises, it naturally stays put; but when held back it is transferred to another. If you hoard it, you won't keep it; if you scatter, you won't lose.[7]

John Calvin was a student of Patristics.[8] One of the authors he quotes most often in his writings, after the Apostle Paul and Blessed Augustine of Hippo, is the work of St. John Chrysostom.[9] Calvin expresses his deep admiration for Chrysostom as Biblical exegete when he writes, "The chief merit of our Chrysostom is this: he took great pains everywhere not to deviate in the slightest from the genuine plain meaning of Scripture, and not to indulge in any license of twisting the straightforward sense of the words."[10] From this foundation, Calvin developed his own theological view of economics.[11] It is no wonder that there is a resurgence amongst Reformed and Evangelical churches in Patristic studies.[12] As Curran D. Bishop notes, "The nature of Calvin's use of Patristic sources changed little throughout his career; in the various editions of the *Institutes*, the changes represent expansions in terms of quantity and familiarity rather than in character."[13]

Calvin's worldview, significantly influenced by the foundational elements of the Bible and the Church Fathers, formed the basis upon which he expanded and evolved these concepts. This development had a profound impact not only on Western Christianity but also on the secular cultures of Western Europe and North America.

Within Western Christianity, disgruntled Roman Catholics were seeking a different path from the corruption and decadence they saw in the medieval Roman Church. Hence, through various disparate circumstances, individuals such as Martin Luther and John Calvin emerged to lead the Reformation.

These events would not only be a religious revolution and renaissance in Western Europe but also usher in a different view of economic theory. Calvin's influence can be found in three key components of thought regarding economics: usury, capital generation, and stewardship. Briefly, let us explore each of these.

The first example of this can be seen in the area of financial money lending, which has come to be seen over the centuries as un-Christian, and thus, the Church placed its members restrictions on their engagement in that industry. As Nathan Dorn explains:

> Traditionally, the Catholic Church forbade Christians to lend money to other Christians at interest, basing its prohibition on the Vulgate's translation of Luke 6:35...The Third Lateran Council of 1179 enacted a proposal of Pope Alexander III to make all those who violated this prohibition subject to excommunication. This situation made it difficult for people to raise capital, and since the need for capital was persistent, many Christians were open to finding ways to work around the prohibition. One solution was to allow non-Catholics to practice moneylending. This seemed viable, because canon law did not ostensibly apply to non-Catholics and non-Catholics were in any case not subject to ecclesiastical punishments. Along these lines, many princes throughout Europe adopted the habit of playing host to Jewish communities so that the local Jews could practice moneylending to the benefit of local trade, industry and war-making without the threat of papal excommunication hanging over the Jews or more importantly over the prince who made use of them.[14]

It is in this economic milieu and backdrop that Calvin is born. Calvin strongly believed in the Providence of God in all matters, including one's financial situation. Calvin is such an influential figure at a pivotal time in European history that his impact on this matter cannot be understated. By Calvin methodically expounding on why Christians could do moneylending, it opened up broader avenues of capitalization, employment, and prosperity opportunities which were not be being seen in the predominantly agrarian society in which he lived.[15]

As Thomas Purifoy, Jr. observes:

The economics of Calvin moved Christian thinking about markets in the right direction. He attacked the medieval usury doctrine, which contained broad (though inconsistently enforced) prohibitions against interest. Calvin argued that interest was legitimate except in the case of lending to the poor, but (inconsistently) also said that a person should not be a professional moneylender...Overall, Calvin's thinking on usury and interest helped the medieval world escape another un-Biblical restriction...the economic policies we regard today as supportive of 'free markets' or 'classical liberalism' have some of their ancestry in Calvin and his followers.[16]

The second example of Calvinistic economic thought can be found in capital generation brought about through honest work and investment. Simply stated, this would be expressed in the theological idea that God has blessed the individual with certain talents and abilities that can be used for His glory and the greater good. The fruits of which could be seen in the accumulation of wealth. Calvin would write about this:

> We should accept the gain that comes to us as coming from God's hand, not using evil means to take away another's goods, but serving our neighbors in good conscience; that we should enjoy the profit of our labor in good conscience; that we should enjoy the profit of our labor as a just salary; that in buying and selling we should not employ fraud, deceitful tricks, or lies, but we should go briskly about our business with honesty, in the same way that we require it of others.[17]

Calvin's emphasis on hard work as a generator of prosperity and this prosperity having its origin in God. This definitely was a catalyst for growth in Western Europe. Still, it would see its even greater fruition in the New World in America when colonists built upon the opportunities they would find there. It was this idea, which was developed by Calvin, that sociologist Max Weber would credit as creating the notion of the "Protestant work ethic" that was the bedrock of societal economic prosperity that sprang from the womb of the Reformation.[18]

The third aspect that Calvin presents to economic thinking is the concept of stewardship. Calvin writes, "by using it moderately he should employ the property that has been given to him in order to help and to provide for his neighbors, seeing himself as God's steward who possesses the goods he has on condition that he must one day render an account."[19] With this, Calvin echoes the Patristic teaching on the matter. Wealth is not to be hoarded but to be shared in generosity for the glory of God and the benefit of others.

The Patristic View as Developed by Calvin as a Model

Calvin's reintroduction of the Patristic idea of wealth and its role in the life of society cannot be understated.[20] He not only did this for the Christian community, but also the broader secular society as well. Purifoy aptly states,

> "Calvin's work has had such a powerful impact on how we live in the freer countries of the world that we should become a little more familiar with what he said about business, economics, and politics.. Calvin's work argued that Christians were perfectly free to engage in 'secular' occupations so that Christian merchants and industrialists need not be regarded as second-class citizens. This was a break from the generally-held medieval perception that commercial activity – particularly moneylending – was suspicious and even immoral."[21]

This re-engagement with commercial economics by Calvin had provided a two-edged sword in the areas of greed and avarice amongst Christians in his day and this he was much aware. Purifoy notes:

> "Calvin recognized the tendency toward graft in the businessmen of his day (at one point, he referred to them as 'robbers'). Nevertheless, he accepted commerce as a beneficial human activity."[22]

In today's secular world, we see this at times unbridled with no presence of the concern and vision that the Church Fathers and Calvin had. The Christian ideal is that capitalistic economics is fine with the understanding that it should be done honestly to give God the glory and for the betterment of God's creation. It is to advance the mission of the Kingdom. It is not an end in itself. That is the problem that one witnesses today. Economics and the pursuit of monetary gain have become idols and an end unto themselves. The Church Fathers, earlier, and Calvin, later, taught economics and wealth-building as a means to the end of advancing the Kingdom of God.

Peter Feuerherd makes the distinction clearly when he writes:

> Both the blame and the credit for capitalism has often been placed at the feet of a 16th-century Christian theologian named John Calvin . . . Though Max Weber gave Calvin credit for sanctifying the Protestant work ethic, he never accepted capitalism unconditionally. Whether seen as an unapologetic capitalist or reformer, Calvin provides a clear example that religious thought permeates beyond church walls, impacting the world of believers and non-believers.[23]

For Calvin, as he learned from reading Patristic writings, it was only within the context of a proper *phronema* of true *oikonomia* that proper economic theory could exist. Otherwise, humanity did and will continue to corrupt it with lawless ruthlessness. Calvin writes, "When a person has the means to increase his wealth, let this be done without doing an injury to others."[24]

As we have seen in this essay, a theology of economics in the Judaeo-Christian tradition begins in the Old Testament and continues into the New Testament. This would be further developed and expounded upon during the Patristic era. The foundation of Christianity's view of money and material possessions is tempered through the lens of *oikonomia* (stewardship) of what God has given the believer because God owns it all; Christians are just managers who have been entrusted with its care.

John Calvin's monumental contribution to the Christian worldview of the theology of economics can be found in his writings, which helped to reintroduce to the Church the practical Patristic ideas on the subject which lay dormant for several hundreds of years. He helped launch a prosperity revolution of capitalistic endeavor that the world had not seen prior and still continues.

Without a proper understanding of stewardship, the individual risks becoming tempted by greed, avarice, and idolatry. God owns everything. Human beings have been entrusted as stewards of God's creation. The secular age distorts and diverts the role of economics from its original mission as being a vehicle of kingdom-building for the glory of God.

Questions for Discussion and Reflection

Individual | Class | Small Group

1. The integration of Economics and Theology is a crucial topic. Considering William T. Cavanaugh's perspective, how should Christians reconcile with the apparent autonomy of economics from theology? Moreover, it is essential to discuss the importance of integrating theological perspectives with economic understanding in today's secular age.

2. John Panagiotou highlights that true stewardship (oikonomia) goes beyond monetary aspects and is deeply rooted in one's mindset and disposition. This broader understanding of stewardship challenges the typical Christian approach to managing resources, especially in a culture that often equates stewardship merely with financial management.

3. The role of money and wealth is a significant biblical focus, as highlighted by numerous verses and Jesus' teachings. It is essential to reflect on how this extensive biblical focus on financial matters should shape the Christian approach to wealth management and its use in everyday life.

4. In today's era, economics is almost entirely dominated by secular thinking. Therefore, it is crucial to explore the specific theological approach or perspective that resonates with Christians today. This has a significant impact on the everyday life of a believer in terms of managing finances and material resources.

5. John Calvin's views on economic theory have contributed significantly to the Christian and secular realms. Calvin's teachings on

usury, capital generation, and stewardship continue to shape modern financial practices and Christian attitudes toward wealth.

6. Given the tendency of today's economy to idolize wealth and view economic success as an end in itself, it is challenging for Christians to maintain a healthy perspective on stewardship. It is essential to explore ways in which believers can engage in capitalistic societies while upholding kingdom-building principles and glorifying God through their economic activities.

Part III
NATIONAL LIFE

Open Borders or Open Hearts?
Are Boundaries Morally Good?
Peter A. Lillback

> Open borders are now becoming institutionalized as a universal right of all humans to immigrate to anywhere they choose. In other words, we are reverting to the world of the pre-citizen and two pre-nation mindset of normalizing migrations in the West, with values and assumptions more similar to those of the seventeenth century than the twenty-first
>
> –Victor Davis Hanson, *The Dying Citizen*[1]

Immigrants (legal or illegal, documented or undocumented) are a national concern. Whether we call them migrants, illegals, strangers, sojourners, pilgrims, foreigners, exiles, refugees, asylum seekers, or aliens, they flood our news and our borders.[2] And the debates they stir are not just between so-called conservatives and the mainstream media. Even former President Obama's recent remarks on immigration policy were censored by ABC.[3]

1. Competing Perspectives

Ironically, shibboleths demarcate an unseen ideological boundary separating adherents of open borders[4] and those who support a rigorous control of national boundaries.[5] One side insists on visas, passports, and the priority of citizenship. To such, the waves of immigrants crossing the southern borders are not caravans but invasion forces. The other side of this contested chasm celebrates the heroism and risky sacrifices of asylum seekers, the compassion of open borders, and the pro-life humanitarian concern for endangered and vulnerable refugees.

Christians on both sides of the debate affirm that these immigrants pressing to enter the United States are image bearers of God and afford an extraordinary opportunity for gospel witness, medical care and humanitarian compassion.[6] Those who have experienced the struggles of immigration and exile have found the biblical genre of exilic and post-exilic literature especially relevant.[7] The venerable traditions of Catholic social thought have also been strained by the exigencies of immigration perplexities as evident in the response of the American Bishops to papal pronouncements.[8] Marxist-influenced hermeneutics also shape biblical texts proffered to support the plight of migrant workers.[9] Recognizing the weighty concerns raised by both sides of this debate attempts at a "third way" are offered.[10]

1. The American Historical Context of Immigration

While the issues of immigration are global concerns, they are particularly pertinent to the United States given our nation's history and unique advantages. The history of immigration in America has moved over time from white-only immigration to essentially global immigration. Driving concerns have been cultural stability, workforce considerations, ability to accommodate, acculturate and assimilate new arrivals as well as the protection of national security. The original Nationality Act of 1790 limited citizenship by naturalization to "free white persons." Starting in 1892, Ellis Island[11] was the primary inspection point of immigrants where the decision to grant entrance or require a return to the point of emigration was determined for millions. The initial immigration policy was ended by the National Origins Formula of immigration begun in 1921 and in force until 1965. This legislation, however, restricted immigration from the Eastern Hemisphere. That Act had the effect of preventing East and South Asians from immigrating and substantially restricted African immigration. While clearly favoring European immigration, it did not limit immigration from North or South America. The Immigration and Nationality Act of 1965, also termed the Hart-Celler Act, ended the National Origins Formula of immigration. The 1965 Act substantially facilitated the migrant worker pipeline of immigration by favoring familial and ethnic relationships, which has come to be known as chain migration. Comprehensive immigration reform legislation has been proposed but remains unachieved by recently divided Congresses.[12]

Perhaps the political volatility of the immigration issue coupled with the alluring potentials of future voters and near-term inexpensive laborers have silenced the political elite on both sides of American politics. Liberals have been accused of furthering illegal immigration to swell voters for their socialistic agendas. Conservatives are accused of turning a blind eye to immigration abuses from a desire for cheap and potentially untaxed migrant labor. Marxist educators decry the perceived impact of capitalism on migrants and their families.[13]

Recent American history, as exemplified by the Biden administration, has allegedly practiced a minimalist control of the southern border in what many have viewed in stark contrast to the Trump administration's efforts to enforce strict policing of the border and to tighten control of international immigration. It has been argued that the suffering at the border has created not only opportunities for human exploitation but political and ideological exploitation as well. John Aman seeks to document how the compassion of Evangelical Church leaders is being exploited for the agenda of the socialist open borders financier George Soros.[14]

The questions are difficult. Is the advocacy for the immigrant a socialistic imposition or humanitarian idealism? Are the so-called sojourners, wayfaring strangers, and pilgrims really a vast trojan horse, the external cover for implanted enemies, terrorist cells, criminal cartels, as well as pawns for sexual abuse and smuggling of deadly drugs? Is the 1965 legislation that accelerated chain migration, coupled with the unchecked entrance of migrants, a dangerous flaw that will eventually destroy the country? Should Christians welcome the immigrants or pray imprecations against the political forces that have organized their seeming assault on our nation's boundaries? Or perhaps both?

Arguments enjoined for a generous posture toward migrants point Christians to Biblical teachings such as Israel's duty to protect the stranger, the widow, and the orphan.[15] Doesn't the New Testament teach the welcoming of strangers, since hospitality can unwittingly be rendered to angels (Hebrews 13:2)? Should not the social conscience of the Christian be deeply stirred to care for "the least of Christ's brethren" as taught by the Lord in His parable of the sheep and the goats and that doing so as unto Christ has relevance for one's ultimate destiny (Matthew 25:31-46)? Surely, every believer must recognize the significance of the fact that the infant Jesus, his mother Mary, and Joseph were refugees in Egypt (Matthew 2:13-15; 19-23).

Proponents of a strong national border are not persuaded. These biblical truths, they assert, do not cancel other Scriptural concerns such as the biblical warrant of governmental authority and the necessity of legitimate order as seen in Romans 13:1-7 and 1 Peter 2:11-17.[16] Their concerns are captured in questions such as: Doesn't the government have a prior duty to protect its own citizens and their families? Doesn't Paul insist that Christians should seek to do all things decently and in good order (1 Corinthians 14:40)? Don't catch and release policies of illegal immigrants at the border facilitate criminality such as sexual exploitation and smuggling of deadly narcotics? Does not uncontrolled immigration exacerbate the spread of diseases like COVID and tuberculosis? Further, should we not be concerned about unchecked criminal activity, and enemy subversives, who exploit the movements and exigencies of immigrants to cover their penetration of the United States' long open borders to weaken national security and ultimately destroy the nation?[17] As a practical matter, shouldn't there first be careful planning for the quantity and manner of caring for immigrants and refugees given the stress already weighing heavily on the indebted national economy? Don't concerns for these matters also reflect the teaching of Christ by a holistic application of the Two Great Commandments, namely, "to love God" and "to love our neighbors as ourselves"?

Such questions are often left unaddressed and the debate may conclude with a swift retort similar to, "Aren't those just pragmatic mercenary concerns instead of lofty prayerful merciful compassion?"

1. Calvin's Geneva: The Historic Reformed Perspective on Immigration

For those who identify with the Reformation or stand in the Reformed tradition, the experience of Calvin and his leadership in Geneva are significant for the immigration debate. Countless Protestant refugees fled to Calvin's Geneva in his lifetime, doubling its size, due to the persecution of Protestants in France and throughout Europe.[18] After Calvin, many more came from France in the aftermath of the St. Bartholomew's Day Massacre (1572) and the sweeping expulsion of the French Huguenots by the Revocation of the Edict of Nantes (1685). The exile of the Huguenots turned them into global refugees. Calvin's perspective on immigration in Geneva clearly warrants consideration.[19]

Jacob's study of Calvin's Old Testament commentaries regarding the use of the Hebrew word *GER* gives insight into the Genevan reformer's understanding of the refugee or stranger. For Calvin, the "stranger" in Israel was a landless non-Israelite, an alien, often lacking the necessities of life, and so, along with the widow and orphan, was justly worthy of legal protection. Jacob summarizes Calvin's understanding of the *GER*:

> Calvin's Old Testament commentaries clearly and consistently reveal he considered the *GER* to be a non-Israelite, who did not have the opportunity to become an Israelite, although these "strangers" were still to be shown the same generosity as the Israelite widows and orphans received. This is because the condition of these three categories of people is similar: they are a most alienated people, destitute and deprived of material relief, while poverty and hunger are two facts of their daily existence. In placing the *GER* alongside the widow and orphans as parties that need the protection of laws for the sake of social justice, Calvin portrays the *GER* as an economically vulnerable person who is most likely landless.[20]

Calvin viewed himself and his ministry as expressions of this concept of stranger.[21] Moreover, Calvin argued that the Scriptures showed the importance of listening to the wisdom and insights of strangers in their midst.[22]

Calvin's ministry was as a stranger, but also a welcomer of exiles and refugees in Geneva. For Rodriguez, Calvin's ministry rebukes contemporary Calvinists whose "moral and political quietism is a tragic betrayal of a long Calvinist legacy of welcoming strangers, resisting tyrants, establishing justice, and stepping across borders and cultures in vulnerability and faith. It will also discredit the common misconception that John Calvin was a cold and pharisaic stickler for the rule of law. Instead, it will offer a more accurate representation of John Calvin as a humanistic reformer whose ecclesiastical and civil polities sought that "every resident of Geneva be integrated into a caring community."[23]

Indeed, as Rodriguez well notes, Calvin's teaching in the *Institutes* theologically warrants acceptance and extensive care for the refugees. Calvin writes,

> Therefore, we have no reason to refuse any who come before us needing our help. If we say that he is a stranger, the Lord has stamped on him a sign that we know [the image of God].... If we allege that he is contemptible and worthless, the Lord responds by showing us that he has honored him by making his own image to shine in him. If we say that we owe him nothing, the Lord tells us that he has brought him before us so that in him we may see the many benefits that we owe to him. If we say that he is unworthy that we take even a step in his behalf, the image of God which we are to see in him is quite worthy that we give for it all that we are and have. Even when it is someone who not only is worthless, but also has insulted and injured us, this is not reason enough for us to cease loving, pleasing, and serving him.[24]

However, immigration is not a simple matter for the host community, even when there is linguistic and religious homogeneity. Rodriguez paints the tumultuous picture of Calvin's Geneva as largely French-speaking immigrants and French-speaking refugees flooded the French-speaking but independent republic:

... one can appreciate the concerns of the native Genevans. One can even understand their resentment. By mid-century, every single one of their local pastors was foreign born. In claiming their city's independence years earlier, the Genevans had liberated themselves from the local nobility. Now they had to watch as nobles fleeing from France and Italy entered their gates and wielded a disproportionate amount of influence in their economic matters.

Anti-immigrant sentiment reached its peak in 1555 under the leadership of Ami Perrin, who called himself a Genevan patriot. Perrin goaded a street mob to threaten foreign-owned businesses in the city. The mob gathered outside the city council to intimidate the magistrates. John Calvin himself stepped into the fray. He stood amid the angry crowd that was chanting, "Kill the French," and proclaimed: "If you must shed blood, let mine be first." Perrin later sought to oust Calvin by force but was defeated and exiled from the city. Calvin's public victory allowed him to consolidate his authority as pastor and direct his political support to better care for the needs of refugees.[25]

Calvin's insistence on the believer's substantial duty to provide for the refugee is thus not only demanding but potentially chaotic. Ultimately, Calvin's teaching on caring for the refugees proved to be both ironic and tragic. This is manifest in light of two significant accounts of refugees associated with Geneva that had fatal endings. The first is Calvin's problematic role in the case of Miguel Servetus' sojourn in Geneva and the second, the tragic demise of the Huguenot settlement in Brazil.

The well-known account of Servetus will not be developed here. However, it is evident that the theological Trinitarian heretic and fugitive/refugee was not welcomed into orthodox Geneva. Nor would he have been in any European city of the Reformation era. To be clear, human rights in general and the specific rights of conscience were then far from acceptance. Servetus with Calvin's support was arrested and executed for his anti-Trinitarian heresy. Earlier however, the intellectual rights of heretics had been asserted by Calvin. Calvin's clemency regarding Servetus, however, was limited to an appeal to the magistrates for his execution to be by the sword rather than by fire, which the magistrates rejected. Calvin was sharply criticized for his support of the execution of Servetus merely on theological grounds by his erstwhile Genevan subordinate and teacher Sebastian Castellio. Castellio anonymously published a work that highlighted Calvin's change of views regarding the freedom of thought that had occurred only after his assumption of leadership in Geneva.[26] The Servetus affair has ever since been one of Calvin's stigmata that also underscores the difficulty of providing care for the refugee given the often-merciless power of law and solemn duties of magistrates to enforce it. Calvin in this instance found that the complexity of welcoming the refugee, already sufficiently challenging when there was theological harmony, was far more difficult when the cohesion of a common religion or theology was not available.

The second tragic account of refugees in the Genevan context concerns Vice-Admiral Nicolas Durand de Villegagnon and the Huguenot genocide at Fort Coligny in Brazil. This history is related by Rodriguez, although he does not engage its relevance to the concerns of an unquestioning welcoming of strangers.[27] The 1555 Huguenot mission to Brazil, named in honor of Huguenot Admiral Gaspard de Coligny, and led by Villegagnon, an appointee of Coligny, was an early Reformed over-seas missionary venture. It remains a testament to the lethal potential of a hasty and careless approach to immigration.

The history of the mission reveals the difficulties of resettling the swelling Genevan refugees, the perils of colonialism, and the sufferings of religious persecution and betrayal. The Huguenot mission to Brazil culminated in further persecution of the Huguenots and the slaying of several of their preachers—all at the behest of the mission's leader, Villegagnon.

Villegagnon was a recent convert from Catholicism to the Reformed faith. He was appointed to lead the mission to Brazil as a seeming friend and supporter of the Huguenots. Initially, he favorably communicated with Calvin but later changed his attitude toward Calvin and the Huguenots due to the sacramental influence of a Lutheran critic. Ultimately, he reaffirmed his Roman Catholicism and became an opponent of Reformed sacramental practices which led to his order for the expulsion of the Huguenots. Finally, Villegagnon ordered the Huguenots to be hunted down and executed as enemies of the state.[28] In hindsight, it may be that Villegagnon only welcomed the Huguenots while their work ethic facilitated the building of the fort he was commanded to build.

To summarize, a recent convert to the Huguenot faith became an enemy of the Huguenot refugees, forcing them again to become refugees and ultimately martyrs for their faith. Greater caution may have changed Huguenot history. The saga of Villegagnon and the Huguenot refugees at Fort Coligny suggests a pointed lesson concerning immigration. If new converts and seemingly friendly refugees are capable of being secret enemies or becoming overt enemies, should not unknown, untested, and unexamined refugees be carefully vetted even as an open-hearted concern for their well-being is being provided?

The magnanimous spirit of Geneva toward the Reformed refugees was a hallmark of Calvin's City, which also had to endure the complexity of Servetus and the tragedy of Fort Coligny. These accounts offer a context to consider if boundaries can be construed to be morally good.

1. The Union of Biblical Wisdom and Compassion Define Boundaries Morally Good

Limitations are inescapable aspects of life. But national boundaries from an open-border perspective are construed as inherently evil. Its advocates address the moral issues surrounding immigration by focusing on the plight of the poor, the duty of the haves for the have-nots, and the unquestionable right of refugees and migrants to penetrate national boundaries, whether legally or not.[29]

Immigration concerns of a previous era considered health, danger, criminal records, political ideology, and religious values which are often dismissed today. Universal human rights have transmuted into universal access and unquestioned entry into the national borders of another country, particularly the boundaries of the United States.

To begin, let us reiterate that the Old Testament perspective on the stranger, Jesus' teaching concerning the Good Samaritan, and His parable on the separation of the sheep and the goats in the eschatological judgment establish the Christian's duty for special care for the needy, poor, endangered, the alien, the orphan, and the widow. The flight of Mary, Joseph, and the Infant Jesus offers a compelling example to encourage a compassionate response toward refugees.[30]

Hence, the contemporary debate should not be about whether the stranger, the alien, the immigrant, or the stranger should be helped. The Biblical record buttressed by Calvin's Reformed legacy clearly shows this ought to be the case. Rather, the question is whether there exists a moral good in establishing national boundaries. These would be boundaries intended to evaluate the claimants of compassion, control the permeability of borders for health and safety, and facilitate the necessary evaluation of the nation's capacity to provide economic, cultural, spiritual, and strategic resources that bless not only the migrant and refugee but the nation's existing needy. Such needy would include the poor, orphans, widows, aliens, minorities, and the underserved. For an effective mercy ministry, rather than a mercenary attitude toward immigrants, the apostolic injunction with its balance of honoring and ordering, of *doing all things decently and in order* (1 Corinthians 14:40), surely applies here. Moral judgment ought not to be unifocal, but multi-focal.

An aspect of such a multi-focal approach must consider the pressing issues of the immigrants' national origins. The legal and moral issues existing within the borders of the countries of emigres are often disregarded by the open-borders perspective. As a result, the concerns for the refugees and the immigrants become almost exclusively matters of the American border. The concerns driving immigrants from their homelands must be addressed as Schaab affirms, "Therefore, the question of immigration cannot be addressed solely through national legislative reform in the United States. International solutions must be sought for those problems that precipitate the decision to emigrate."[31] The duties of immigrants' home countries should be considered and carefully addressed prior to opening borders. Foreign policy review is a legitimate moral prerequisite for establishing immigration policy.

Several biblical perspectives can be enumerated to support wise boundaries motivated by open hearts, as a superior alternative to open borders. The following provides a framework for compassionate wisdom at national boundaries.

1. **The Duty to Care for the Poor.** The Old Testament affirms care for the impoverished (Leviticus 25:35; Psalm 82:3-4; 140:12; Prov. 22:22-23; 31:8-9; Isaiah 25:4; 58:6-7; Jeremiah 22:16; Ezekiel 16:49), even as it recognizes that there are no utopian solutions to solve poverty (Deuteronomy 15:11). There are blessings, however, for caring for the poor (Deuteronomy 15:10; Prov. 14:21).
2. **Jesus' Realistic Teaching on Caring for the Poor.** Jesus urged generosity to the poor (Matthew 5:42; 19:21; 25:31-46; Luke 3:11; 6:20-21, 38; 12:12-14, 33-34; Isaiah 61:1 with Luke 4:16-21). Yet, the complexity of caring for the poor is recognized by Jesus' teaching. While the poor are precious and should be cared for, they are not the only concern of Christians (Matthew 26:6-13) as He affirms that poverty will not be eradicated in a fallen world (Deuteronomy 15:11).
3. **Jesus Taught that Care for the Poor Can Be Abused for Unjust Gain.** Further, Jesus' ministry also demonstrates that concern for the poor can be used as a ruse for unjust self-enrichment (Matthew 26:6-13; John 12:1-8). Accordingly, Jesus reminded His followers that they must hold those entrusted with funds to a high level of accountability as seen in the parable of the dishonest steward (Luke 16:1-13; *cf.* 1 Corinthians 4:2).
4. **Boundaries Are Not Inherently Evil as God Is Sovereign Over His Boundaries**. God's word declares He is sovereign over boundaries (Exodus 23:31; 34:24; Deuteronomy 32:8; Nehemiah 9:22; Psalm 74:17; Proverbs 15:25; Acts 17:26). God is sovereign over boundaries and is not unjust in doing so, as God cannot be unjust. This is significant for the leader under God whose duty is to exercise his authority to protect life, property, and boundaries (Romans 13:1-7). In fact, various aspects of the magistrate's moral duties flow from the Ten Commandments given by God in Exodus 20 and Deuteronomy 5. The Ruler is just to exercise wise authority

as this is an implication of the Fifth Commandment. The Authorities are right to protect life by protecting against the loss of life implicit in illegally breached boundaries, as the sanctity of life is established by the Sixth Commandment. The King supports the Eighth Commandment when he prevents the theft of his and his subjects' land. When rulers exercise just authority over their boundaries, they are even termed "gods" in Scripture and by Christ (Psalm 82:6; 138:1; John 10:35). If God, who is inherently good and compassionate, has nevertheless chosen to set boundaries, then nations setting boundaries and limitations are not inherently evil.

5. **God Exercises Grace and Providence Particularly Providing a Model for National Compassion** God as a Sovereign Lord oversees His domains and their boundaries, opening and closing them as He determines to be best (Revelation 3:7-8). Thus God, who has infinite resources, deigns to redeem particularly (Ephesians 1:3-11; 2 Tim. 1:9). Similarly, He cares particularly by His providence as seen in His provision for the widow and the leprous officer in the times of Elisha and Elijah (1 Kings 17:1-9; 2 Kings 5:1-14; Luke 4:24-30). There are many biblical examples of God establishing and defending the boundaries of His domains: Eden (Genesis 3:23-24), the ark of Noah (Genesis 6:18; 7:1, 4-6, 13, 16), the Tower of Babel (Genesis 11:7-8), the Abrahamic covenant (Genesis 12:1-3; 17:1-9), the Davidic dynasty (2 Samuel 7:11-17). Similarly, Jesus taught that not everyone who says, "Lord, Lord" will enter the Kingdom (Matthew 7:21-23; 25:11-12). He declared that the gate is wide that leads to destruction, but narrow is the gate that leads to life (Matthew 7:13-14; Luke 13:22-30). Thus, choosing to care for a particular number or group of people at national boundaries if done with integrity, reflects divine particularism and is not immoral as God is perfect in His nature, word, and deeds. Love by nature is specific and particular regarding family and spiritual relationships

(Exodus 20:12; Galatians 6:10; Ephesians 5:25). Nevertheless, these truths do not diminish the requisite concern for the needy by those who have been blessed since the Lord also taught, to whom much is given, much is required (Luke 12:48).

6. **The State Only Has Finite Resources and Cannot Rescue Universally.** The universalism of open borders has rejected the notion of particularity in the care offered to the immigrant. Yet realistically, a state has only finite resources and can only rescue and care for, particularly in terms of the material needs of immigrants. Accordingly, specific care administered by wise borders is not immoral, if it is coupled with compassion shaped by love and wisdom to maximize the impact of finite resources (Proverbs 10:4; 17:16; 21:5; Luke 14:25-33; 15:11-31). The analogy of sovereign particularism provides wisdom to the immigration debate. If God who has infinite resources and is inherently good and compassionate has nevertheless chosen to act with particularity, then a policy of caring particularity cannot be inherently evil. Planning to do an act of love is not only wise but also compassionate (Luke 10:33-35).

7. **True Justice Is Classless, While Social Justice Limits Justice by Economic Reductionism.** Whereas open borders limit justice to the poor through their conception of social justice and refuse to limit the borders with wisdom, the open hearts of wisdom approach governs borders by love's broad calling and by not limiting justice to only a certain class. Love recognizes that all are worthy of justice and that commitment determines the right way to deal with the exigencies of the borders. Hence, issues of justice are for all— both rich and poor, citizen and alien, stranger, pilgrim, and refugee (Leviticus 19:15; Micah 6:8). Care must be extended to the needy, and there are special promises for those who do so (Proverbs 14:31; 19:17; 22:9; 28:27; Isaiah 58:10; Acts 20:35). While the duties and blessings of justice extend to all, not just to the poor, the duty of sharing

worldly blessings especially rests with those to whom much is given, for from them much is required (Luke 12:48; 1 Timothy 6:17-19; 1 John 3:14-18). Those with greater resources are called to minister by love (Matthew 7:12; 22:39; 1 Timothy 6:17-19; 1 John 3:14-18).

8. **Justice in Caring for the Needy Recognizes the Distinctive Roles of the Church and the State.** Scripture interprets Scripture. This principle reveals that the roles and functions of the church's compassion are not the same as the state given the state's primary duties of justice. Biblical justice affirms that property rights are divinely sanctioned in the eighth commandment and that authority is to be recognized as a divine gift to be exercised under God in the fifth commandment. Property and authority are especially the duties of the state's justice system. The distinctive responsibilities of the church and state are underscored by Jesus (Matthew 22:21) and the Apostles (Romans 13:1-8; 1 Peter 2:13-17).

9. **Christian Compassion Recognizes the Need for Prioritization and Rejects Marxist Wealth Redistribution.** There are expanding concentric circles of biblical Christian compassionate care according to Galatians 6:10 that begin with the believer and move outward to all men as capacity allows. Social justice from a Marxist ideology focuses on wealth and its redistribution and silences biblical justice that seeks to give every man his due. The Scriptures simultaneously affirm that the life of the poor is precious even as the property of the economically blessed is to be protected. Biblical justice opposes Marxist ideology. Marx denied the right to private property, but God has decreed its protection in the Eighth Commandment. Justice to both the poor and the economically blessed are called for by the Moral Law of the Ten Commandments. Wisdom does not and will not defend injustice. Rather, it is folly to confuse justice by reducing it to only economic considerations. A biblical approach that takes seriously the

obligation of grace and mercy to the poor will count the cost, make wise plans, and work with open hearts to do the most good possible for those in crisis and deep need. In providing such resources of health and wealth, wisdom will also seek to prevent and to address rampant abuse, crime, and poverty that occur at all phases of immigration and are often exacerbated by open borders. This approach Christians believe is far more effective and lasting as caring and planning are united. Suffering is often not diminished but only redistributed by the uncoordinated and illegal activities associated with open-border immigration. Blind compassion is folly.

10. **Compassionate Actions May Appear to Be Good Yet Be Cruel and Conducive to Evil**. Wisdom recognizes that the compassion of evil is cruel (Proverbs 12:10). Evil leaders and enemies can manipulate good for evil ends. Evil men can cleverly exploit the good intentions and actions of people to cause them ultimate harm as seen in the lives of Joseph, Daniel, Mordecai, and Esther by making good actions illegal or unseemly. Those who seek to do well by wise open-hearted compassion should not let their good be evil spoken of (Romans 14:16).

11. **God's Judgment upon Sin Is Manifest and Cannot Be Eradicated in This World**. While we are to show Christ's love to the needy in this world, we can never entirely remove the curse upon humans due to the fall (Genesis 3:15-19; Romans 8:18-28). Divine judgment rests upon all mankind which means that there will be refugees from just and unjust wars (Matthew 24:6), thus calling on believers in their good works to be salt and light (Matthew 5:13-16), resisting enemies in conflict (Hebrews 11:32-38) while loving enemies in relationships (Romans 12:17-21). There will be occasions for believers to pray imprecatory psalms (Psalm 7, 35, 55, 58, 59, 69, 79, 83, 109, 137) while seeking to love their neighbors and their enemies (Matthew 5:43-48; 22:34-40; John 13:31-35). The judgment of God is on human folly

and sin in their manifold forms (Romans 1:18-32). When believers pray the Lord's Prayer, "Thy Kingdom Come", we are praying for the final judgment that closes the doors of heaven, purifies the earth of sin in all its forms, and creates a new heaven and new earth where only righteousness will be allowed to enter (Matthew 6:10; Revelation 21:1-8; 22:14-15). That is the ultimate border closure.

12. **Sinfulness and Total Depravity Impact All—The Poor, the Rich, the Citizen, and the Refugee.** Total depravity does not disappear if one becomes a refugee or an immigrant. The perfectibility of man in a fallen world is impossible (Genesis 6:5-7; Matthew 15:13-20; Romans 3:23; Ephesians 2:1-4). Thus, just laws may be broken by refugees and immigrants due to evil desires to deprive other refugees, immigrants or poor citizens of their needed support and social care. This may occur through misrepresentation of the truth in violation of the Ninth Commandment. Are open border advocates encouraging false witness and the normalization of the same to gain refugee status for many for whom it is unwarranted? Open border advocates make immigrants immune to moral scrutiny and unaccountable to authorities who seek to honor the rights of others. This has the effect of limiting compassionate caregivers from exercising wisdom.

When the range of biblical teaching is considered, it manifests that the Gospel's call for an open heart of love harmonizes with a just border policy that is shaped by wisdom.

1. **Practical Proposals for Addressing Immigration Practices and Their Impact**
2. Pierce the veil of socialistic moral superiority by asking those who demand open or unaccountable immigration for examples of their own actual personal investment in the needs of others.

3. Find a ministry that cares for the needy and graciously and mercifully do your part.
4. Ask your pastor to preach a sermon series on the godly right of property, the duty of rulers to exercise godly wisdom on behalf of their subjects, the duty to love one's neighbor, and the Christian's privilege to exercise and to model the Golden Rule as well as to live with wisdom.
5. Pray for the persecuted and the true refugee and consider what you might do to ameliorate their authentic suffering. Should your church adopt a refugee family and minister to them?
6. Call on your legislators to exercise the same standards for health, family, safety, and anti-criminal behavior for immigrants, refugees, and aliens as they demand for documented immigrants and residents in their own legislative districts.
7. Review the ideology and pleas of various refugee advocacy groups before you support them to determine if they make one-sided demands for the unmeasured growth of non-national populations or if they are truly showing humanitarian compassion that accounts for the requisite costs and services to meet the need.
8. Invasion can occur by war and by excessive migration. Is there evidence that the movement or ministry you are considering supporting enables the assimilation of the immigrants? Will they "balkanize" the nation catalyzing conflict, or enrich it by preserving the immigrants' cultures as they enjoy the rights of their new home and learn its language, culture, and values strengthening the national social fabric and thereby preserving unity and peace?
9. Pray for a revival among those who enter our land whether legally or illegally, whether documented or undocumented as Christian ministries willingly and sincerely preach the gospel and meet the needs of those who cross their paths.
10. Affirm in discussions that boundaries are inescapable in all of life and that wisdom demands wise boundaries be set for

the nation. This is just as true as boundaries are necessary for your home, relationships, friendships, schools, churches, businesses, and community services.
11. Consider what role you should play to improve the abuses facilitated by current immigration legislation or enforcement.
12. Pray for personal and community fiscal faithfulness lest the influx of unplanned immigration cause the failure of the national economy through unchecked spending, national debt, and socialistic exorbitance.
13. Pray for selfless compassion to share with those in need if the grocery shelves post-COVID and post-immigration excesses result in long lines, empty shelves, rising hunger, or deprivation.
14. Prepare for living on less through longer periods should national financial decline occur causing previously enjoyed blessings to become less available than previously.
15. Pray for the ability to speak the truth in love regarding these polarizing issues in this politically charged era when argumentation and evidence are often trumped by emotion.
16. Rejoice that God is sovereign even should we enter a season of judgment for national sin and folly, remembering that loving care is the Biblical way and is consistent with justice, mercy, and the law of God.

Conclusion

National boundaries are morally good. In affirming this, two distinctions are in order. First, it is clear that what a nation does at its borders is far beyond what the church is able to do let alone an individual. Individuals and churches have voices and votes, but not vetoes. Direct change in policy requires securing authority to do so through governmental office and legitimate power. The individual and the Church should encourage people to get involved to secure such a role to make a difference. Second, whatever may be the positive or negative current practices of government leaders at the border, the duties of believers to seek to offer compassionate care coupled with responsible administration of that care honors the spirit of Christ and the teachings of Scripture. Open borders, however, in a fallen world are contravened by wisdom, godly authority, and biblical justice for all. Wise biblical compassion opposes immigration policies advocating open borders that are unregulated and unaccountable.

To be sure, there is potential for hypocrisy on all sides of the border debate. The open borders movement can be practiced from behind a gated community and exercised by a socialistic abuse of the tax system making others pay for what one would not do on his own, perhaps all the while enriching themselves. Believers in support of open-hearted compassion, may talk a good game, but not engage the issue in a meaningful way, allowing others to do the work and to provide the generosity. Ideally, believers are called to heed the divine call to love and to use wisdom in decisions and actions. This is liberality tempered by wisdom when emotions do not trump truth.

Finally, is wise self-interest for the Church to show Christian liberality. As Clark writes, "The reality is, as we face increasing exile in our land, we'll need to rediscover the necessity of hospitality for the gospel. Church attendance will likely continue to wane and with it pulpit evangelism. Meanwhile, Christian witness could be all but silenced in the workplace or classroom. Public spaces could suddenly become 'safe,' off-limits to proselytizing or any religious conversation. But our private homes will long remain a haven for free speech, the perfect place for reasoning with others about the gospel."[32]

Let us look forward to the day when each can say, "We are no more strangers and aliens but fellow citizens in Christ" (Ephesians 2:19). In the meantime, national boundaries will likely remain a contentious battle zone. But God's redeeming grace and over-ruling providence will not fail to accomplish His saving purposes for His people on all sides of national borders. Should ours be a season of judgment, let us remember too that God's discipline leads to mercy and grace for His people (Hebrews 12:5-14).

Questions for Discussion and Reflection

Individual | Class | Small Group

1. How can Christians balance compassion for immigrants and the necessity of national security, given the biblical mandate to care for the stranger and the governmental responsibility to protect citizens?

2. What are the variables or factors in play when discussing immigration reform from a historical context?

3. Discuss the ethical implications of open borders in light of biblical teachings. How does the concept of open borders align or conflict with Christian principles of stewardship, community welfare, and hospitality?

4. How can Christians balance biblical wisdom and compassion when addressing immigration? Discuss the potential for boundaries to be morally good, as opposed to the notion of open borders, in the context of Christian ethics and biblical teachings.

5. Explore John Calvin's approach to immigration in Geneva, particularly his views on caring for refugees and integrating them into the community. How can Calvin's example inform the Church's response to modern immigration challenges?

6. What is the Scriptural perspective on immigration reform, and how does the ongoing debate around immigration tie into broader discussions about the New Heaven and the New Earth?

The Thanatos Syndrome
What the Bible Says about Euthanasia
Michael A. Milton

> Please do this one favor for me, dear doctors. If you have a patient, young or old, suffering, dying, afflicted, useless, born or unborn, whom you for the best of reasons wish to put out of his misery—I beg only one thing you, dear doctors! Please send him to us. Don't kill them! We'll take them—all of them. Please send them to us! I swear to you you won't be sorry.
>
> — Walker Percy, *The Thanatos Syndrome*[1]

We cannot deny it; the Bible doesn't. Human suffering can metastasize into an inconsolable despair that causes a person to prefer death over life. The Apostle Paul admitted as much when he wrote,

> For we do not want you to be unaware, brothers, of the affliction we experienced in Asia. For we were so utterly burdened beyond our strength that we despaired of life itself (2 Corinthians 1:8 ESV).

To be so burdened by pain, sorrow, weakness, or some other merciless affliction led even St. Paul to despair of life itself. So, we are not alone if we find ourselves in such a situation. The Bible is not silent about agony or the sense of despair that it breeds.

But what do we do with suffering?

In Horace McCoy's 1935 novel, the title of this quintessential Postmodern story is established in the closing scene. The female lead of the story, Gloria, a bitter, angry, and ultimately miserable creature, asks Robert, the naïve, anti-hero-protagonist of the book, to end her life:

> "'I had the pistol in my hand.'
> 'All right,' I say to Gloria. 'Say when.'
> 'I'm ready.'"[2]

Robert compliantly shoots Gloria in the side of her head, as directed by the pathetic creature. The police arrive. Robert is detained. On the way to the police station, one of the cops asks the murderer, "Why did you kill her?" Robert replies without the slightest evidence of guilt or immorality, "She asked me to." The policeman, baffled at such a thoughtless obligation to Gloria's distraught demand, responds with contempt and incredulity, "Is that the only reason you got?" Robert replies, "They shoot horses, don't they?"[3]

"They Shoot Horses, Don't They?" is the definitive Darwinian rejoinder to the persistent angst of humanity.[4]

Let us be clear: no one is immune from the helpless feeling of watching another person spiraling downward, trapped by the sinister force of the black hole of despair. We intuitively want to help. To the book *cum* film, "Yes, we do, indeed, shoot horses to put them out of their misery. But your Gloria was not a horse. And we are not animals. Indeed, *that* essential fact is at the heart of a worldview debate. Gloria was wrong in her demand that Robert put her out of her misery. We can, at least, understand the physical and mental forces that drive her to such irrationality. Yet, Robert is culpable, too, for committing—not a "mercy killing"—but rather a homicide.

The decline of Western values born out of and nurtured in our Judeo-Christian foundation stones is inevitably accompanied by observable symptoms of such decline.[5] One of those symptoms has persisted throughout world history and has only recently been popularized to the point of legalization in some countries and U.S. states.[6] That symptom has a name: *euthanasia*. But precisely what is euthanasia? And what does the Bible say about euthanasia? In this chapter, we will seek to answer these questions as well as provide a scripturally sound and mercifully compassionate response to the existential pain that causes humankind to consider euthanasia as a solution.

Therefore, let us construct a response to the question, "What is euthanasia?"

Euthanasia is a contradiction of terms by definition

Euthanasia is an English word derived from a Greek compound meaning "good death."[7] Euthanasia is mainly associated with the voluntary or patient-consented ending of life through the assistance of another. The act is sometimes referred to as "mercy killing." The concept originates not only in the ancient Greco-Roman world, often cited as such, but also extends back to the time of David and King Saul. The practice has been universally banned in the Western world until recently. The twentieth century, in particular, witnessed a movement for the legalization of euthanasia. The Netherlands remains the most liberal in its legislative allowance of euthanasia.

Euthanasia is a symptom of the Thanatos Syndrome—the Culture of Death

The act of euthanasia is part of the *cult* of death and is an act condemned in Scripture not only by principle but by example. In principle, we gather the truths from the word of God that touch upon the subject, and we can conclude that life and death belong solely to the Creator, Almighty God. The Bible says that there is a time to be born and a time to die. The Lord Jesus talked about Paul's suffering and reminded him that when he is weak, he is strong. The Apostle Paul taught the Philippians that he would identify his suffering with Christ so that he might attain the resurrection. Even as advocates of euthanasia sought to normalize such voices as Dr. Walker Percy, the prodigious author-philosopher-psychiatrist-Christian apologist from Covington, Louisiana, penned his final novel in 1987 to call out the culture of death and it consequences.[8] The title of the work is *The Thanatos Syndrome*.[9] "Thanatos" is the Greek word for *death*. In the story, Thomas Moore—a quite interesting Catholic name assigned to the protagonist in *The Thanatos Syndrome*—is a psychiatrist who returns to Feliciana (based on the real East Feliciana and West Feliciana parishes where Dr. Percy once resided) to practice medicine after some severe mistakes in his life. The remnant of a "decrepit empire" of Spain, the Feliciana parishes became a refuge for "all manner of malcontents," from Tories who opposed the American Revolution to deserters, criminals, and smugglers.[10] Upon his return, he notices bizarre behavior in his patients and even in his wife. Through the means of sabotage of the water system by malevolent forces, the residents of this Louisiana parish began to act like chimpanzees, i.e., mere animals. Even those called to be helpers and caregivers became participants in this strange culture. Through the voice of his character in the Thanatos syndrome, Walker Percy wrote,

> "You are a member of the first generation of doctors in the history of medicine to turn their backs on the oath of Hippocrates and kill millions of old useless people, unborn children, born malformed children, for the good of mankind —and to do so without a single murmur from one of you. Not a single letter of protest in the august New England Journal of Medicine."[11]

Walker Percy was precisely correct. Sadly, *The Thanatos Syndrome* is not just a novel. The Thanatos syndrome is an invasive cancer choking out the living conscience of a civilization forged on the teaching of St. Paul and St. Peter, that is, upon the very teaching of our Lord and Savior Jesus Christ.

What does the Bible teach us about euthanasia?

Let us gather several salient Scriptures that are unmistakable signposts in these days of Biblical ignorance. Let these signs guide us to the truth. Let us compare Scripture with Scripture to see the indisputable evidence: God hates the murderous taking of human life. Therefore, God abhors that wicked and deceitful deed that men call "The Good Death." Our unequivocal statement is derived from many places in God's Word. Let us mark well our pathway to this knowledge, this wisdom, this revelation that euthanasia is incompatible with God's will.

Seven Biblical Categories of Revealed Truth that Guide Our Response to the Question of Euthanasia

Systematic theology—the categorizing of similar Scriptural citations that unveil God's will—supports our research in locating the answer to the question of euthanasia. In approaching God's inerrant and infallible Word, one may discern at least *seven categories* of Biblical truth that instruct us in our quest to understand God's will about this difficult subject:

1. Scriptures that reveal *the image of God* in humanity;
2. Scriptures that reveal *the value of life;*
3. Scriptures that reveal *the Law of God;*
4. Scriptures that reveal *the Providence of God;*
5. Scriptures that reveal *the love of God;*
6. Scriptures that reveal *the destiny of the believer;* and
7. Scriptures that reveal *an appropriate response* to human suffering.

Thus, in these blessed Biblical star clusters of divine truth, we are granted God's ineffable light to make our way through the admittedly dark space corridors where unbearable human suffering cries out for relief through death. And what is the verdict of Holy Scripture on euthanasia?

1. Euthanasia destroys the image of God.

"Then God said, 'Let us make man in our image, after our likeness. And let them have dominion over the fish of the sea and over the birds of the heavens and over the livestock and over all the earth and over every creeping thing that creeps on the earth.' So God created man in his own image, in the image of God he created him; male and female he created them" (Genesis 1:26-27).

"Do you not know that you are God's temple and that God's Spirit dwells in you? If anyone destroys God's temple, God will destroy him. For God's temple is holy, and you are that temple" (2 Corinthians 3:16-17).

2. Euthanasia devalues human life.

"And for your lifeblood, I will require a reckoning: from every beast I will require it and from man. From his fellow man I will require a reckoning for the life of man. 'Whoever sheds the blood of man, by man shall his blood be shed, for God made man in his own image'" (Genesis 9:5-6).

"Whoever takes a human life shall surely be put to death. Whoever takes an animal's life shall make it good, life for life. If anyone injures his neighbor, as he has done it shall be done to him, fracture for fracture, eye for eye, tooth for tooth; whatever injury he has given a person shall be given to him. Whoever kills an animal shall make it good, and whoever kills a person shall be put to death" (Leviticus 24:17-21).

3. Euthanasia desecrates the Law of God.

"You shall not murder" (Exodus 20:13).

"Because the people have forsaken me and have profaned this place by making offerings in it to other gods whom neither they nor their fathers nor the kings of Judah have known; and because they have filled this place with the blood of innocents" (Jeremiah 19:4).

"Bear one another's burdens, and so fulfill the law of Christ" (Galatians 6:2).

4. Euthanasia disregards the divine prerogative of our Creator.

"And he said, 'Naked I came from my mother's womb, and naked shall I return. The Lord gave, and the Lord has taken away; blessed be the name of the Lord'" (Job 1.21).

"Then Saul said to his armor-bearer, 'Draw your sword, and thrust me through with it, lest these uncircumcised come and thrust me through, and mistreat me.' But his armor-bearer would not, for he feared greatly. Therefore Saul took his own sword and fell upon it" (1 Samuel 31:4).

"Then David said to the young man who told him, "How do you know that Saul and his son Jonathan are dead?" And the young man who told him said, "By chance I happened to be on Mount Gilboa, and there was Saul leaning on his spear, and behold, the chariots and the horsemen were close upon him. And when he looked behind him, he saw me, and called to me. And I answered, 'Here I am.' And he said to me, 'Who are you?' I answered him, 'I am an Amalekite.' And he said to me, 'Stand beside me and kill me, for anguish has seized me, and yet my life still lingers.' So I stood beside him and killed him, because I was sure that he could not live after he had fallen"

5. Euthanasia denies the divine ownership of our bodies by Almighty God.

"Then the Lord God formed the man of dust from the ground and breathed into his nostrils the breath of life, and the man became a living creature" (Genesis 2:7).

"And he said, 'Naked I came from my mother's womb, and naked shall I return. The Lord gave, and the Lord has taken away; blessed be the name of the Lord'" (Job 1:21).

"In his hand is the life of every living thing and the breath of all mankind" (Job 12:10).

"Your eyes saw my unformed substance; in your book were written, every one of them, the days that were formed for me, when as yet there was none of them" (Psalm 139:16).

"For 'In him we live and move and have our being'; as even some of your own poets have said, '"For we are indeed his offspring"' (Acts 17.28).

"Do you not know that you are God's temple and that God's Spirit dwells in you? If anyone destroys God's temple, God will destroy him. For God's temple is holy, and you are that temple" (1 Corinthians 3:16-17).

6. Euthanasia distrusts the providence of God.

"Many are the plans in the mind of a man, but it is the purpose of the Lord that will stand" (Proverbs 19:21).

"For everything there is a season, and a time for every matter under heaven: a time to be born, and a time to die; a time to plant, and a time to pluck up what is planted; a time to kill, and a time to heal; a time to break down, and a time to build up" (Ecclesiastes 3:1-3).

"And just as it is appointed for man to die once, and after that comes judgment" (Hebrews 9:27).

7. Euthanasia diminishes Christ's redemption of body and soul.

"More than that, we rejoice in our sufferings, knowing that suffering produces endurance, and endurance produces character, and character produces hope, and hope does not put us to shame, because God's love has been poured into our hearts through the Holy Spirit who has been given to us" (Romans 5:3-5).

"I appeal to you therefore, brothers, by the mercies of God, to present your bodies as a living sacrifice, holy and acceptable to God, which is your spiritual worship" (Romans 12:1).

"For this light momentary affliction is preparing for us an eternal weight of glory beyond all comparison" (2 Corinthians 4:17).

8. Euthanasia devalues the mystery of redeemed suffering.

"He who did not spare his own Son but gave him up for us all, how will he not also with him graciously give us all things" (Romans 8:32).

"So we do not lose heart. Though our outer self is wasting away, our inner self is being renewed day by day. For this light momentary affliction is preparing for us an eternal weight of glory beyond all comparison, as we look not to the things that are seen but to the things that are unseen. For the things that are seen are transient, but the things that are unseen are eternal" (2 Corinthians 4:16-18).

"For to me to live is Christ, and to die is gain" (Philippians 1:21).

"That I may know him and the power of his resurrection, and may share his sufferings, becoming like him in his death" (Philippians 3:10).

9. Euthanasia discredits the promises of God.

"Even though I walk through the valley of the shadow of death, I will fear no evil, for you are with me; your rod and your staff, they comfort me" (Psalm 23:4).

"For I know the plans I have for you, declares the Lord, plans for welfare and not for evil, to give you a future and a hope" (Jeremiah 29:11).

"Who shall separate us from the love of Christ? Shall tribulation, or distress, or persecution, or famine, or nakedness, or danger, or sword" (Romans 8:35)?

"Come to me, all who labor and are heavy laden, and I will give you rest" (1 Corinthians 11:28).

"But he said to me, 'My grace is sufficient for you, for my power is made perfect in weakness.' Therefore I will boast all the more gladly of my weaknesses, so that the power of Christ may rest upon me'" (2 Corinthians 12:9).

10. Euthanasia demands that God must bow to our supposed better wisdom.

"Then his wife said to him, 'Do you still hold fast your integrity? Curse God and die.' But he said to her, 'You speak as one of the foolish women would speak. Shall we receive good from God, and shall we not receive evil?' In all this Job did not sin with his lips" (Job 2:9-10).

"For with you is the fountain of life; in your light do we see light" (Psalm 36:9).

"O Lord, make me know my end and what is the measure of my days; let me know how fleeting I am" (Psalm 39:4).

"But Peter and the apostles answered, 'We must obey God rather than men'" (Acts 5:29).

11. Euthanasia disallows the possibility of healing.

"No temptation has overtaken you that is not common to man. God is faithful, and he will not let you be tempted beyond your ability, but with the temptation he will also provide the way of escape, that you may be able to endure it" (1 Corinthians 10:13).

12. Euthanasia disavows the love of God in human suffering and death.

"Precious in the sight of the Lord is the death of his saints" (Psalm 116:15).

"Casting all your anxieties on him, because he cares for you" (1 Peter 5:7).

"He will wipe away every tear from their eyes, and death shall be no more, neither shall there be mourning, nor crying, nor pain anymore, for the former things have passed away" (Revelation 21:4).

Our Conclusion

Euthanasia is prohibited by the entire testimony of God's Word. But back to the person in agony. What can we do to alleviate the suffering of those who are dying? Mercifully, God directs us how to care for the dying.

The Biblical Case for Palliative Care of the Dying

Palliative care is defined by the World Health Organization:

"An approach that improves the quality of life of patients and their families facing the problems associated with life-threatening illness, through the prevention and relief of suffering by means of early identification and impeccable assessment and treatment of pain and other problems, physical, psychosocial and spiritual."[12]

Palliative Care is a relatively new approach to end-of-life care. The concept is not new, however. God has called us to provide "palliative care" (holistic care) to those who are suffering and who are in the process of death. This care for the suffering and the dying includes medications that can alleviate pain and reduce discomfort (Proverbs 31:6-7).[13] Whether emergency means are used to sustain human life beyond death caused by the body's own decline is a private decision that deserves the respect of others. The Bible supports doing all to support and sustain human life. However, when maintaining life introduces new extraordinary suffering, there is every right to reject such intervention. I had a friend, one of our elders, and a physician who had lived to almost ninety years of age. When he learned that he had cancer, he decided against heroic treatments. He told me that from his experience, the pharmaceutical intervention was going to "take him out" for whatever time the Lord had given him. So, he lived for another six months or so. He cherished his days and went about life the way he wanted: tending his garden, going to church, writing the remaining chapters of his book on family history, listening to his symphony records, and giving counsel to younger physicians. He died looking forward to seeing the Savior face to face.

Without question, such a decision is a very private and uniquely personal decision. When we are under extreme stress it is good to seek the godly counsel of trusted others. Sometimes family members are not the best at that. There is a time for warm, loving speech, and there is a time when we just need the unvarnished data, the clinical opinions of those who would administer any potential drug. Speak with the doctors of the physique, e.g., your oncologist, and speak with the physicians of the soul, your pastors. Then, speak with your loved ones.

The Bible teaches us that while suffering itself has no spiritual value, suffering that is identified with the suffering of Jesus Christ on the cross becomes a remarkable pathway to spiritual strength, rivers of healing grace, and, ultimately, for the believer, a doorway into the presence of our Lord (Romans 8:17; 2 Corinthians 1:5; Philippians 3:10):

> "But rejoice that you share in the sufferings of Christ, so that you may be overjoyed at the revelation of His glory" (1 Peter 4:13).

God speaks to us in Psalm 116:15 about His love of His people in death: "Precious in the sight of the LORD *is* the death of his saints."

The Thanatos Syndrome in our day is a culture predisposed to death. Such a foolish denial of God logically devolves into a denial of God's image in humankind. This erroneous thinking cultivates a prevalent mindset that fails to distinguish between human and beast. Therefore, we fall into the ultimate denial of the *imago Dei (the Image of God in Man)* and the predictable response to humans in misery: If we kill dogs in pain, why not each other? What is wrong with putting someone out of his misery? It all sounds effortless and yet horrendously inhuman when we leave God out of the equation. The thing is, one *cannot* remove God from the equation. He is the giver of life and the Lord of life. We must give honor to the human body as honor unto God. Suffering is inevitable in a fallen world. Thus, give strong medicine to the suffering (Proverbs 31:6), viz., employ medical therapies that relieve pain and suffering.

Loved ones, healthcare providers, and others do not murder or assist in the suicide of humans in distress in the same way as a farmer might "put down" a poor animal in misery. Neither do we add to their misery by introducing such means that will lengthen their suffering. "Do no harm," is a Biblical truth embedded in the Hippocratic Oath.[14] No, we care for them. We give them medication—a gift of God—to alleviate pain and suffering. We do all we can, and if we err, *we must err on the side of life.* Hold the suffering. Show them love in the name of our Lord Jesus. And whisper the promises of Jesus to the suffering saint who longs for Christ: "I will never leave thee, nor forsake thee" (Hebrews 13:5).

We who follow that One who is always with us must not only define and announce the doctrines that frame the matter of taking human life before birth or before death. We must continue to provide a place of dignity for those poor souls that an increasingly lost world says, "You are not worthy to live." We must say with Percy's symbolic Father Smith of fictitious Feliciana Parish, the frail and mentally faltering priest, "We'll take them—all of them. Please send them to us! I swear to you you won't be sorry."

Then, and only then, when we have done all, we will entrust those who suffer unto death to God's loving arms. And He who made us, yea, He who agonized on the cross for any who turn to Him, will receive the sufferers unto Himself.

———

Questions for Discussion and Reflection

Individual | Class | Small Group

1. The Dilemma of Despair: Paul speaks of being "utterly burdened beyond our strength" and despairing of life itself in 2 Corinthians 1:8. How can we reconcile the presence of such deep despair in a believer's life with hope and assurance in God's sovereignty? Discuss the church's role in providing support and guidance during such despair.

2. The Sanctity of Life: Discussing the ethical implications of euthanasia from a Biblical perspective and the sovereignty of God over life and death. How does the concept of euthanasia challenge or contradict the principles of the sanctity of life as taught in the Scriptures?

3. The Thanatos Syndrome and Christian Worldview: In Walker Percy's "The Thanatos Syndrome," the protagonist witnesses a decay of moral values and the blurring of ethical boundaries. How does this novel reflect the challenges faced by the modern Christian in upholding Biblical values in a secular age? What lessons can we draw from this narrative for our current cultural context?

4. Biblical Response to Suffering: The Bible does not ignore the reality of suffering and pain. Discuss how the Scriptures guide us in responding to personal suffering and the suffering of others. What Biblical principles should shape our approach to dealing with pain and despair?

5. Palliative Care from a Christian Perspective: Considering the Biblical case for palliative care, how should Christians view and practice end-of-life care? Discuss the balance between alleviating suffering and

respecting the sanctity of life as we care for those nearing the end of their earthly journey.

6. Witnessing to the Culture of Death: In a world where concepts like euthanasia are increasingly accepted, how can Christians effectively witness to the sanctity of life and offer a hopeful alternative to the culture of death? Share practical ways in which the church can engage with and minister to those struggling with issues of life, death, and suffering.

―――

The Course of Nations

Is the Decline and Fall of Nations Inevitable?

Michael A. Milton

> Today, in Rome, neither Hadrian's mausoleum nor the *Pons Aelius* commemorate the man who built them. They bear witness instead, on the summit of the mausoleum, to the appearance of the archangel Michael, who in Revelation is described as throwing down Satan to the earth.—Tom Holland, *Pax: War and Peace in Rome's Golden Age*[1]

Subjective experience precludes objective analysis. In other words, as one experiences life at any given moment, one is either unaware or unable to evaluate the significance of the moment. Once there was a train clerk and a landscape artist who did. Their insights can help us assess the possible meaning of our moments as we live them today.

Einstein's Train and Turner's Angst

Before being the great theoretical physicist at Princeton, the famous Dr. Albert Einstein (1879-1955) was a poor student and a clerk at a train station in Austria—but a very curious clerk. Young Albert noticed that as the train sped by, the passengers seemed uninterested and unaffected by the forces around them. A refined lady of leisure sipped tea in a first-class car. She was the picture of decorum as she was encased in the 150-ton iron horse, snorting scalding steam and charcoal smoke at 100,000 pounds-force and rumbling across steel tracks, sparks a-flying! Of course, Einstein would develop his theory of relativity from this initial observation. We may derive some further wisdom from the "relativity train" ourselves.[2] We recognize ourselves as the lady in first class. The heavy, black-iron locomotive is a picture of our times. No one used this image to express the angst of modernity more brilliantly than the inimitable and irascible English landscape artist J. M. W. Turner (1775-1851). His *Rain, Steam, and Speed – The Great Western Railway* (1844) depicts a train moving across the English landscape on the new Great Western Railway. The engineering marvel of Isambard Kingdom Brunel (1806-1859) seems to shame the other would-be wonders of the Thames Valley (surpassing the glory of nature as a hare is unable to compete and even overshadowing Brunel's own Maidenhead Railway Bridge in the atmospheric distance). Turner's usual Romanticism recedes at his disapproval. With a dirty brush and quick strokes, Turner masterfully creates an impressionistic squinted-eye blur of a scene. The resulting creation is both breathtaking and disturbing.

Many of us are riding through life comfortably as postmodernism screams through time, rushing headlong past the quaint and the familiar to a destiny unknown. Melodramatic? Maybe. Maybe not. Step outside. The wind lashes at you like a Category 5 hurricane.

Moreover, you are abruptly overwhelmed by the deafening sounds of a discordant city in turmoil. The soot and steam engulf your senses, wrapping you in the creepy embrace of a strange new decadence. You are moving at breakneck speed. The familiar country blurs into a hazy, distant memory. Then, in a whirlwind, you hear child-like voices from a Sunday School class, morning Pledge of Allegiance recitals, and the black-and-white image of a family bowing in prayer before Thanksgiving dinner. Before you can whisper, "Wait, that is my past," the scenes become dust in the wind, as if they never existed. The cover of Walker Percy's "Signposts in a Strange Land" appears like a ghostly image, a prophetic explanation for the chaos, and then it is gone. The train has passed a point of no return, yet you didn't even know you were on a train, much less one speeding for disaster. You want to scream, but you no longer possess a voice.

Welcome to the Secular Age.

The Signs and Symptoms of Decline and Fall

It is true, as Turner expressed, and Einstein calculated: We journey through life mostly unaware of the significance of the moment. However, those who have studied the rise and fall of civilizations, such as Edward Gibbon (1737-1794) and Will Durant (1885-1981), and more recently, Dr. Tom Holland (b. 1968), and Dr. Iain McGilchrist (b. 1953), have identified critical factors in the decline and fall of a civilization. Each variable is inexorably tethered to the other and represents an integrated economy of diverse forces. Nevertheless, we can identify a few of those features within the constraints of this article. To wit, I would point to signs and symptoms of societal decline in three words.

The first is *complexity*. Civilizations grow and become quite tangled. Complexity is inevitable in economics, domestic affairs, foreign affairs, defense, social welfare, or any other necessary functions of national order. The network of people, features, functions, and unplanned events expands exponentially, becoming unmanageable. Bureaucratic classes emerge to control the chaos, only exacerbating it.

The next sign and symptom of decline and fall is *entropy*. Much of our lives is spent defending ourselves against entropy. Entropy is the universal law of decline and decay. In theology, entropy is the consequence of *the fall* of mankind and the introduction of sin into Creation. But we need not appeal to theology or philosophy to make our point. Consider your life and those around you. Your gym membership might slow "the decline and fall" of your physique but it cannot stop the entropic reality of this age. Grim? Terribly so. Real? Gym memberships are soaring as highly as the national debt. So, "Yes, quite real."

The third value that we consider is *apathy*. We all know that one generation gives way to another in the hope that the sons and daughters will maintain—and deepen—the virtues and values that established their society. However, apathy results from the human propensity to take things for granted. The businessman on the train, making a deal with a customer in Hong Kong via the now-mundane familiarity of his iPhone, has no thought of gratitude to the philosophical and theological ideas that made such a feat possible. And why should he? But, you see, that is the problem. *Unintended ingratitude may be forgiven, but the effect is the same as deliberate disdain.* Like countless others, our subject leaves his Connecticut mini-mansion for work in Manhattan (or on Zoom), oblivious to the immense benefits he's inherited. Whenever Benjamin Franklin said, "You have a republic if you can keep it," he conceded the reality of human apathy.[3]

These are a few tangible factors weaving through civilization, like yeast through dough or, more aptly, like termites within a foundation.

And then the Good Part, Right?

"It is a tale told by an idiot, full of sound and fury, signifying nothing." Macbeth's exasperation is apropos.[4] You might respond, "Okay. You have given us a diagnosis, but what is the cure?" Many historians say that there is no cure.[5] Among these, the more sanguine believe that at least we can provide a sort of palliative care to the dying. They mean that while we cannot restrain or reverse the decline and fall of a civilization, we can nevertheless care for those going through the awful descent. Of course, such a concession is a little more than having your favorite meal delivered to you on a golden platter right before your hanging. Others believe that decline can be halted, and fall can be averted. We have known such miraculous intervention in our own lives that we have a hope born not of this world. So, whether believers or not, let's turn our attention to this hope. Honestly, what do you have to lose?

So, let's start at an unusual place for hope: *Harvard*. No scholar in American Studies has done more to highlight the importance of the Puritan covenant with God than the late Dr. Perry Miller (1905-1963) of Harvard University. Miller, an uneasy agnostic, invested a lifetime of scholarship in researching and demonstrating the uniqueness of the American experiment.[6] Specifically, Miller posited that the Puritans' covenant with God (that they and their progeny would be a nation of missionaries to spread the Gospel) deposited the most prominent spiritual strand in the national DNA.⁷ Others, from the chronicler of the new nation, Alexis de Tocqueville (1805-1859), to the eminent Oxford historian Dr. Paul Johnson (1928-2023), also wrote about this peculiar and observable energy in the American experience. The received understanding is as follows: The English (and Dutch) Pilgrims who settled in New England and the mid-Atlantic did so out of a Reformed (Calvinistic) Christian impetus. These Puritan adventurers formed covenantal relationships with each other and God. They prayed that God would establish them and look out for their descendants and that they would, whether blest or not, seek to proclaim the Gospel of Jesus Christ to the ends of the Earth. Thus, John Winthrop in 1630: "We are entered into covenant with Him for this work (of establishing a new colony)."⁸ This covenant becomes a unifying principle for national identity expressed in civic contexts. Thus, we have Ronald Reagan's use of John Winthrop's "City on a Hill."⁹

Therefore, throughout the history of the United States, there is an unseen but genuine spiritual power at work. This dynamic confirms and convicts the American conscience, guiding Americans back to the original covenant with God. Paul Johnson explains the First and Second Great Awakenings (and similar experiences in American history) as examples of the spiritual vicissitude inherent in the American psyche. Interestingly, the civic expression of this covenant provides unprecedented liberty for people of all backgrounds and all religions. Paul Johnson wrote, "The Americans originally aimed to build an otherworldly 'City on a Hill,' but found themselves designing a republic of the people, to be a model for the entire planet."¹⁰ This was not an accident. For *the freedom of religion is the first great right enumerated in the Bill of Rights. All the other rights flow from the first God-given right.* Such rights are inherent in the Judeo-Christian worldview. That is the paradox: the religious heritage of our founding is there for all to see. Yet, the principles enumerated achieve freedom for all religions or no religion.

If historians such as Perry Miller and Paul Johnson are correct, the spirit of the Pilgrim's Covenant subtly yet profoundly influences the American narrative. Meld this notion with biblical teachings, and you will find a resilient hope that shines brightest during our nation's darkest hours. Thus, just as Jonah, the hesitant prophet, delivered God's truth to Nineveh, the Assyrian Empire's imposing capital, leading to its reprieve from judgment, so too can today's waning nations call upon God with repentance and faith. When they do, the ticking of the clock of divine judgment stops. Life, blessing, renewal, and hope are rejuvenated among the people. Such optimism finds its foundation in theological and biblical grounds. It is for, at least, this historical and biblical truth that we can continue to have hope.

Conclusion

In Ephesians 2:11-22, the Apostle Paul illuminates the believers in Ephesus about the divine miracle of transformation. He beckons them to recall a time when they stood without hope, as highlighted in Verse 12.

> But now in Christ Jesus, you were once off have been brought near by the blood of Christ. For he himself is our peace, who is made us both one and has broken down in his flesh the dividing wall of hostility (13, 14).

As civilizations decline, like the Ephesians before God's gracious intervention, every individual also faces spiritual decay. However, just as no culture is beyond the reach of God's grace, no individual is too lost for divine salvation. Societies or civilizations scale up from individuals to families and then to nations, encompassing the broader family of mankind. Terms like "civilization," "society," and "culture" essentially describe humans in relation to one another. The heartening message of the Gospel is that neither an individual nor any collective is outside the bounds of God's mercy.

So, yes, there is hope. No, the decline is not a fatalistic fix. "But now" remains the hope for human beings at every stage of life, every generation, and every place along the spectrum of the rise and fall of nations. The Cold War poet Czeslaw Milosz (1911-2004), wrote, "'Christ is risen.' Whoever believes that Should not behave as we do."[11]

It is no wonder that one of the leading lights among our Pilgrim founders, Governor John Winthrop, ended his sermon on the *Arbella* in 1630 with a Mosaic appeal to the new citizens of the American colony:

> Therefore, let us choose life,
> > That we and our seed may live,
> > By obeying His voice and cleaving to Him,
> > For He is our life and our prosperity.[12]

Whether Western nations will return to the mindset of America's founders, who uttered such wisdom, is an open question. To deny or ignore the presence of God in our public life will undoubtedly lead to further decline and eventual fall. The most cynical unbeliever must admit the Roman emperor is no more, but Christians remain. As historian Tom Holland wrote of Christ and believers' relationship to oppressive empires,

> Today, although church attendance in the West may not be what it used to be, our society remains as stamped as it ever was by the legacy of the early Christians' hostility to the Whore of Babylon.[13]

Someone once asked Dr. Martin Lloyd Jones (1899-1981) if people change. Dr. Lloyd Jones answered that if he did not believe that people could change, he could not believe the Gospel. However, if by "change" one means the transformation of one's very nature, then people cannot change themselves.[14] Only God can transform human nature. Therein, hopelessness becomes hope. The Lord can cause even a man like Saul of Tarsus, a persecutor of the people of God, to become the great Apostle Paul, the preacher to the Gentiles. So it is with civilizations. And so it is with you and me. That is the course of human beings and, thus, with their families and with their larger communities called nations.

Questions for Discussion and Reflection
Individual | Class | Small Group

1. Reflecting on Historical Perspectives: Considering Tom Holland's observation about the transformation of Hadrian's mausoleum from a Roman commemoration to a Christian symbol, discuss how Christianity has historically recontextualized cultural and historical symbols. How does this ability to transform and imbue new meanings into existing structures reflect the transformative power of the Christian faith?

2. Einstein, Turner, and Modernity: Einstein's observation on relativity and Turner's artistic representation of the Industrial Revolution provide insights into the human condition amidst rapid societal changes. Discuss how these perspectives help us understand our own experiences in today's fast-paced, technology-driven world. How should Christians navigate the challenges of modernity while maintaining their faith and values?

3. Understanding Civilizational Decline: Reflect on the signs and symptoms of societal decline as discussed in the chapter, such as complexity, entropy, and apathy. How can these insights inform the Christian response to the challenges faced by contemporary societies? What role can the Church and individual believers play in addressing these issues?

4. Hope in Decline: The chapter suggests that while civilizations may decline, there is hope for rejuvenation and renewal through divine intervention and repentance. Discuss historical instances where spiritual revival altered the course of societal decline. How can these examples

inspire contemporary Christians to seek spiritual renewal in their communities?

5. The Pilgrim's Covenant and American Identity: Analyze the impact of the Puritan covenant on the formation of American identity, as discussed by historians like Perry Miller and Paul Johnson. In what ways has this covenant shaped the spiritual and civic life of the United States, and how can this legacy be preserved and applied in today's context?

6. The Role of Faith in Transforming Societies: The chapter concludes with the idea that faith can transform not just individuals but entire civilizations. Discuss practical ways in which Christian faith can influence and transform contemporary societies, particularly in light of challenges such as secularism and moral relativism. How can the church effectively communicate the transformative power of the Gospel in a secular age?

Part IV
TRIGGERS

Repaving the Pathway to Poverty
An Urgent Warning Against The New Socialism

Michael A. Milton

> The fundamental error of socialism is anthropological in nature. This makes it much more difficult for him to recognize his dignity as a person and hinders progress towards the building up of an authentic human community.
>
> — John Paul II[1]

Introduction

I wonder: Are we trying to become the very thing that we defeated?

David Miller writes in *Debating Critical Theory*, "Socialism appears to have crept back on to the mainstream agenda in that most unlikely of places, the United States . . ."[2] The incredible reemergence of such a gruesome human catastrophe in such a brief period of time is less bewildering as it is frightening. The failure of Socialism on the world stage was nothing short of breathtaking.[3] Forgetfulness is the instinctive defense of the hopeful. However, that common disease of the human mind that we might call "selective amnesia"—i.e., *willful ignorance*— is a verifiably dangerous intellectual maneuver when dealing with history.[4] I have argued in other places that social criticism's deconstruction of everything, *viz.*, Postmodernism, is the progenitor to socialism.[5] With the West passing from Postmodernism to "a Secular Age," the virus of inhumanity is not only passed along to another generation but finds a most fitting environment in which to grow.[6]

The Cold War

I will never forget what I witnessed in the Cold War — the War that was not a war—and I could never imagine any nation wanting to build a house out of ashes.

From 1947 until 1991, the United States, Great Britain, and the British Commonwealth nations (along with the war-weakened Western European countries), still recovering from the unimaginable sacrifices made to defeat Nazism and Fascism, faced a new menace, one that had been strengthening on the blood of its people since October 1917 (the Russian Revolution).[7] Thus, the (primarily) Anglo-American civilizations were called upon to defend human liberty against the encroaching dark and evil night of Socialist and Communist regimes: the Soviet Union and Communist China and their puppet states.[8] George Orwell coined the term for the global post-WWII crisis: "The Cold War."[9] The Austrian-British economist F.A. Hayek (1899-1992) predicted that centralized state powers were, in fact, powers of darkness that would lead to prison states and utter poverty.[10] Noting that wartime realities forced emergency consolidation of powers reserved for the governed, Hayek warned the West against politically expedient temptations to keep and assume even more centralized controls. F.A. Hayek's classic book of warning, *The Road to Serfdom,* was released in March 1944. The London School of Economics (LSE) scholar leveraged a life of research and writing to issue a dire warning: *viz.*, nations that seize power from the people during emergencies, like WWII, had to return those emergency powers to the People.

Centralization of governance (and, in some cases, a suspension of rights) was necessary to support the national war efforts against Nazi Germany and Imperial Japan.[11] However, Hayek warned that when formidable interests get a taste of the intoxicating liqueur of power, find it difficult to "return" self-governance rights to the People. Thus, the

West began the struggle against Sino-Soviet Communism and the Cold War while striving against domestic political parties, e.g., the British Labour Party and the Democratic party in the United States, that introduced Socialism within the great Western nations.[12] It was an incredible period of history as Socialist-Communist states and Western Allies conducted a complex geopolitical chess match under the threat of nuclear annihilation. The Communists were clear in their end goal: world domination. The US and Britain were equally clear about defending liberty but had to do so with one hand tied behind their backs (viz., leftist movements at work within both countries).[13]

Leaders on all sides assured the People that the Cold War was not a war. It was a hard pill to swallow for the more than seven million Cold War grieving survivors. Dr. Joshua Goldstein, in the Journal of Foreign Policy, documented close to 180,000 lives lost each year from 1950 to 1989 due to the "conflicts," "crises," and "skirmishes."[14] If the Cold War was just a "long peace," as has been suggested, it certainly was a blood-stained peace with all the marks of war. [15]However, The War that wasn't a war was not only a day-to-day fear of the Apocalypse but a period of enormous societal disruption; and that fact leads one back to the agitators from within. As Dr. Paul Kengor has documented with irrefutable research, the Soviets "duped" American liberal politicians throughout the Cold War.[16] Covert operatives from the Soviet carried out successful disinformation campaigns by infiltrating Western institutions. Bastions of Western Civilization such as the university, the media, government, and even Christian denominations, were weakened by a foolish fascination with Marxism, French deconstructionist social theories, and anti-Christian philosophers (such as the Postmodernist professor Michael Foucault). Let anyone doubt Foucault's position, they need only to read his self-identity prior to his death (1984):

> I think I have in fact been situated in most of the squares on the political checkerboard, one after another and sometimes simultaneously: as anarchist, leftist, ostentatious or disguised Marxist, Nihilist or secret anti-Marxist, technocrat in the service of garlands him, new liberal, etc.... none of these descriptions is important by itself; taken together,

on the other hand, they mean something. And I must've missed it I rather like what they mean.[17]

Popular influencers like Hollywood, the Stage, and the music industry quickly caught up with their higher art and letters comrades and merrily, unthinkingly, carried the Socialist messaging to America. Thus, with our institutions emaciated, our economy in shambles, and our people disrespecting law enforcement, the military, and most any authority, the United States of America became a wounded eagle, down but not out, hunted by the ferocious Moscow bear. To quote one Cold War scholar, the West suffered from a "failure of ideological cohesion."[18] Meanwhile, The Soviets and their satellite states persecuted Christians and other groups, racking up murders in the millions.[19]

Many of us in America today lived through those days. I served as a Top-Secret Naval Intelligence interpreter in the 1970s. Our Naval Security Group gathered intelligence, sifted through propaganda, and interpreted data from the Communist enemies worldwide, 24-7, 365 days a year, in the air, on land and sea, deep beneath the ocean surface, and even in outer space.[20]

My point is not to repeat a portion of my curriculum vitae. I share this background with you because I know, personally, what Socialism and Communism can do to a nation.

Our nation was built upon the foundations of moral government. The names of Samuel Rutherford, John Locke, and Edmund Burke may be unknown to many Americans. However, these intellectual (and spiritual giants) were able to discern, display, and classify the rights of the governed and the limitations of the government according to Scripture and to the laws of God embedded in human beings by virtue of the *imago dei*.

Samuel Rutherford (1600-1661) was a Scottish Presbyterian divine who had been a commissioner on the Westminster Assembly. Rutherford's *Lex, Rex* (The Law is King, 1644) is undoubtedly one of the most influential documents to the American founders.[21] Rutherford's rebuttal to an Anglican bishop about the divine rights of kings laid bare the absolute monarchists' errors from Scripture. Rutherford argued from Scripture, reason, and natural law that the law of God is not only supreme but prescriptive for human government. Thus, with a nod to the Magna Carta, Rutherford argued vigorously for the divine rights of the governed. Whether Constitutional Monarchy or a Constitutional Republic, Rutherford held that the laws of God, rightly interpreted and applied for the good of Man, are the defining articles of a moral government.

John Locke (1632-1704) was a learned man, a Christian man, and a physician of the body as well as the mind and the soul. Like Rutherford and Burke, Locke's writings, including his *Two Treatises of Government* (1689) and his involvement with the Glorious Revolution of 1688 (in which earlier 1640s Puritan concerns for Parliamentary strength, as representatives of the People, placed the monarchy in an honorable but less authoritarian position). Lock's landmark lessons on private ownership are good examples of his reasoning:

> [John] Locke was the first to make a case for property of unlimited amount as a natural right of the individual, prior to governments and overriding them. Many others had made a general case for limited government: Locke's great innovation was to justify it as necessary to protect unlimited property. Since men formed themselves into civil societies in order to protect their individual properties, no civil society could conceivably wish to take away any part of any man's property except in so far as necessary to protect property as an institution (that is, by such taxation as was necessary to maintain law and government); and governments, whose rightful powers were only those delegated to them by the whole civil society, could therefore never have the right to interfere with anyone's property beyond what was required to protect property.[22]

Edmund Burke (1729-1797) was a member of Parliament during the crisis that led to the American Revolution. Burke recognized the consent of the governed and, in letters and speeches, appealed to the teachings of Christ as "superior," and the moral efficiency of Christ's message must shape human government.[23] Burke was an unreformed critic of the French Revolution as he saw the rebellion as a criminal act.

His voice became especially important in debate over the American Revolution. Burke supporting the American cause.

For Rutherford, Locke, and Burke, the intellectual and moral foundations of the United States of America are antithetical to the base intrusion of socialism and communism. Communism seeks to replace Almighty God with Statism; self-reliance and human dignity with governmental dependence; and representative government with totalitarianism.[24] The Socialist State seeks to replace meritocracy with identity politics, the American Puritan work ethic with equal outcomes, upward mobility with elitism, the family with the collective, the university with indoctrination camps, and the protection of the vulnerable with the survival of the fittest. The Socialists seize intellectual pressure points in culture. Then, having deconstructed and desecrated the older order, they wait. The *new socialists* wait until events converge to create a decisive moment, a turning point. "Never let a good crisis go to waste" is an accurate if not detestable and insensitive philosophy worthy of the most loathsome beasts.[25] "Emergency measures" remain Socialism's main play for seizing permanent power.

The Beast

As Kurt Aland noted in his *The Relation Between Church and State in Early Times: A Reinterpretation*. "The relation between Church and State is one of the central themes of Church history in every period."[26] Thus, The discussion of Communism, Statism, Socialism, and the history of the centralization of governmental powers is not unrelated to the Holy Scriptures. Not only did such oppressive powers exist in the Old Testament accounts of God's People—"every prophetical book in the OT, with the exception of Hosea, contains oracles against non-Israelite nations (e.g., Amos 1:1-23; Isaiah 13-23; Jeremiah 46-51; Ezekiel 25-31)—but the pattern of successful or intended sabotage by state powers unwittingly carried out diabolical objectives against the Kingdom of God.[27] The frequency of the incidents forms a recurring motif. The many instances of persecution against God's chosen people is a singular occurrence that is expressed in "many different avenues of approach."[28] Using Biblical theology—"the discovery of the unity of biblical revelation is the concern of biblical theology—the reader is able to discern this antagonistic struggle throughout the sixty-six books of the Bible.[29] However, The Revelation of Our Lord Jesus Christ to the Apostle John names this recurring theme through symbolism.[30] Unlimited government indirectly undermining or directly undoing the right of faith in life, speech, and private property or economic self-determination (and other God-given rights) is a tyrant in the economy of God's universal laws, and thus, is a "Beast." The earthly reality is but a mirror of the spiritual warfare of the cosmos in which Satan uses ". . . agents, instruments, or tools which the dragon uses in his attack upon the Church.[31] The beast of the sea (13:1-10) and the beast that came up from the earth (13:11-18) are symbols of human governments operating by "brute force" to trounce the rights and, thus, the lives of the saints.[32] Mounce writes that the second beast, the Beast of the Earth, or land, is the symbol of "ideology" or political philosophy that sustains the irreverent acts of the Beast of the Sea.[33] The second beast polices the activities of the Beast of the Sea. The Beast of the Earth is the enforcer. There is both a philosophical-intellectual think tank to support the Statist policies, and a powerful agent to carry out the deadly campaign of persecution. As the dragon gives power to the Beast of the Sea (13:4), we see how Lucifer wages a proxy war against Christ and the Church through the authoritarianism and totalitarianism of Statism.[34] As "symbolism plays a major role in apocalyptic . . . giving free reign to the imagination, [in which] symbols of the most bizarre sort become the norm," we approach the Beasts of Revelation with interpretive humility. However, some of the symbols are quite transparent. None less so than the Dragon-empowered beasts.

The first beast as an insatiable monster arising from the sea. The sea, in Revelation, "belongs to the old fallen order and represents, like the experience of Israel at the Red Sea, the barrier which the redeemed must pass through in the new exodus from earthly experience to the redeemed world of God."[35] So, this corrupted colossus from the deep and the dark appears to crush the Church and prevent the rule of Christ is not only a description of the troubles during John's day but is "the ongoing state of the world."[36]

In summary, there is a ruling motif of warfare against the saints in the Word of God: A Beast of the Sea—dictators, tyrants, and entire governments—seeking to restrict and ultimately destroy the rights of believers; and a Beast of the Earth, a second power, that gives both authority and police action to support the inhumane campaign of the first beast. Behind it all is a dragon, Satan, that is influencing the Beast of Statism (whether Edom, Babylon, Rome or the innumerable successor beasts that have waged a similar campaign) . The literal war on earth, appearing in each generation, and apparently gaining in both breadth and scope, as the ages wind their way to climactic events, is a manifestation of the unseen but very real spiritual warfare waged in the spiritual realm.

Of interest to our paper is how the beast secures the power? We propose a story from the example of beasts to discover our answer. The laughing hyaena is an appropriate example of how Socialism ascends to dominance, even in the presence of ostensibly greater creatures.

The Antelope and the Hyenas

Trailing a weakened antelope, a savage clan of spotted hyenas slobber, snarl, and scream, but *wait*. The maniacal monsters wait for a crisis. With a growing sense of dread, a weary, aging antelope is aware of his stalkers. The distraction paves a deadly path for the noble creature. Indeed, the antelope under duress makes one wrong move, then another. He takes chances. The antelope is resilient, and he knows he can ordinarily defeat the demented beasts of prey. However, the sum of his small mistakes equates to a great and fatal conclusion. The mighty Lord Derby Eland antelope, disturbed by the growing threat of the pillaging predators, gets bogged down in the mud while seeking shelter in a shallow river. This is what the maddened monsters have been waiting for: *a crisis of opportunity.* Several of the faster hyenas lunge to tear at the rump of the immobilized antelope. The impressive two-feet of twisted-antlers are daunting weapons of the wild. When his head is down and in fighting stance, a one-ton male charges at twenty-five miles per hour. Even imperiled, the great eland is dangerous. Several hyenas lay dead, gorged and stomped by the massive animal. However, the remaining hyaenas are unmoved. They know: "We have more than enough to get the job done." The vicious rabble encircle the prey ever closer. Their numbers grow. The piercing yelps reverberates through the wild like an invitation to the impending blood games at the Colosseum.

Other predatory species, eager to join a blood-feast, now, arrive. The wait intensifies. The younger male warriors are quivering with nervous anticipation to ambush the compromised six hundred pounds of flesh in the mud. "Bel," the prince of the spotted hyenas, calms the quivering cackle of hyenas, "Patience my lads, patience . . ." says the Alpha-male. "For what?" A young lieutenant asks. The devilish older beast answers the eager underling with the wisdom of the Serengeti: "For the inevitable *tipping point* in the game," says the conniving conquistador: "We wait for that moment when our incremental, smaller attacks escalate to a *crescendo*, and then, my boy—then—there is no way out for the once-mighty hind! A crisis, catastrophe, or an emergency will hit. There is *always* a crisis! We will use whatever upheaval that fate sends us as the cover for our decisive, final, and fatal take-over!" Then, the beast has lost, and the fool's flesh is ours!" This strategic postponement of hostilities may last through the day. As the shadows of darkness approach, the ravenous hyenas are ordered to strike intermittently. The disease-laden dogs and hyenas howl in a dizzying cacophony of hellish, eardrum-splitting noises, like a war tribe shrieking, with incessant sounds of drums pounding, evil laughter, and screams from the netherworld. The hyaenas are now drunk on anticipation. Suddenly, the assurances of the Alpha jackal are justified. Suddenly, a lioness appears. She strikes at the antelope. Then, another. This is what the hyenas and jackals have been waiting for: *a bifurcation of time.* The equilibrium of norms, chipped away by smaller attacks, is, at that moment, upended by a singular event. *This is the long-awaited apocalyptic tipping point from which there can be no return.* This is the midnight hour, the climactic moment when the lazier afternoon hours are recognized for what they were: not a reprieve from the attacks, but the final countdown to sudden death. The act only needed one crisis, one emergency, one spark, one pandemic of mayhem, to allow the antelope to fall to the dominance of the demonic predators.

We need not recount the gruesome events that followed. It is enough to say: *once the crisis appeared the catastrophe was inevitable.* By morning the scattered bones of the once magnificent antelope are strewn as silent tombstones in a battlefield. A few younger antelopes approach the devastating scene. They sniff at the scene of death. It is alarming, and, for a second, even confusing if not foreboding. However, the strong young antelopes are healthy, free, and easily distracted by the promise of youth. They move on to graze without further thought of the witness of history. The yearlings have fooled themselves with the dependable lie of history: "It could never happen again."

And shall we, too, move past the ominous reminders of the Cold War?

When I see the increasingly dangerous consolidation of power by one party in Washington—not by democratic processes but by a confederacy of political machinations—the escalation of lawlessness in the land, unbridled racism that incites the lower instincts to retreat to tribes, and the replacement of national identity around the ideas of the Constitution with the prejudicial interests of groups, the immorality in so-called entertainment, the widespread naïveté and uncritical acceptance of poisonous new cultural norms, then, my mind returns to the Cold War. I see the bones of a struggle that left millions dead, and I cannot pass unmoved and uninterested.

Mercifully, the Lord gave us a Ronald Reagan, a Margaret Thatcher, and John Paul II, along with Rev. Billy Graham, and many others, who not only recognized the threats, but named them, challenged them, and, by God's grace, defeated them.[37] Some say that the Cold War ended when the Berlin Wall came down. Others recognize that there was an earthquake-event that sent a fault line running through the length of the Berlin Wall and split the Iron Curtain.

In June 1979 John Paul II touched down in Poland. Against every order, the Pontiff conducted a great Communion Service. The people even saw the secret police abandoning their shadows and taking their place in the line to receive the Bread and the Cup.[38]

The late Dr. Lee Edwards, the renowned American historian, was unequivocal in his assessment: "The Pope's historic pilgrimage set in motion 'a revolution of the spirit' that resulted—a mere decade later—in the collapse of communism in eastern and central Europe."[39]

I was there as Communism collapsed—not in Poland or East Germany,—but the most Stalinist-Communist regime on earth: Albania.[40]

The Persecuted Priest

Albania was the last Communist nation to break free from the diabolical grip of totalitarianism. In 1991 I was there, preaching through the country and serving as a journalist for World Magazine. One evening, my Albanian host, a young man who was a student at university, asked me to join him at Skanderbeg Square. He informed me that there would be a significant student gathering in that main public space in the capital city—a demonstration to celebrate freedom. "We want you to preach the Gospel." So, that night, we gathered with hundreds of students in Skanderbeg Square. The liberty-loving young people had toppled the 30-foot-tall bronze statue of the infamous and ruthless dictator, Enver Hoxha (1908-1985; pronounced "Ho'-Jah"), in February 1991.[41] The students had removed the disgraced figure to a location at the University of Tirana. I must only assume that the statue's head came loose from the body and was brought to the square (or another dictator's head was available). For that unforgettable night, I preached the Gospel of Jesus Christ to Skanderbeg Square's masses from atop the severed metallic head of a dictator who vowed to wipe out Christianity once and for all time.

I preached a message on true freedom in Christ from whom flows all other liberties in life.

The following day, in the hotel (a ramshackle turn-of-the century room with water available, "When the shepherd boy can fix pump at the river"), I conversed with a Roman Catholic Bishop and an Albanian priest. The two Christian clerics were seated next to me, having coffee. The Bishop recognized me from the night before, at Skanderbeg Square. He leaned over towards my table, smiling and speaking English in a heavy native Italian accent, said, "Pastor, thank you for your message last night." I thanked him for his encouragement. He smiled and continued. "I want to introduce you to a great Christian hero." I turned my interest to an unusually thin, middle-aged man, wearing a Roman collar, and seated across from the Bishop. His face was noble though his cheeks seemed hollowed by disease or hunger, or, perhaps, both. Yet, rather diminish his overall countenance, the obvious suffering that he had borne added to the depth of his presence. The priest's deep-set eyes made shadows in the excess skin wrinkled beneath. Oddly, the shadows served to paradoxically highlight his sparkling eyes of faded cornflower.

There was sunlight in the dark recesses of pain. Here was joy. Here was suffering; and one attribute did not cancel the other, but, instead, formed the full measure of this man's countenance. His head was shaved clean, though I noticed he had not shaved that morning. "Mirë dita, Pastor!" ("Good day, Pastor) the priest smiled and radiated what I could only describe as sincerity, and contentment. "I am *Father John," he said.[42] The priest's unbridled smile revealed more gum than tooth. The Bishop asked the Albanian priest to stand and raise his shirt to reveal his bareback. Father John moved sprightly at the bishop's behest, though it appear to me that the priest moved at great personal cost. The priest stood with an apparent favoring of one leg over the other, crippled by force of some brutish power. He looked, with modesty, to see if there were others around. Seeing none, he raised his arms backwards, across his shoulders, to hoist his frayed and fading black clerical shirt from oversized slacks held in place by piece of leather leash. As Father John raised the shirt, gingerly, as if to minimize an incredible pain, it suddenly occurred to me that the scene was like a dramatic lifting of curtains at a county fair, to reveal a scene of horror. To be clear, the drama of the unveiling was not contrived, but inherent. Both the bishop and the priest looked at me to see my reaction. They knew from experience that *I would* experience a reaction.

I can never banish the gruesome visage that I witnessed that day. The conception before me was encoded in my brain as *explicit memory*. As such, the vision was seared through the thin membrane separating matter and spirit. The sight metastasized into emotion and became experience. It is as disturbing at this moment as when I saw it on that summer morning in 1991. The flesh on the priest's emaciated back looked like a veritable mountain range of lesions, welts, and wounds that had, over time, melded together to create a grim testimony to inhumanity. I was invited to observe his wounds more carefully—which I took as somewhat odd but followed the guidance. So, I continued to gaze in horror at Father John's mangled flesh. The Bishop, wanting me to experience the depth of suffering of the priest before speaking, at last, spoke.

"You see this, Pastor? Is this not horrible? I will tell you what happened. I will tell you about 'Utopia' in the Peoples Socialist State of

Albania! This good man was in a hard labor prison for five years. His crime? Father John had been caught by the secret police baptizing children in an underground church in Albania's northern mountainous regions. What you see, Pastor, is the price of following God in a godless system."

The People's Socialist Republic of Albania, officially atheist by constitution, having purged the land of clergy in 1968—I have a book of photographs of the hangings in my study—considered expressions of faith in God as a class of crime most seditious. The Socialists believed, "You cannot love God and the State." So, the Communists got rid of God, or so they supposed.

There was an uninterrupted silence as I looked upon Father John's back, as if to honor the presence of one who had suffered for Christ. The Bishop fixed his eyes upon mine as if to demand silence at the sight, and, to seal his words and sear my view into my consciousness. At a moment he calculated to be unbearable to see any more, the bishop turned to the priest, and instructed him in Albanian, "Tell this Presbyterian minister about how God used that time." The priest with his arms turned backward, holding his black clerical shirt to his shoulders, his naked back of fused flesh fully exposed, spoke to me in his native northern dialect: "The Communist guards beat me because I would not deny my Savior, the Lord Jesus Christ. I love Him more today than I have ever loved Him. God was at work, Pastor. You must believe me! I know I look terrible, but God is in this!"

As I listened, my eyes filled with tears. I tried to speak, but the wounds were to me a holy thing, a place where God dwelt. I was in awe even as Isaiah before the Lord. I heard the Lord speak in His Word to my spirit, "This is My body . . ." (Luke 22:19) I recognized the lacerated flesh as reminders of the crucified and risen Christ. I sensed the presence of the holy: "But the LORD is in His holy temple. Let all the earth keep silence before Him" (Habakkuk 2:20 NKJV).

"Pastor . . ." the Catholic bishop spoke, as if he were a psychologist brining me out of a hypnotic state. "Pastor, I know it is hard to see. Can you believe this?" I couldn't. The level of hatred of God, and the depth of a faith in God were juxtaposed and intersecting at the same time. At first, the encounter was difficult to process. But there it was. Father

John, still presenting his wounds, spoke matter-of-factly and without any sign of emotion as if he had cried so often that he had depleted his tears. Still gazing upon the mutilated soft tissue covering unseen bruises and breaks, I heard this Christian shepherd speak once more, softly, without remorse or resentment, as he expressed theological reflection on the persecution:

> "God was in the prison with me. You see, the guards were changed out every few weeks. The sadistic ritual became too gruesome for one man. Pastor, you must understand I do not hold them accountable. I forgave them as they carried out their orders from that 'Beast,' the Socialist State. Some of the guards who lashed me and demanded that I renounce Jesus Christ became Christians. Some would even show up to perform their ghastly duty and only pretend to whack me. Then, those guards would gather with the others and attend my secret services in the forest." At that sentence, the priest, heretofore unbreakable, began to weep. "Oh, I miss them so: my parish in the woods."[43]

Like many Americans, Canadians, British, Western Europeans, and others, I have watched and listened to the voices of those seizing power by all necessary means, discrediting — "canceling" — any voice of dissent and requiring that the population not only do as they say but also believe what they believe. In Romans 1:18-32, St. Paul' description of the downward cycle of unbelief, the normalizing and codification of sin is the final ring of the Inferno of atheism (vv. 28-32 in NASB).:

> And just as they did not see fit to acknowledge God any longer, God gave them over to a depraved mind, to do those things which are not proper, being filled with all unrighteousness, wickedness, greed, evil; full of envy, murder, strife, deceit, malice; *they are* gossips, slanderers, haters of God, insolent, arrogant, boastful, inventors of evil, disobedient to parents, without understanding, untrustworthy, unloving, unmerciful; and although they know the ordinance of God, that those who practice such things are worthy of death, they not only do the same, but also give hearty approval to those who practice them.

Conclusion

President Biden, in his inaugural address to the American nation, promised "unity."[44] Yet, the furiously busy agenda that unfolded looked more like "uniformity."[45] Unity is a virtue built on the foundation of love. Uniformity is a ruthless agenda to forcefully silence all critics, reeducate all others so that the party line is protected, and centralized power is maintained.

I sense jackals and hyaenas in our midst. The bleached bones of fallen antelopes are scattered across human history. The great Eagle is in danger. Apathy and immorality, mixed with the incessant, mind-numbing, soul-searing cult of entertainment, and the Mad-hatter's world of Postmodernism, a Foucault-induced anti-Christian mindset that deconstructs every sacred idea and replaces it with nonsensical words and imaginary concepts.[46] Up is down. Down is up. Women are men. Men are women. Children are objects. Right is wrong and wrong is right. Only power and control remain free from deconstruction. Power and control are the currencies of the Socialist State.

But there is still the Lion—the Lion of Judah, the Lamb of God who takes away the sins of the world. He lives. He is, to borrow from Lewis, "on the move." He is more powerful than all the jackets and hyenas in the world. He has shown that each time the beast has sought to devour His people, *He arrives.* As with His arrival at Lazarus's funeral, He appears in His own time and for His own purposes. He uses the very things that seek to destroy His kingdom to become the paradoxical power that destroys the enemies. It is *always* only a matter of time.

I, for one, would prefer the wounds from being beaten daily for telling the truth rather than the eternal shame of living a lie. For, mark my words, the day will come when the Socialist State that is now being constructed in our country *will fall* to the ground, toppled by the masses who were denied their God-given right to "life, liberty, and the pursuit of happiness." The mighty Lion will roar from the holy mountain, His voice reverberating across the plains of time, "And ye shall know the truth, and the truth shall make you free" (John 8:32).

Out of the ruins of another crumbled wall will arise the great bald eagle, his wings fully extended in renewed strength, soaring freely, high above the fresh growth of fruited plains and the city on a hill.

Questions for Discussion and Reflection

Individual | Class | Small Group

1. Compare socialism's view of human nature with the Christian understanding of human dignity and the Imago Dei. How does this difference impact society's structure and governance?

2. The chapter emphasizes the danger of forgetting historical events like the failure of socialism. Discuss the importance of historical memory in shaping a society's future. How can Christian communities ensure that lessons from the past concerning human dignity and freedom are not forgotten?

3. Reflect on how ideologies like socialism and communism perpetuate oppression and undermine the church's mission. How can Christians resist ideologies that contradict Biblical teachings?

4. The author's personal experiences from the Cold War offer a unique perspective on the dangers of totalitarian regimes. Explore the power of personal narratives and testimonies in communicating the impact of political ideologies on faith and freedom.

5. How can Christians use Biblical theology to respond to political ideologies that usurp God's authority and violate human dignity?

6. How can the Church respond to the rise of ideologies that threaten religious freedom and human dignity in today's world?

Loving God, Loving Others
The Evil of Hatred by Accidental Differences in Humankind

Michael A. Milton

That human beings have rights, that they are born equal; that they are owed sustenance, and shelter, and refuge from persecution: these were never self-evident truths.

– Tom Holland, *Dominion*[1]

Let's begin with two statements, two thoughts, two convictions, and one set of diametrically opposite worldviews:

If someone says, "I love God," and hates his brother, he is a liar; for he who does not love his brother whom he has seen, how can he love God he has not seen? And this commandment we have from Him: that he who loves God must love his brother also" (1 John 4:20–21 NKJV

Here is the other statement:

I had fantasies of unloading a revolver into the head of any white person that got in my way, burying their body and wiping my bloody hands as I walked away relatively guiltless with a bounce in my step.[2]

The distance between the two statements born out of divine love and the other out of mortal hatred is as far as heaven is from hell. The psychiatrist's Freudian "id" is as bloated with self as her soul is depleted by sin. Even if she chose this wish narrative as a shamanic therapy to excise the accumulated infection from a spiritual pathology, the effect is the same: self-satisfaction by homicide.

The former? Healing. Hopeful. Redemptive. The latter? Troubling. Chilling. *Inconceivable*. How does a human being come to such a place?

The (Hopefully) Obvious Concern

That a physician and scholar should hold a lecture, "The Psychopathic Problem of the White Mind," in a prestigious school of medicine (Yale) to express her innermost *feelings* (not tested hypotheses, as one might expect from a scientist) about *race* through *rhetorical exclusion* is to underscore the dissimilarities between two groups of people for the purpose of denying the benefits of community, *viz.*, a degree of life, liberty, and happiness would be *almost* inconceivable.[3] *Almost* -because that same physician is actively (even if unwittingly) fermenting social anarchy based on the well-honed strategies of pitting people against people of the same nation using skin color (and a predictable sociohistorical revisionist history to go with it, e.g., the 1619 Project).[4] Division by identity hatred is a well-documented *m'ethode de succ`es* (in the same way that the destruction of the Twin Towers on 9/11 was a *success* for the murderous terrorists who planned and executed the atrocity). The doctor's advocacy of murder as a sort of self-prescribed amphetamine to quench her homicidal yearnings (and, by her admission, to overcome her intense anxiety provoked by a perceived incorrigible presence of "whiteness"), is based on a group of people of the same skin color, is, at once, repulsive and appalling. There is absolutely no fear of *cliché* in deducing, "If a medical doctor teaching before an elite graduate school audience can openly share her 'dream' of murdering other human beings based on their genetically predisposed and comparatively lower levels of melanin, how many other madmen will carry it out?"[5] Skin color has been demonstrated to be the product of a complex genetic journey that involves both human migration, generations of genetic dynamics, and the adaptability of human beings to live in certain environments.[6]

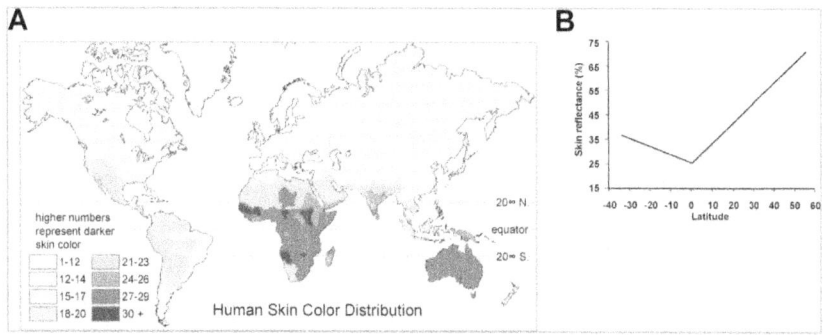

Figure 1: Summary of 102 skin reflectance samples for males as a function of latitude, redrawn from Releth-ford (1997). https://doi.org/10.1371/journal.pbio. 0000027.g002.

The human pigmentation journey continues as globalization disperses highly isolated skin types. Melanin pigmentation types, *eumelanin* (darker) and *pheomelanin* (lighter), produce skin color in individuals, but much work remains in learning about *why* we should care. For instance, the abundance of pheomelanin could increase cancer rates in lighter-skinned, freckled individuals of, e.g., Irish descent.[7] Those with increased levels of eumelalin tend to have greater resistance to malaria and related health benefits by settling near the earth's equator. What unique health concerns do these families of Man develop in northern climates? What about the death rate of the Boers (Dutch farmers in South Africa) from melanoma? These are some of the *more critical questions* of "race," if you prefer that term for the various people groups of humankind. Ethnicity, or "color," as the psychiatrist chose to describe the differences in human beings, is not only a social construct but is also a physiological reality; a reality that deserves scientific inquiry for the greater flourishing of our *one race* of Mankind. If the Yale School of Medicine is interested in race and medicine, perhaps inviting a researcher to lecture on the latest work being done on pigmentation and disease would be better than hosting a practicing racist. Of course, such subject matter would be scientific rather than social, or political. However, the Dean of Yale Medical School could be spared the embarrassing optics, and questionable association with a psychiatrist dreaming of killing white people. Or, maybe hosting an alleged racist just doesn't matter anymore.

So, the concept of moral depravity or superiority by the observation of melanin measurements is incredibly naïve if not downright ignorant. However, Dr. Aruna Khilanani, who lectured at the Child Study Center at Yale School of Medicine, confirmed to all (including, regrettably, our future pediatricians) a sobering maxim: *Yesterday's conspiracist is today's voice of reason.*

The Biblical Truth about Race

None of the *scientific* observations we have noted contradict the record of Scripture.

Even a cursory survey of the Old and New Testaments reveals a unified truth: God created Mankind ("ad-am" in Hebrew), male and female. Sin and rebellion against God led to the first great migration away from Eden. This was, as John Milton (1608–1674) famously retold the biblical story in *Paradise Lost* (1667). Through several significant events in world history (the global Flood and aftermath), God made from the remnant of Mankind, viz., Noah, his wife, his sons and their wives, various families, nations, ethnicities, and other categories of human beings. These varieties of the one "species" came about, in large part, when God divided humanity into families and dispersed them across the earth. Though Mankind sinned against God, the Lord God is gracious and intends for a *Paradise Regained* (John Milton, 1671). God loves His creation. Human beings thought about time as cyclical until Christ. As Tom Holland described it, Christianity reconfigured time.[8] *Christ has died, Christ is risen, Christ will come again.* Or, Eden to New Heaven and New Earth—Creation, Fall, Redemption, and Consummation.

However, the Bible is clear that God has prioritized His most sacred creation, Mankind. For Mankind has the image of God, the *Imago Dei*. Humanity, all of us, have communicable attributes of God (we lack and can never attain the incommunicable attributes, e.g., *omniscience;* We are not and can never be a god). Yet, we carry a reflection of His image, marred as that image may be by sin. People, *all people,* are precious to God. He promised that through Abraham, God would bring blessing to the entire earth, that is, to the one human race. God accomplished this through Israel, ethnic Jews of old, some faithful to God and some not; who became the birthing nation to the Messiah, our Lord Jesus Christ, who came to fulfill the Covenant, meet the demands of God's holy law, and live a sinless life offered up for our sins on a cross. By faith in Jesus Christ, any human being who calls on the name of the Lord Jesus will be saved. By the grace of God alone and without human contribution to salvation, Jesus Christ's righteousness is imputed to our account, and Christ's atonement on the cross is sufficient to pay for our sins.

Here is a brief on the Bible and Race (with the author's emphases):

ONE RACE (GENESIS 1:26 KJV)(NORTON 2005)

> So God created **man** [$'\bar{a}\,\bar{a}m$] in his own image, in the image of God *he created him; male and female he created them.*[9]

PARADISE LOST (ROMANS 8:19-23 ESV)

> For the creation was subjected to futility, not willingly, but because of him who subjected it, in hope that the creation itself will be set free from its bondage to corruption and obtain the freedom of the glory of the children of God. For we know that the whole creation has been groaning together in the pains of childbirth until now. And not only the creation, but we ourselves, who have the first fruits of the Spirit, groan inwardly as we wait eagerly for adoption as sons, the redemption of our bodies

GLOBAL CATASTROPHE (GENESIS 10:1-5 ESV; THE FLOOD AND THE REBIRTH OF HUMANITY)

> These are the generations of the sons of Noah, Shem, Ham, and Japheth. Sons were born to them after the flood. The sons of Japheth: Gomer, Magog, Madai, Javan, Tubal, Meshech, and Tiras. The sons of

Gomer: Ashkenaz, Riphath, and Togarmah. The sons of Javan: Elishah, Tarshish, Kittim, and Dodanim. From these, the coastland peoples spread in their lands, each with his own language, by their clans, in their nations.

Babel and Human Migration (Genesis 11:4, 6, 8 ESV; The building of a great structure, prior to the rebellious desire for a unified front against God)

Then they said, "Come, let us build ourselves a city and a tower with its top in the heavens, and let us make a name for ourselves, lest we be dispersed over the face of the whole earth."

And the Lord said, "Behold, they are one people, and they have all one language . .

So the Lord dispersed them from there over the face of all the earth, and they left off building the city.

A Divine Covenant to the Earth (Genesis 12:3; John 3:16, 17 ESV)

. . . and in thee [Abraham's nation, Israel, and the land (their earthly home) that will bring forth the Messiah] shall *all families of the earth* be blessed.

For God so loved *the world,* that he gave his only Son, that *whoever believes in him* should not perish but have eternal life. For God did not send his Son into the world to condemn the world, but in order that *the world might be saved through him.*

People Groups (Jeremiah 13:23; Acts 10:28; 17:26; Romans, 2:11; 10:12-13; Galatians 3:28; Colossians 3:11 ESV)

Can the Ethiopian change his skin or the leopard his spots? Then also you can do good who are accustomed to do evil.

And he said to them, "You yourselves know how unlawful it is for a Jew to associate with or to visit anyone of another nation, but God has shown me that *I should not call any person common or unclean.*

And he made *from one man* every nation of mankind to live on all the face of the earth, having determined allotted periods and the boundaries of their dwelling place,

For God shows no partiality.

For there is *no distinction between Jew and Greek* ; for the same Lord is Lord of all, bestowing his riches on all who call on him. For "everyone who calls on the name of the Lord will be saved."

Here there is not Greek and Jew, circumcised and uncircumcised, barbarian, Scythian, slave, free, but *Christ is all and in all.*

Racism is Condemned (Leviticus 19:33-34; James 2:4; 8,9 ESV)

When a stranger sojourns with you in your land, you shall not do him wrong. You shall treat the stranger who sojourns with you as the native among you, and you shall love him as yourself, for you were strangers in the land of Egypt: I am the Lord your God.

Have you not then made distinctions among yourselves and become judges with evil thoughts? If you really fulfill the royal law according to the Scripture, "You shall love your neighbor as yourself," you are doing well. But if you show partiality, you are committing sin and are convicted by the law as transgressors.

Have you not then made distinctions among yourselves and become judges with evil thoughts?

The Future of Race (Romans 8:20-23; 1 Corinthians 12:13 ESV)

> After this, I looked, and behold, a great multitude that no one could number, from every nation, from all tribes and peoples and languages, standing before the throne and before the Lamb, clothed in white robes, with palm branches in their hands, and crying out with a loud voice, "Salvation belongs to our God who sits on the throne, and to the Lamb!"

> For in one Spirit, we were all baptized into one body—Jews or Greeks, slaves or free—all were made to drink of one Spirit.

Diagnosing and Treating the Sin of Racism

The practice of assessment, diagnosis, and spiritual treatment of the human soul through the prayerful and studied application of Word, Sacrament, and Prayer remains the most potent method for human transformation.[10] Such a practice is called *pastoring*. *The cure of souls is the* God-ordained vocation and central mission of the Christian shepherd. For instance, we witness evidence of a veritable *Balkanization* (i.e., fragmenting) of America (and other Western and English-speaking nations, e.g., Australia).[11] Sadly, division and other pathologies of human society are an undeniable result of the poisonous presence of original and residual sins -the physical and metaphysical consequences of creaturely rebellion against the Creator are well-known to the Christian shepherd and pastoral theologian. There is a particularly virulent and vicious strain of the sin of division: the degrading, dangerous, and highly infectious fracture between human beings because on based on *accidental, non-contributing* factors. We use the word *accidental* to describe those features, traits, and characteristics beyond one's control (we are certainly not asserting that life is an *accident* in the usual first meaning of that word).

One cannot choose certain physical features, one's bloodline, or even one's socio-economic or geographic place of origin. Therefore, to isolate and harass, or to hate a person or group in any way, based on the offended party's disdain for accidental causes in one's life is not only cruel but illogical. One's boorish behavior might put us off at a party. Still, such a factor is not accidental or inherited (though it is possible that no one ever taught the poor fellow about social etiquette). While possibly cruel or insensitive to the plight of another, we would, at least, be protesting a malleable factor. The poor fellow can change his ways. If, on the other hand, you were offended by the indelicacy of the man at the party because he was born with physical deformities, e.g., an irregular nervous system that caused him to spill his drink, you would be a fool. The man is incapable of choosing his physical qualities. Shout, jump up and down, or leave the party in disgust, but you cannot expect the poor fellow to change. Yet, you can do something. You could help him. Alternatively, you can ignore the man. You could even gather together a society for the hatred of those born with irregular nervous systems. However, your organization can never change the individual. Your club is only capable of prejudicial treatment of another based on disgust spawned by pure, illogical hatred. The example is admittedly shallow. Yet, human beings routinely hate others based on their disdain for accidental factors: socio-economic classifications, sex (i.e., gender), religion, ethnicity, viz., *race*. Most New Testament epistles had their genesis in responding to the sin of division. Whether Corinth or Galatia, Rome or Ephesus, Christian communities fragmented because of external or superficial differences. Apostolic letters were then drafted and dispersed to the churches to correct the behavior and warn of God's wrath against such division.

Racism and other prejudicial actions result from sin and the complexities of converging pathologies of the human soul. The cure is the open-hearted, forgiving love of God in Christ. Consider this one passage citing the desire of Jesus, the Son of the Triune God, to leave His royal robes in heaven in order to abide with Man: (Philippians 2:5-8 NKJV).

> Let this mind be in you which was also in Christ Jesus, who, being in the form of God, did not consider it robbery to be equal with God, but made Himself of no reputation, taking the form of a bondservant, *and coming in the likeness of men*. And being found in appearance as a

man, He humbled Himself and became obedient to *the point of* death, even the death of the cross.

This is how we come to the passage that inaugurated our journey in this article, 1 John 4:20–21 (NKJV):

> If someone says, "I love God," and hates his brother, he is a liar; for he who does not love his brother whom he has seen, how can he love God whom he has not seen? 21 And this commandment we have from Him: that he who loves God must love his brother also.

Removing Racism

So, the Bible teaches that we are all of one race: the human race. There are differences, varieties, and adaptations within the species, but we are all human beings. Therefore, for one person or group to ridicule, isolate, or injure another group of human beings because of accidental characteristics—variables within the human species they were born with—is a cruel and irrational response. Such tribalism promotes widespread division of people degradation of humanity itself and makes the civil community at any level - from the family to the city, to the nation – an impossible vision. Since such prejudicial language and hostile actions against people flow from the accidental traits they carry from birth, there can be no other assumption that the source of such prejudice is pure hatred that leads to division and division that leads to violence. Such societal confusion that breeds national fragmentation is a well-known chapter in the Marxist-Socialist- anarchist's playbook. Books by communists in America have never hidden their agendas: "Make no mistake about it: we intend to keep bashing the dead white males, and the live ones, and the females too, until the social construct known as 'the white race' is destroyed-not 'deconstructed' but destroyed."[12]

When we hate each other enough, an oppressive force steps in to "heal" the breach. In thirty-two years of military service, including top-secret naval intelligence gathering and analysis in the Cold War and the Chaplain Command of all Military Intelligence Readiness Command (MIRC) Army Chaplains posted around the globe, I have seen the devious plan at work. I have also witnessed the consequences. As a theologian and curator of the human soul, I know the damage done by racism and its wake of burning fuel for generations.

The Bible condemns racism as an assault on the image of God in humanity. For those who say that the clergy should keep quiet in the sanctuary, I would remind us all that Dr. Martin Luther King, Jr. was forced by history to make the matter the centering place of his vocation. Though a scholar, a Ph.D. in Religion, and a shepherd of souls, he sacrificed the life of a "vicar" for the role of a "prophet." It was the great John Donne, the preacher-poet of St. Paul's Cathedral, who reminded us,

> No man is an *Island*, entire of itself; every man is a piece of the *Continent*, a part of the *maine*; if a Clod be washed away by the *Sea*, *Europe* is the lessee, as well as if a *Promontorie* were, as well as if a *Manner* of thy *friends* or of *thine owne* were; any man's *death* diminishes *me*, because I am involved in *Mankind* ; And therefore never send to know for whom the *bell* tolls; It tolls for *thee*.[13]

Our love of God causes us to love others. Our calling as Christians causes us to speak. and act for those in danger. The unique vocation of the clergy requires that we "cry aloud and spare not" (Isaiah 58:1) when the vile threat of racism threatens humanity. Unfortunately, critical race theory, and books such as Ibram X. Kendi's 2019 book, *How to Be an Antiracist*, have become mainstream. The views are not only immature, poorly stated, and riddled with historical errors but are also contrary to God's Word and, thus, harmful to human existence. Yet, their horrendous ideologies are being taught in grammar schools through professional postgraduate courses. There can be only one conclusion to normalizing hatred grounded in *accidental* differences in humankind: the loss of necessary, rational, civil discourse, which invariably leads to civil violence and violence which leads to self-destruction. What is that conclusion? What must we do?

Offer the life of Jesus Christ who forgave us to others. Release the divine *Word from Another World* and the Spirit of God will convert, or, by judicial hardening of those who refuse Him, judge. I will challenge you to see how hatred of others withers when we see that we are of a race of sinners, under the judgment of our Creator, and desperately in need of a Savior. Therefore, I urge:

> Receive God's love in Jesus Christ, and you will not only be protected from such corrosive ideologies as racism, but God will use the very thing that you used to stop God's love, to advance it. For good is stronger than evil, and the God who sent His Son to save one race, the race of humanity, will transform you.

How did your mother sing it to you when you were a child? Perhaps, the words are dated or unintentionally focused on color, suspect to stereotypical latent tendencies of an older, less sophisticated era. Nevertheless, the mother who would sing this to her wee lad or lass knew that the more prevalent sins of the heart that could strike at her child *had to be faced,* and *had to be defeated* on the most decisive battleground: the child's heart. Her chosen weapon for this spiritual warfare is the one we need now, more than ever: *the love of God in Jesus Christ.* Remember? I do.

> Jesus loves the little children, all of the children of the world; Red and yellow, black and white, they are precious in his sight; Jesus loves the little children of the world.[14]

God's love in our hearts yields a harvest of love for others. This is how otherwise uncontrollable weeds of racism wither, and the new growth of life emerges, bringing peace, creating unity, and releasing the power of life as it was meant to be lived.

QUESTIONS FOR DISCUSSION AND REFLECTION
Individual | Class | Small Group

1. Contrasting Worldviews on Love and Hatred: Reflect on the stark contrast between the Biblical command to love one's neighbor and the expression of racial hatred cited in the chapter. How do these opposing views reflect the fundamental differences between Christian teachings and secular ideologies? Discuss the implications of these worldviews on individual behavior and societal norms.

2. The Role of Forgiveness in Addressing Racial Hatred: Considering the chapter's mention of Dr. Aruna Khilanani's statements and the Biblical emphasis on love and forgiveness, discuss how Christian principles of forgiveness and reconciliation can be applied to address deep-seated racial animosities and heal societal divisions.

3. Christianity's Influence on Human Rights and Equality: Tom Holland's quote suggests that human rights and equality are not self-evident truths but have been shaped by historical and cultural influences. Do you agree or disagree? Why? Discuss how Christianity has contributed to the development of these concepts. What role can the church play today in promoting and defending human rights and equality?

4. Scientific and Biblical Perspectives on Race: The chapter explores both scientific and Biblical perspectives on human diversity and race. How can these perspectives complement each other in promoting a deeper understanding and appreciation of human diversity? Discuss the importance of acknowledging both scientific findings and Scriptural teachings in conversations about race.

. . .

5. Addressing Racism from a Pastoral Perspective: Consider the chapter's discussion on diagnosing and treating the sin of racism. As Christians, how can pastoral care and Biblical teachings be utilized to combat racism and promote reconciliation and unity within communities?

6. The Power of Love in Overcoming Division: The chapter concludes with a focus on God's love as the solution to hatred and division, exemplified in the children's hymn about Jesus' love for all children. Discuss practical ways in which the church and individual believers can demonstrate this love in a divided world and how this approach can contribute to healing and unity.

The Final Hope
On Spiritual Awakening
Michael A. Milton

> I shall see no hope until individual members of the church are praying for revival, perhaps meeting in one another's homes, meeting in groups amongst friends, meeting together in churches, meeting anywhere you like, and praying with urgency and concentration for a shedding fourth of the power of God, such as he shed forth one hundred and two hundred years ago and in every other period of revival, and of reawakening. There is no hope until we do.
>
> — Martyn Lloyd-Jones, *Revival*.[1]

You have heard it said. You have undoubtedly said: "The only hope, now, is God to send true revival." Of course, you are not speaking of an annual event in a local church, a spring get-together that focuses on reaching the lost and stirring up spiritual strength in believers (however laudable and Gospel-obedient such an event might be). Instead, when we say there is "no hope for America unless God sends revival," we are speaking of a supernatural in-breaking of the Spirit of God that produces sorrow over sins, repentance, and a turning to God by receiving Jesus Christ as Lord and Savior and enjoying the blessing of his Lordship in every area of our lives. *That* is a genuine spiritual awakening of people wrought entirely by the divine activity, eternal purposes, and out of the fathomless, compassionate nature of our sovereign and loving Creator.

What are the Manifestations of Spiritual Awakening

The spiritual awakening and either an individual or a Community — whether that community is a village or an entire hemisphere —has specific identifiable characteristics.

Signs of Genuine Spiritual Awakening

Spiritual awakening produces a fresh recognition of the holiness of God and the simpleness of mankind. As the great Dr. Martyn-Lloyd Jones put it in his essential work on Revival:

> "The essence of a revival is that the Holy Spirit comes down upon a number of people together, upon a whole church, upon a number of churches, districts, or perhaps a whole country. That is what is meant by revival. It is, if you like, a visitation of the Holy Spirit."[2]

Spiritual awakening creates a healthy sense of introspection, leading to the discovery or confession of pockets of sin and, consequently, sinful behavior.

Spiritual awakening causes the individual or the community to cry out to God for forgiveness. To come before an omniscient, omnipresent, and omnipotent God of the universe, one is left unable to speak. This person may have been worshiping God all of her life, but she realizes she has been going through the motions at that moment. Now, in the gift of God reviving her soul, she sees the cancerous deposit of rebellion against God. She recognizes that the cancer of sin has metastasized into every area of our being. The hideous site is too much for her. The revived believer recovers a voice for the only possible response before a holy God: she cries out for forgiveness with a rare and utterly authentic contrite Spirit.

Spiritual awakening cultivates a supernatural and visceral need for prayer: private prayer, family prayer, prayer in public worship, and prayers throughout the days of one's life. Spiritual awakening is such a profound event that the wake of its presence can and often does last a lifetime (e.g., the First Great Awakening; British Colonies in America, 1740s and 1750s; and the Welsh Revivals of 1904-05).

Spiritual awakening stirs a burden to reach others with the pure Gospel of Jesus Christ (salvation by grace alone through faith alone in Christ according to the Scriptures alone and all unconditionally and unreservedly to God's glory). In the First Great Awakening that stirred the Colonies from Vermont to Virginia from New Hampshire to North Carolina, missionary movements emerged in New England. Under the guidance of men such as Jonathan Edwards and David Brainard, tidal waves of missionary groups washed across the British colonies, testifying, witnessing, and preaching the holiness of God, the sinfulness of Man, and the only way to God through His Son, Jesus Christ. No less than the U.S. National Humanities Center had to admit the enormous sway that the spiritual awakening had upon a People who would, in only a few decades, forge a new nation:

> These early revivals in the northern colonies inspired some converts to become missionaries to the American South. In the late 1740s, Presbyterian preachers from New York and New Jersey began proselytizing in the Virginia Piedmont, and by the 1750s, some members of a group known as the Separate Baptists moved from New England to central North Carolina and quickly extended their influence to surrounding colonies. By the eve of the American Revolution, their evangelical converts accounted for about ten percent of all southern churchgoers.[3]

Another mark of true spiritual awakening is the emphasis on biblical truth, viz., right doctrine. This may sound counter-intuitive to some who have misunderstood revival. However, an authentic act of revival from on high that leads to spiritual awakening always—*always*—seeks the truth of God in God's Word, the Holy Bible. The doctrines of grace preached by the Reformers never shine more brilliantly than when proclaimed in the light of the true revival. To assume that revival and its consequent blessing of spiritual awakening is *only* a divine visitation upon the heart *and not the head—i.e., the emotions but not the intellect—* is a seriously flawed supposition based upon notorious examples of demonic abuse of the heavenly intervention (more on that in a few paragraphs), or historical ignorance. A Cornell University publishing house sponsored a journal article on spiritual awakenings. The content contains embarrassingly shallow observations about spiritual awakenings: "Spontaneous Spiritual Awakenings (SSAs) are subjective experiences characterized by a sudden sense of direct contact, union or merging with a perceived ultimate reality, the universe, or the divine."[4] The peer-reviewed assertion may accurately describe certain pagan rituals and even some accounts of outlier Christian sects. Still, it is not descriptive of the spiritual awakenings of, e.g., the First Great Awakening.

True revival transforms *heart and head*. Indeed, it may be stated without reservation that the great confessions of Christianity—often composed, like the New Testament epistles, under the threat of false teaching or doctrinal apostasy—were studied and articulated during times of historic and widespread spiritual awakening.

Along these lines, we should add those genuine spiritual awakenings, whether in one person or larger populations, have inspired the building of hospitals, new churches, and special attention to the oppressed, the marginalized, the physically handicapped, and those who are wounded of mind or soul. Moreover, old wounds are healed. Centuries-old breaches are repaired. The desert of human sinfulness begins to bloom. Never was this more apparent than in the growth of African-American denominations, missions, schools, and cooperative Gospel work between whites and blacks in the days leading to the American Revolution. Thus, biblical "social justice" follows revival as spring follows winter. An organically God-designed power at work renews all things in some way.

Spiritual awakenings often initiate movements to repent and remove injustices. Shameful entertainment permitted in the days before divine visitation becomes a scandal to the one who has known the holiness of God. Legislation, the courts, and law enforcement work together to reform their respective systems for the good of all. Inequities are addressed. License leading to crime is confronted. The body politic is awakened to the responsibilities of citizenship. Thus, associations begin to form for every conceivable public interest.

Spiritual awakenings also profoundly affect family life, exalting motherhood and calling for manly responsibility in caring for the home physically, materially, and morally.[5] Role relationships in the home and the public square are reassessed. What we think of as traditional roles are no longer an embarrassment. The winners? Women and children, who were promised such liberty in days of sensuality and disobedience, are again valued as the highest essence of our humanity. Homemaking is not disparaged but cherished. Lessons learned even in the dark days before the revival, respecting (and deploying) women's unique contributions to every area of life and paying attention to, e.g., the respective stages of childhood, are not merely reassessed but eagerly embraced and incorporated into the post-revival "turning." Yet, the unfounded stigmas, e.g., those that led to sneering at women in the home, women as primary caregivers of children, are happily deserted.

The present-day fixation on gender fluidity is unable to have public support when a large part of the population has come into the presence of the Creator who made Mankind male and female (and the glorious complimentary gifts and graces that are innate in male and female). When a people (a person, a family, an institution, or a nation; that is, any community on any point of the spectrum) loses its way, it defaults to the most base post-Edenic urges at work within them. With this loss of a sort of societal magnetic field emitted by the proper "fear of God," people revert to what Dr. Walker Percy assessed as "genital sex and violence."[6] Ultimately, even "genital sex" becomes an act of violence. Thus, in the end, there is only violence against each other. Such conditions are the reason for God's judgment of the earth before the deluge.

Conversely, when revival visits those communities of people, the compass is reset. Illicit sexuality and wanton violence—never the diagnoses but the symptoms (the diagnosis is a loss of humanity in a denial of God)—are, after authentic revival, like a flesh-eating microbial disease that withers for lack of oxygen. Human intercourse, Buber's "I and Thou," finds expression. The planets return to their places in orbit.

It should be added that genuine spiritual awakenings attract demonic opposition. This has often appeared in the form of excess, as noted in the phenomenology of "Spontaneous Spiritual Awakening." Barking like a dog, climbing a tree like a squirrel, or laughing uncontrollably are not signs of God's visitation but of demonic presence or human perversion. Yet, each act of genuine spiritual awakening has often attracted parasitic phoniness. Do not be duped into believing that the work of God produces hysteria or insanity.[7] Similarly, do not doubt the ship's seaworthiness because some barnacles become attached. Scrape away the parasites by prayer, fasting, and wise application of the Gospel to all parts of the Church.

Can We Anticipate Spiritual Awakenings?

Is the supernatural outpouring of God's Holy Spirit and subsequent spiritual awakening an event we can anticipate? Is it still even possible? I want to demonstrate that according to God's Word in the book of Jonah and the fourth chapter of St. John's gospel, we may see that a spiritual awakening is not only possible but that we should always pray for and anticipate the outpouring of God's Spirit upon his people and even upon a city, nation, or a hemisphere of the world or more.

Two passages, one in the Old Testament and one in the New Testament, provide a wealth of guidance concerning the large-scale converting ministry of the Holy Spirit.

Spiritual Awakening in the Book of Jonah

The book of Jonah describes the compassion and love of God for his creation. Rabbis used this ancient text to remind Israel that the covenant of God's grace was not limited to Israel. Jesus referred to Jonah as history and applied the events to His ministry (his resurrection).[6] In a real way, God's activities recorded in the book of Jonah demonstrate that the Lord has compassion on all areas of his creation — from the human beings in the city of Nineveh to pagan mariners who end up calling on Almighty God to save them, to the marine life under the sea, and even to a gourd. The last challenge of God to Jonah echoes through the age in the enigmatic conclusion to the book: "Should I have spared a plant but not spared these people who do not know their right hand from their left, and also much cattle?"

Everyone and everything in the book of Jonah responds to God except for the Hebrew prophet, Jonah. Nineveh is, of course, converted

— from the king on down. The book has an enigmatic and powerful ending. This one question, put to Jonah and the reader, challenges covenantal smugness ungodly sectarianism, and condemns a privatized faith. The gift of faith that we enjoy is not exclusive to ourselves. How does the old axiom go? *We have been blessed to be a blessing.* Sometimes such says are banality. Sometimes, old sayings are new to each generation because they are true. We should have a heart like God's and desire genuine revival amongst those who do not know the Lord. When revival comes to individuals or communities, missionary impulses are reanimated.

What lessons do we take away about a tremendous outpouring of spiritual renewal in our day?

1. God calls us to pray for a supernatural outpouring of his spirit. Just as he called Jonah to go to Nineveh, "that great city," and proclaim the word of God, so the Lord, also, the Lord God is calling for us to pray for our country in peril, for the Western nations who once knew God but to a phone them off in favor of a secular age. Is there anything in the passage that indicates this is a one-time event and not reproducible in the lives of the people of God? The answer is clearly and most certainly "no." God calls us to pray for genuine revival from on high and for that to come to the very worst of places. But unlike Jonah, we must pray for ourselves first. We must pray that God would send revival in our hearts so that we may proclaim the unsearchable riches of Christ to a lost nation of people.

2. God is calling us to go and share the gospel of Jesus Christ to those in need. It is important to see God send revival to Nineveh through the means of his prophet, Jonah, despite Jonah's despicable behavior. Could Almighty God unleash the powers of heaven in a display of supernatural conversion en masse? Of course. However, in his sovereign love and inscrutable design for the universe, God chose that men and women, boys and girls, should receive the good news of the gospel through the testimony of others who had been saved. If we are so compassionate to cry out, "Oh God, save us! Send the supernatural outpourings of your Holy Spirit upon this nation!" Then, we should also be courageous enough to go and proclaim that word in whatever way we can wherever God has placed us.

The Samaritan woman at the well

The other vital passage to guide us in our question, "Can we still expect the supernatural outpourings of the spirit of God?" is a New Testament example. I believe that is one of the most important examples of revival in all of the Bible. John 4:4 is a critical juncture in the ministry of our Lord. Some went around the graveyard of the Gadarene, some avoided the little children, and some, even the disciples, avoided the Samaritans. Yet, Jesus went to each of these. John provides the hint that something was coming when he wrote, "But He needed to go through Samaria" (John 4:4).

He needed to go through Samaria. In other words, he, like his disciples, could have avoided this pagan, mixed-blood, synchronistic religious area by taking another route. But we see that Jesus was intentional. The King James Version puts it memorably, "And he must needs go through Samaria"). This divine intentionality noted by John demonstrates God's desire to reach all peoples upon the earth and that he will use the testimony of one person to open hearts to a tremendous outpouring of the spirit of God, a genuine revival from heaven.

It is essential to understand that the Samaritans were a singularly segregated people living among the Jews.[8] They were, in fact, the offspring of both Hebrews and neighboring pagan peoples.[9] As the marauding enemies of Israel occupied the northern kingdom, a result of Israel's disobedience and persistent waywardness, they took Jewish wives to themselves. The children of these mixed marriages undoubtedly located a familial and not unfamiliar compromise: to ostensibly follow the God of Israel while retaining the worship of the idols of their pagan ancestry. Thus, there arose a widespread Samaritan syncretism of a religion based on the Torah, with pagan practices and demonic doctrines of idolatry. Not only were the Samaritans treated as halfbreed kindred to be avoided, they were also considered, with justification if not compassion, to be thoroughly converted to pagan deities with just enough biblical truth sprinkled through to say that they, also, were children of Abraham and spiritual disciples of the one true God. Beyond these historical facts, they were the object of the ubiquitous human tendency towards racism and spiritual pride. In a word, many of the Jews believe the Samaritans had once known the truths of the Bible and worshipped the one true God but had rejected him in favor of a pluralistic religion. I share these things with you in this article because it is crucial to see that God's compassion resulting in a genuine revival from on high is not limited to pagan people who have never heard the gospel. It is also for those who have heard the gospel, received it, welcomed Christ's teachings into all of their culture, and later rejected God for a less demanding, more socially acceptable religion, or (so they imagine) no religion at all. This is particularly important in our study of true revival comes to the nations of the West, including the Anglo-sphere nations such as Great Britain, the United States, Canada, Australia, and New Zealand, and the Commonwealth nations scattered across the earth. I have heard the argument posited that Western nations, particularly the English-speaking nations which had so much to do with the spread of the reformed faith — that is, Bible-believing, Christ-centered, Great Commission-motivated Protestant faith — can never know genuine revival because they have had the blessings of God and have rejected them in favor of the shiny idols of the secular age. The problem with that opinion is that it lacks biblical support. Even more, such a denial of God's willingness to pour out his Holy Spirit on the people flies in the face of John chapter 4 and the incredible case of the Samaritan woman at the well.

Rather than focus on the first part of this remarkable story, the interview between Jesus and the Samaritan woman at the well, a dialogue which is replete with teaching on evangelism to those who have once known the gospel and then rejected it, I draw your attention to the last part of John chapter 4. You will undoubtedly remember that the Samaritan woman was converted to the truth that Jesus Christ is the Messiah of God. Yet, do you recall the response of this newborn Christian? She ran into the town where she lived, where she was known, and, despite her inferior credentials as both a woman of unscrupulous morals and a woman — unable to give testimony in that culture because of the backward view of Genesis 1 and two in the fall of mankind without the redemption that God offers through Jesus Christ — she proclaims that she has met one who knows everything about her. She preaches that this is the Messiah. In a demonstration of the spirit of God's proleptic play embedded in her message, many receive her testimony and removed to repentance and faith. John chapter 4 tells us that a great revival broke out because of this woman's testimony.

As I write these words, I cannot help but pray to Almighty God to send his spirit upon the world of sinners. In John chapter 4, we learn of the universal spiritual principles of God concerning revival amongst those who had heard and rejected God in their history.

1. The sin of rejecting God does not preclude genuine revival.

That a revival came to a Samaritan village, the dwelling place of those who had known God in their history and who had rejected God in favor of pagan deities, where is much the object of God's love as Nineveh, a people who had not heard the good news of God. I am thankful for this revelation is it means that those who have grown up hearing the gospel, as I had, and who had taken a prodigal turn, also, as I had done, were nevertheless candidates for the outpouring of the Spirit of God. Revival in mass is but a greater manifestation of the outpouring of the spirit of God upon an individual and how we thank God for this truth.

2. The cacophony of religious voices, the pantheon of pagan idols, is indefensible when the Spirit of Almighty God comes down in sovereign mercy upon God's people.

There is hope for Nineveh. There is hope for Samaria. There is hope today for those who have never heard the gospel. And thank God there is hope for the nations in the West that once formed what was known as Christendom. This also means that there is hope for you — whatever you have done, wherever you have traveled in your prodigal journey away from God — the Lord can and will pour out his spirit upon you when you cry out to him in repentance and faith in Jesus Christ as the resurrected and raining son of the living God.

Conclusion

There is no hope for America except for revival from God. Yes, that is a true statement. Moreover, it is something that we may anticipate. No biblical teaching precludes such a glorious event. Some passages warn that there is a judicial hardening of the heart when one repeatedly ignores or denies the spirit of God, humanly speaking. But if anyone cries out to God for salvation, God will hear and receive them.

The great Welsh preacher and physician Dr. Martin Lloyd Jones, pastor at Westminster Chapel in London, reminded us of the truth. I was so transformed by his preaching of this truth from John 4 that I preached hope for revival for my ordination examination. I remember a line from that sermon, inspired by Lloyd-Jone's insights on revival: "We should not be surprised when we pray for revival, and it comes; we should be surprised when the supernatural outpourings of God are not present."

I believe a great awakening can come upon our nation and even Western Europe, those other nations that have known God and rejected. It will mean, however, that our churches will put first things first. We have been, in large part, abandoned solemn and reverent worship. There are no tear stains on the pews in our churches. The church doors are closed in many places except for one Sunday morning service, which is often nothing more than a musical concert. Instead of the exposition of the word of God, which brings down the spirit of God upon his people, we have witnessed the watering down of preaching in the many sectors of the church. The prayer meeting of old is all but gone. We have so privatized our faith that we dare not mention the names of our loved ones who need the Lord. So the hope of genuine revival — and let me be clear to say there is no human calculation or man-made formula to leverage the blessings of God — undoubtedly begins with a reluctant witness going to share the truth of the gospel with those who had never heard; or with one who determines to take the hard road, go a long way, to present Jesus Christ as Lord and Savior to those who might have heard of God, and even enjoyed the residual benefits of a formally Christian nation. Out of the belly of our burdens, we cry with the Psalmist:

"Will you not revive us again?
   That Your people may rejoice in You?
   Show us Your mercy, Lord,
   And grant us Your salvation" (Psalm 85:6, 7 NKJV)?

Revival is the vision that lifts the burden. And that is a vision that brings a sure hope and, in our understanding, a final hope.

Questions for Discussion and Reflection
Individual | Class | Small Group

1. Exploring Personal Transformation: In what ways can a spiritual awakening challenge and transform our personal understanding of sin and holiness? Reflect on how this transformation might manifest in one's daily life and relationships.

2. Community and Revival: Consider the role of community in experiencing a spiritual awakening. How does a community's collective pursuit of holiness and repentance contribute to or hinder a genuine revival?

3. Historical Perspectives vs. Today's Secular Age: Reflect on the historical instances of spiritual awakenings, such as the First Great Awakening, in ohtoday's secular age. How do these movements contrast with the spiritual and secular dynamics of our current society? What insights can be drawn from these historical revivals to address the spiritual challenges of our time?

4. Prayer and Anticipation of Revival: Discuss the significance of prayer in anticipating and preparing for a spiritual awakening. How can individual and communal prayers act as catalysts for revival?

5. Doctrine, Awakening, and Secularism: Explore the relationship between doctrinal truth and spiritual awakening within the framework of a secular age. How does a robust understanding of biblical doctrine counteract the challenges posed by secularism? Discuss how doctrinal depth can foster a genuine spiritual revival in a society that often marginalizes religious truths.

6. Revival's Societal Impact in a Secular World: Consider the broader social and cultural impacts of a spiritual awakening, especially in a secular society. How can genuine revival influence societal norms, values, and legislation in an age often indifferent or hostile to religious perspectives? Reflect on historical examples and contemplate how a contemporary revival might reshape the social and cultural landscape in our secular age.

Part V
FAITH

Between Bethel and Ai

Isaac Watts and Oswald Chambers and a Christian Worldview

George Grant

> The language of this world is no longer our own, but the language of heaven is not yet our mother tongue. As a result, we are only able to speak in heavily accented phrases pitched somewhere between the two. —Isaac Watts, *The Improvement of the Mind*
>
> Bethel is the symbol of communion with God; Ai is the symbol of the world. Abraham pitched his tent between the two. —Oswald Chambers, *My Utmost for His Highest*

Sometimes, we grasp the profoundest truths in the most peculiar ways and in the most unexpected circumstances. Among the toughest lessons for any believer to learn is what it means to be in the world but not of it (John 17:15-18). Making the connection between heavenly concerns and earthly responsibilities is never easy. We are all constantly tugged between piety and practicality, between devotion and duty, between communion with God and calling in the world. Honing a balanced Biblical worldview is no easy task—not the least because our attention to spiritual things is integrally bound to material things.

My reading and learning from Calvin, Owen, Chalmers, Spurgeon, Schaeffer, Packer, Sproul, and a host of other luminaries of the faith over the years have helped to lay the foundations for a coherent and balanced Biblical worldview, but perhaps surprisingly, I have gained the most striking insights from a hymn writer and a devotional author: Isaac Watts and Oswald Chambers.

Widely recognized as the unrivaled father of English hymnody, Watts wrote more than a thousand hymns and psalm settings including *O God, Our Help in Ages Past, When I Survey the Wondrous Cross, Alas and Did My Savior Bleed, Jesus Shall Reign, How Sweet and Awful Is the Place,* and *Joy to the World.* Church musician Mike Cosper has aptly called him "the reformer you know by heart but perhaps not by name."

In addition to being a prolific poet, Watts was a scholar of wide reputation. A contemporary of Samuel Johnson, Cotton Mather, Isaac Newton, George Whitefield, John Locke, John and Charles Wesley, Daniel Defoe, and Jonathan Edwards, Watts was a successor to the great John Owen at the Mark Lane Chapel, just around the corner from Tower Hill and the All Hallows spire where Samuel Pepys watched in horror as the Great Fire of London devastated the city. He was a gifted preacher, a careful theologian, and an ardent apologist. He published more than two dozen theological treatises; essays on psychology, astronomy, and philosophy; three volumes of sermons; the first children's hymnal; seven pioneering works on educational pedagogy; and a treatise on logic that served as the standard university text at Oxford, Cambridge, and Harvard for generations.

That he was quoted by Charles Dickens in *David Copperfield,* Herman Melville in *Moby Dick,* Lewis Carroll in *Alice's Adventures in Wonderland,* Charles Haddon Spurgeon in *The Treasury of David,* and by a host of others in classic literature across a wide range of genres is a testament to how large, how deep, and how wide his ongoing legacy has been.

One of the things that has always struck me about the hymnody of Watts is how easily his phrasing and syntax can be understood. Though he was contemporaneous with many other Puritan writers that we moderns struggle to comprehend, the prose and poetry Watts is clear and explicable. Avoiding the prevailing temptations of both theatrical ornateness and debased crassness, his rhetorical flourishes are unerringly elegant but always understandable. They are richly imaginative yet unapologetically simple. They are substantively reverent, incisive, and theological while simultaneously accessible, personal, and practical.

"Where the flights of faith and love are sublime," he wrote, "I have often sunk the expressions within the reach of an ordinary Christian. I have used words of greater latitude and comprehension suited to the general circumstances of men." Thus, according to Samuel Johnson, "He was the first who taught the Puritan Dissenters to write and speak like other men, by showing them that elegance might consist with piety."

Watts was able to accomplish this rare feat because he had a carefully worked out theology of language: he believed that believers could no longer speak with worldly tongues but were not yet sufficiently sanctified to speak with the tongues of angels. As a result, we must stake out ground somewhere between. The implications for grammar, logic, and rhetoric, for worship, discipleship, and pastoral care, for theology, apologetics, and evangelism, for beauty, goodness, and truth, enabled Watts to articulately bemoan the devastating effects of the fall, where "sins and sorrow grow" and "thorns infest the ground." But he also joyously celebrated the fact that Jesus has come. Indeed, "He rules the world with truth and grace," and not in just a few isolated corners, oh no: "fields and floods, rocks, hills, and plains" all bear testimony to the fact that "He makes His blessings flow as far as the curse is found." Watts could not have said it any more simply, nor could he have said it any more profoundly.

Watts sparked in me the beginnings of a fuller understanding of our calling in the world, this side of heaven.

It was nearly half a century ago that I began to make my way through the classic *My Utmost for His Highest*. It was the very first daily devotional I'd ever read. And it had an immediate, powerful, and enduring impact. Oswald Chambers was not exactly a paragon oar exemplar of Reformed theology with his Keswickian view of sanctification—though he was converted under the ministry of Charles Spurgeon and was profoundly shaped by the sermons of Thomas Chalmers.

In any case, very quickly, I found a host of his memorable phrases making their way from the pages of that little red hardcover book into my daily conversation: "broken bread and poured out wine," "not knowing wither," "prayer is the greater work," "the strain of waiting," "we are made for the valley," "do what is not your duty," "listening in the dark," and "unhasting and unresting." Day after day, I found his wisdom to be pungent and picturesque—enabling me to taste and see the profoundest truths of the Gospel with a potent practicality.

One entry particularly bolstered my faith, emboldened my vision, shaped my thinking, and gave trajectory to my calling. It is from the January 6 entry on "Worship," based on Genesis 12: 8. Abram, called by the Lord out of Ur of the Chaldees made his way first to Haran, then to Shechem, and finally to the hill country between Bethel and Ai where he pitched his tent under the oak of Mamre. Chambers commented "Bethel is the symbol of communion with God; Ai is the symbol of the world. Abraham pitched his tent between the two."[1]

Explaining, he wrote, "We have to pitch our tents where we shall always have quiet times with God, however noisy our times with the world may be. There are not three stages in spiritual life—worship, waiting, and work. Some of us go in jumps like spiritual frogs; we jump from worship to waiting and from waiting to work. God's idea is that these should all go together. They were always together in the life of Our Lord. He was unhasting and unresting."

When I first read that passage so many years ago now, I was struck by the rare wisdom it contained. Finding a proper balance between heavenly concern and earthly responsibility is never easy. We are all constantly tugged between piety and practicality, between devotion and duty, between communion with God and calling in the world. Honing a balanced Biblical worldview involves both the drudgery of daily labor and the high ideals of faith, hope, and love. It involves the certainty that we are called to work and serve in this poor fallen world while simultaneously acknowledging that we are merely pilgrims journeying to the celestial city.

To pitch our tents between Bethel and Ai is thus a Biblical way of describing our call to be in the world but not of it, to never quite be home until we're all the way home, to never bifurcate or dichotomize our callings into upper story leaps or lower story slumps. It is a metaphor for describing a genuinely Biblical worldview.

The word "worldview" is a poor English attempt at translating the German *weltanshauung*. It literally means a "life perspective" or "a way of seeing." It is simply the way we look at the world. We all have a worldview. It is our perspective. It is our frame of reference. It is the mindset shaped by our assumptions and presuppositions. It is the means by which we interpret the situations and circumstances around us. It is what enables us to integrate all the different aspects of our faith, and life, and experience.

According to James Sire,

> A worldview is a map of reality; and like any map, it may fit what is actually there, or it may be grossly misleading. The map is not the world itself, of course, only an image of it, more or less accurate in some places, distorted in others. Still, all of us carry around such a map in our mental makeup and we act upon it. All our thinking presupposes it. Most of our experience fits into it.

Thus, our worldview is simply our way of viewing the world. The truth is though, the Christian view of the world and all the things of the world is fraught with evident paradox—an appreciation for both the potentialities and the liabilities of fallen creation.

We know for instance, that the world is only a temporary dwelling place. It is "passing away" (1 John 2:17) and we are here but for a little while as "aliens and sojourners" (Acts 7:6). Because we are a part "of God's household" (Ephesians 2:19), our true "citizenship is in heaven" (Philippians 3:20). Our affections are naturally "set on things above" (Colossians 3:2).

In addition, the world is filled with "dangers, toils, and snares" (Jeremiah 18:22). In tandem with "the flesh and the devil," it "makes war" on the saints (John 15:18). "All that is in the world, the lust of the flesh, the lust of the eyes, and the pride of life not of the Father" (1 John 2:16). The world "cannot receive the Spirit of Truth" because "the cares of this world choke the Word, and it becomes unfruitful" (Matthew 8:22).

Thankfully, Christ "overcame the world" (John 16:33) and then "chose us out of the world" (John 15:19). Thus, we are not to be "conformed to the world" (Romans 12:2), neither are we to "love the world" (1 John 2:15) because "Christ gave Himself for us, that He might deliver us from this present evil world" (Galatians 1:4). Though we once "walked according to the course of the world" (Ephesians 2:2) now we are to keep ourselves "unspotted by the world" (James 1:27). Indeed, "friendship with the world is enmity with God" so that whoever is "a friend of the world is the enemy of God" (James 4:4).

Thus, warnings against worldliness, carnal-mindedness, and earthly attachments dominate Biblical ethics. Elsewhere, Chambers said, "The counsel of the Spirit of God to the Saints is that they must allow nothing worldly in themselves while living among the worldly in the world."

But then, that is the problem, isn't it? We must continue to live in the world. We must be "in" it but not be "of" it. And that is no easy feat. As John Calvin wrote in his little *Golden Booklet of the True Christian Life*,

> Nothing is more difficult than to forsake all carnal thoughts, to subdue and renounce our false appetites, and to devote ourselves to God and our brethren, and to live the life of angels in a world of corruption.

And to make matters even more complex, we not only have to live in this dangerous fallen world, but we have to work in it (1 Thessalonians 4:11), serve in it (Luke 22:6), and minister in it (2 Timothy 4:5). We have been appointed ambassadors to it (2 Corinthians 5:20), priests for it (1 Peter 2:9), and witnesses in it (Matthew 24:14). We even have to go to "the uttermost parts" of it (Acts 1:8), offering "a good confession of the eternal life" to which we were called (1 Timothy 6:12).

The reason for this seemingly contradictory state of affairs—enmity with the world on the one hand, responsibility to it on the other—is simply that "God so loved the world that He gave His only begotten Son" (John 3:16) Though the world is "in the power of the evil one" (1 John 5:19) and "knows not God, neither the children of God" (1 Corinthians 1:21), God is "in Christ reconciling the world unto Himself" (2 Corinthians 5:19). Jesus is "the light of the world" (John

1:12). He is the "savior of the world" (John 4:14). He is the "lamb of God who takes away the sin of the world" (John 1:29). Indeed, He was made "the propitiation for our sins; and not for ours only, but also for the whole world" (1 John 2:2). Through Christ "all things are reconciled to the Father" (Colossians 1:20) so that finally "the kingdoms of this world shall become the kingdoms of our God and of His Christ" (Revelation 11:15).

A genuinely integrated Christian worldview must be cognizant of both perspectives of the world—and treat them with equal weight. It must be engaged in the world. It must be unengaged in worldliness. It must somehow correlate spiritual concerns with temporal concerns. It must coalesce heavenly hope and landed life. It must coordinate heartfelt faith and down-to-earth practice.

And that is just what Chambers had in mind when he charged that, like Abraham, we should "pitch our tents between Bethel and Ai." A vision of life and faith that is both unhasting and unresting, that has ready access to both the busy, noisy world and the quiet refreshment of Heaven, will enable us to walk in the midst of this poor, fallen world, fully invested in our daily callings yet with our eyes firmly fixed on the prize of eternity. It is our sojourn between Bethel and Ai that enables us to fulfill our responsibilities here without ever being altogether at home. Thus, the high ideals of a Biblical worldview are happily instituted by the grace of God in our lives, our work, and our ministries.

In a sense, this is also what Watts was describing when he worked out his theology of language—a language camped out somewhere between our worldly sojourn and our celestial home.

Between Bethel and Ai: that is where I pray the Lord would enable me to pitch my tents—until that glorious day when I am brought all the way home, where tents will be exchanged for mansions "Oh, how grateful I am that Watts and Chambers were both able to articulate so clearly this balanced vision of what it means to be "in the world, but not of it."

---

1. In "Practical Faith in a Fallen World," Dr. Grant explores the challenge of balancing spiritual beliefs with earthly responsibilities. How can Christians navigate this tension in their everyday life, particularly in secular professions?

2. Reflect on Oswald Chambers' metaphor of pitching our tents between Bethel and Ai. How can this analogy guide Christians in their daily spiritual practice and help them stay grounded in their faith amidst worldly distractions?

3. Discuss the impact of hymnody and devotional literature, as exemplified by Watts and Chambers, on shaping a Christian's worldview. How do these forms of expression complement more formal theological study?

4. How can Christians apply the principle of living between Bethel and Ai to address current social, political, and ethical challenges in light of Dr. Grant's insights? Also, discuss the church's and individual believers' role in engaging with the world while maintaining a distinct Christian identity.

Enslavement by Category
The Wisdom of Dorothy Sayers
Michael A. Milton

> Though they know God's righteous decree that those who practice such things deserve to die, they not only do them but give approval to those who practice them.
>
> — St. Paul, Romans 1:32 ESV

Dorothy Sayers (1893-1957) should be remembered as one of the great 20th-century novelists. However, despite her remarkable literary achievements, Dorothy Sayers is frequently recognized as a Christian apologist. That may be so because she was so good at both, but she was especially noted for her role as a female theologian. Located in "the same section of the library" as CS Lewis and, perhaps, closer to GK Chesterton, Sayers distinguished herself by calling "balls and strikes" as she saw them in a day of increasing compromise by the Church. I believe her words have proven prescient. Her pearls of cultured wisdom and doctrinal insight are gifts for our time. Oh, that we would receive them. Oh, that we would even bother looking for them. For we desperately need her clarity of thought.

However, I do recognize that her logic is so precise and the calculations of her Christian theological reflection so sharp that many of our contemporaries might find her insights doctrinaire or, more probably, quite indecipherable. For ours is a gutted age, an era of T. S. Eliot's "hollow men," and a time marked by spiritual (and, thus, real) regression, outlined with Spirit-inspired accuracy by Paul the Apostle in Romans 1:18-32. These people resist the light and slowly move into the darkness of unbelief. In the darkness, the blind man wanders unprotected across the unforgiving moors and mountains until, inescapably, he trips into a sudden point-of-no-return, the gravitational pull of self-incrimination, and incurs an over-the-edge, steep plummet into the sharp-edged rocks of utter madness.

Nevertheless, for those who will "hear, read, mark, learn, and inwardly digest" (Cranmer, BCP, 1549), the clarion call of the Gospel, a gift of a branch, appears, stopping our fall. Such ragged mercy protrudes from the craggy mountainside and snags us to safety despite ourselves. That is the prevailing context for the Gospel, "despite ourselves," or as Scripture puts it, "but God." "They would have slipped, but God." Lord, send Thy grace to stop our fall. Save us from ourselves. Κύριε, ἐλέησον.

Χριστέ, ἐλέησον. Κύριε, ἐλέησον. "Lord have mercy. *Christ, have mercy.* Lord have mercy."

Because of her prominent position, Dorothy Sayers was invited to speak at a women's gathering and address the matter of feminism. Sayers produced a characteristically provocative title for her presentation: "Are Women Human?"[1] Her talk was nothing short of ideological feminism turned upside down. She rejected any further category than male and female. I would argue that in this thinking, she was supremely feminist and irreducibly human.

Given the inability of a Supreme Court nominee (now Justice), a woman by the way, to define her sex in United States Senate confirmation hearings, and the propensity to celebrate sin-sick men dressing as women, practically emasculating themselves, or, worse still, masquerading as women to diminish women in sports, or traumatize children in "reading times" at school, we need to hear from Sayers. This princess of the pen resisted the term "feminist" in the same way an intuitive gazelle avoids the apparent refreshing bath in a calm river that conceals the stealthy crocodiles. Indeed, the ladies might have been surprised – they should not have been — but Dorothy Sayers took the opportunity to remind them that human beings are images of God. To go beyond man and woman—that is, male and female within mankind—young and old, adult or child—is to create cases that not only dehumanize but also leave an open door for crouching totalitarianism, dictatorships, despotism, and other forms of State bondage (viz., *Statism*, that beastly power described in Revelation). For this reason, I have chosen to publish part of her speech on this blog. Thus, Dorothy Sayers and her word for today:

Hardening of the Categories and the Death of the Individual

> "Indeed, it is my experience that both men and women are fundamentally human and that there is very little mystery about either sex, except the exasperating mysteriousness of human beings in general… If you wish to preserve a free democracy, you must base it—not on classes and categories, for this will land you in a totalitarian State where no one may act or think except as a member of a category. You must base it upon the individual Tom, Dick, and Harry, on the individual Jack and Jill—in fact, upon you and me."[2]

Arbitrary and artificial categories will have a greater and more devastating effect on the human condition than COVID-19 ever could. Everyone seems to want to get in on their game of dividing people, even deciding which creature is more worthy of life than another (uncanny fulfillment of George Orwell's metaphoric analysis of the origins of the Soviet Union, *Animal Farm, 1945*). From corporations to advertising and even to federal forms, one *must* ostensibly agree with someone's cracked idea of categories of human beings, even when the ideas are insanely wrong. Those who advocate such distinctions within humanity have cleverly assigned a moral value to this subversive initiative, showing that the one who denies the categories is unfairly labeled as "mean." But let us be clear: One is not impolite or "mean" because one refuses to entertain a madman with his lunatic ideas. Proverbs 26:4-14 reminds us, "Don't answer the foolish arguments of fools, or you will become as foolish as they are" (NLT).

Are Ethics Possible?

Public service posters featuring Miss Ellen Degeneres are taped on painted cinder block walls of public schools nationwide. The message? "Don't be mean." *Don't be mean.* When we planted a church in Weddington, North Carolina, a town and country suburb of Charlotte, we first worshipped in a high school. So, we saw the posters each week. A biblical verse is outlawed from public schools, but Ellen's sainted secular wisdom is welcome. I would pass the oversized poster of the lauded lesbian pointing at me like Uncle Same. "Don't be mean, YOU." I always thought, "So, *there is* an ethic at work" in so-called progressive ideologies. Of course, we know all too well that the *meanies* are the "traditionalists" who still believe and, thus, live out of the centering power of a theistic, specifically Judeo-Christian, worldview. Who are these mean people? These are the anachronistic ones who refuse to admit ridiculous categories such as third or fourth genders, menstruating males, or other such dangerous nonsense. They not only practice these things but demand that you approve (from Romans 1:32). We don't. However, because of an understandable but misplaced open butterfly valve in the conscience, some believers feel compelled to go along with this farce out of a nod to Christian manners. I would respond that admitting lunacy as normative is the opposite of kindness.

Moreover, coddling confused characters fosters delusional thinking and catastrophic societal degradation. We are under no moral or civic duty to concede absurdity. We have mentioned Romans chapter 1, verses 18 through 32. Furthermore, we do so again because the passage is relevant to the crisis of fast-moving currents of polluted canals threatening the *polis*—*Study* St. Paul's teaching in Romans chapter 1, verses 18 through 32. There, the great Apostle to the Gentiles accurately depicts the downward spiral. The depiction of the broad highway from unbelief to insanity is painted with the bristly brush of a stubborn refusal to acknowledge the plain and undeniable evidence of a Creator.

The runaway train engine picks up steam through the noxious fuel of willful denial of God (creaturely rebellion). At length, the suicidal engineers exhibit a deranged disregard for God's law (creaturely anarchy) and, finally, codify the pathway to madness. The [Apostle of the Heart Set Free](#) describes a devastating human regression triggered by the rejection of God and, therefore, absolute truth, triggering an inevitable breakdown. The warning signs from the denial of God to the deification of self are unmistakable: "God gave them up (24)" "God gave them over (26)" and "God gave them over" (28). By the third sounding of the warning bell, the tragic end becomes inescapable.

Responses

Polemical responses to the downward spiral are almost certainly ineffective. The reason is apparent: In the latter stages of the Romans 1:18-32 scenario, the God-denier is delusional. So, arguments are not the answer to such a self-induced judgment. There is a reversal of the condition and remedy of the disease only in the name of the Lord Jesus. "Jesus, save me" is a plea made not in meaningless incantation but in voicing the only Truth capable of reaching through the hardened layers of atheistic sap and the diabolical guanos. I say again, "But God." Salvation by divine conjunction is our only hope. For with God, nothing is impossible.

We will increasingly need to talk together to help save our loved ones from the centrifugal forces of the downward spiral. Recovering and reading spiritual guides such as Dorothy Sayers is an excellent place to start.

So, Then

"Are transvestites human?" Yes, they are. "How about Republicans?" I hope so. Wait. I know. "Are elderly people on their last breath human?" The truth is that even human bodies devoid of the breath of life are human. The human body bears the image of God and deserves honor and respect. The idea of a "decent Christian burial" is grounded in the Imago Dei, viz., the image of God in mankind. This is why believers in the early Church ran into the Tiber to "rescue" human bodies thrown away by Romans.

Back to the present dangers of suspending reality to advance an ideology. We owe those sad men pretending to be women (and vice versa) our prayers and *unapologetic disapproval* of their mindless charade. We also owe humanity our voices: Leave our women alone. Cavorting in drag is hurting not only the perpetrator but especially our women and children. Aberrant sexuality invariably seeks to diminish motherhood and femininity and, thus, assaults all that is pure and lovely in life. If I could speak to someone reading this who may be engaged in cross-dressing, homosexuality, adultery, polygamy, and similar sins, I would plead: Let us help you find the healing for whatever it is that hurts you. I would say to those who enable their behavior, "Stop demeaning our girls with unisex locker rooms, competing with males in athletics, and dismissing the beauty of authentic femininity." I add, "Leave our boys alone and let them grow to be strong men who will use their strength to be husbands, fathers, and leaders." We need boys to be men who leverage their God-given male attributes to guard the sanctity of the family against the vile forces of evil. Strong men will exalt womanhood and protect childhood. There is nothing toxic about what God created as good.

It's time to say we are human and will not play along with those who seek to deny it. It is the opposite of unkindness to assert the truth. Not only that, but it is the antithesis of virtue to signal the approval of foolishness.

A Prayer by Thomas Cranmer

Blessed Lord, who hast caused all holy Scriptures to be written for our learning, grant us that we may in such wise hear them, read, mark, learn, and inwardly digest them; that by patience and comfort of thy holy Word, we may embrace, and ever hold fast the blessed hope of everlasting life, which thou hast given us in our savior Jesus Christ (*The Book of Common Prayer*, the Collect for the Second Sunday in Advent).

Reference

Calvin, Jean. *Calvin's Commentaries.* Grand Rapids: Baker Books, 1999.

Cranmer, Thomas. "The Collect for the Second Sunday in Advent." *The Book of Common Prayer of the Church of England,* 1549.

Orwell, George, and George Orwell. *Animal Farm, and Nineteen, Eight-Four.* 2021.

Sayers, Dorothy L. "Are Women Human?: Address Given to a Women's Society, 1938." *Logos: A Journal of Catholic Thought and Culture,* vol. 8, no. 4, 2005, pp. 165–178., doi:10.1353/log.2005.0040.

Field Notes from Babylon
Faithful Gospel Witness in the Secular Age

Michael A. Milton

> [In present] secular explanations . . . the vessel of the liturgy is punctured, so that the contents spill out across the floor.
>
> — Roger Scruton, *The Soul of the World*

Imagine, if you will, a cold wind sweeping through the hallowed halls of our revered institutions. This wind carries the icy chill of secularism, a blistering gust threatening to extinguish the remaining embers of a Christian past. Sheared window glass flies like shrapnel. The foundations are shaken. Darkness descends like a plague. A fool in the deserted streets stands looking heavenward, shaking his fist at God and crying, "I don't believe in You! You don't exist!" Cosmic dystopia is only one unfaithful generation away.

Our people are often exposed to these harsh northern winds. However, the fire of faith will never be extinguished. It is Christ who builds His Church, and not us mere mortals. Nonetheless, we must remember that the Lord who ordains the end has also mandated the means. To think otherwise would be to embrace pagan fatalism. Even if

Canaan or Babylon become dystopian, they will not ultimately triumph over the whole earth. The Creator has different plans for His creation.

As pastors and church leaders, we navigate an increasingly Orwellian landscape while holding fast to our gospel mission as the world around us sways under uncontrollable gusts of iniquity. As shepherds, our duty is to guide the flock of Christ and seek out those who are lost. We must continue to carry out our duty even in difficult times, just like how shepherds tend to their sheep in all kinds of weather. Although the seasons may change overnight, we must not lose sight of our goal of reaching out to the lost and caring for the lambs even in the midst of a storm. We take inspiration from the well-known verse from Daniel, "Those who are wise shall shine like the brightness of the sky above, and those who turn many to righteousness, like the stars forever and ever" (Daniel 12:3 ESV). But the question remains, how can we do this?

In this crucial moment, it is imperative that we pinpoint and address the afflictions plaguing the human soul, followed by a contextual pastoral response.

The Secular Age Through a Pastoral Lens

We can, of course, assess and diagnose the prevalent conditions of man in the secular age. Yet, one of the blessings of cultivating a life of the mind in Christ is to isolate the work of others in the service of our mission.

In his seminal work "A Secular Age," Charles Taylor paints a picture of our times that demands our attention. As scholarly as those Gifford lectures that brought about his book, we must find access to the ideas and then distill and share the helpful insights. I am not saying that I have run the barley and hops of my fieldwork in Taylor through a flawless brewery. Far from it. These are just a few other possible helpful ideas from Charles Taylor's *A Secular Age*.

Nevertheless, these fragments of another's wisdom might help us in our mandate: "We destroy arguments and every lofty opinion raised against the knowledge of God, and take every thought captive to obey Christ" (2 Corinthians 10:5 ESV). We are not destroyers of worlds like a morbid Oppenheimer. We obedient ranch hands clearing brush, or more biblically put, faithful shepherds building a bridge over the streams with the debris we have picked up from the storm.

Our goal is not to study Taylor or any other contemporary or ancient thinker for their sake. Instead, all intellectual undertakings of this kind are intended to feed our efforts for the biblical Christian strategic operation before us. Our strategic mission is to make disciples of the nations, baptizing them in the name of the Father, Son, and Holy Spirit, teaching them to observe whatsoever our Lord Jesus Christ taught. Insights from analyses—from intelligence gathered by trusted observers—that originate from sources operating within a biblical worldview aid us in the tactical work of destroying Jericho walls, proclaiming the rightful Lordship of our Joshua, the Lord Jesus, and "taking" each camp and city in the land. Militaristic language may disturb some, but we ask you to remember that we conduct campaigns within the revealed metaphors God gave us. Now. Let's pause to keep this in mind: In each phase of missional operations, we must remember whether scholarship or praxis, activities are always the servants of the greater mission. Always.

No scholar is a scholar for his private interests—no laborer labors for only herself. We serve at the King's pleasure and for His Kingdom's good. We also do all for the sake of the elect. Whoever the elect of God are (some are enemies today but brothers and sisters tomorrow), we serve obediently by reaching all. We seek to occupy all the land, every sphere of human existence or endeavor. We claim the earth for Christ. This is not a theonomic manifesto. This is a Gospel mandate. Saved men and women will seek God's truth and apply it to their world. Therefore, while we wish to see nations governing on the teaching of Christ and citizens responsibly advancing their vocations with Christ-honoring objectives, we know that the way to achieve that is through the human spirit. Structures are, mainly (not wholly), human creations intended to secure the greatest good (in malevolent cases for a tyrant and his court, or, in beneficent instances, for the greater good). Political structures, whether in government, the market, or religion, are ideas in organizational expressions. So, we neither flatter nor fear governments and other power structures, however beast-like or welcoming. We know that the human soul is the area of operation. For as the Holy Spirit blesses the announcement of the Gospel and human beings are transformed, we know that Jesus Christ is now and shall be victorious. The cross and the empty tomb prove that fact. History is witness to the irrepressible power of the Gospel time and time again.

Neither do we fret as we assess the features of the land, the unholy settlements of this present evil age. Remember Caleb: "But Caleb quieted the people before Moses and said, "Let us go up at once and occupy it, for we are well able to overcome it" (Numbers 13:30 ESV). Caleb's courage is our command. Use any insights to forward the movement of Christ in our generation for His glory and others' good. Be not afraid. God goes before us. His victory is certain. His presence is our strength. The star that led foreign nobility to the manger, the light that lit up the sky to poor shepherds to know God's will, guides us still. That star, those angelic hosts, generate their same faith-building luminous rays of strength from the Word of God. This is a word made more sure.

This is the situation before. So, we begin to spy out the land, consider the costs, estimate the materials needed, and plan to enter the land. Let us begin. Each day, each generation, each tradition or strain, and each tribe within Israel prepares to enter the land for the glory of God and the good of His Creation.

Thus, we isolate pathogens in our day so that we might address them with Gospel truth, not run from them. So, let us use some of the ideas we find in contemporary scholarship on behalf of the people living in Canaan. These field notes from Babylon will help us to assess, diagnose, and treat the wounds with the balm of Gilead, even the life of our God and Savior, Jesus Christ.

Features of the Secular Age Gleaned from Charles Taylor

The Buffered Self: This concept speaks of a world where individuals are islands unto themselves, adrift in a sea of privatized spirituality. This isolation prevents people from a productive engagement with each other. Forgiveness, patience, and other virtues honed in the context of community are slow to develop, if at all, in home to office, office to home, home to a restaurant or concert, and back again. This secular circuit insulates the secular man from not only *belonging*, as Roger Scruton said was a vital expression of faith, but from Martin Buber's "I-thou." The "subtraction" (to use Taylor's appropriate word) of *belonging* and *practicing* humanity (the ongoing dialogue of person to person) is like removing essential vitamins from one's diet. This becomes a journey of a ship filled with victims of scurvy. And that creates tumors of the soul. As nutrients are lost when a bodily organ fails to function correctly, the Imago Dei suffers from want for the divine. Ultimately, such a trajectory becomes a ghost ship unleashed from its own power and tossed to and fro by the elemental forces of the wind and the sea.

As shepherds, our challenge is to build bridges to these isolated souls, guiding them back to the communal harbor of faith. But how? Hold the question.

The Nova Effect: Our society offers a diverse range of spiritual paths, competing for dominance like a cosmic explosion. It is our responsibility to maintain the singular truth of Christ among a multitude of alternatives in this celestial dance of ideologies. How can we achieve this? There has never been a more crucial time to be both innocent as doves and wise as serpents.

Cultural Malaise: We have witnessed a shift towards overt antagonism against Christian values, which has created a cultural fog that obscures the once-clear lines of moral and spiritual truth.

Excarnation: In contrast to the Incarnation, this age appears to move away from the sanctity of the human person. Our message should counter this by affirming the divine imprint on every soul.

Navigating the Secular Landscape

Our journey through this secular age mirrors that of Daniel in ancient Babylon.

So, the assessment is in. We live in a secular age, a new and harsh season of human existence. The symptoms of self-destructing ideas and behaviors point to the continuing diagnosis. We are sinners in need of a Savior. Whether in Canaan, where people had rejected the light of God that shone after Eden, or in Babylon, where pagan deities were preferred, or in the Great Babylon of John's day, when Nero and a ferocious Roman Empire persecuted the Church, or today when so many of our fellow travelers in this age have turned from God to godlessness and have come to, in some places, insanity; the diagnosis remains unchanged. "People need the Lord." Without Him, we are like disobedient children playing in the shallow waters of the Amazon. The evening comes. The indigenous village mother cries, "Where are you, my children?" Her voice is overcome by the innocent laughter of the little ones splashing and laughing with delight in a backwater pool. A large log rises to the waterline just a few yards from the water party. The log moves stealthily toward the children. At the waterline, it appears as if the log has eyes.

How?

Other insightful voices have added insight to the treatment plan, viz., our response to those trapped by the secular age. Undoubtedly, each response carries questions, some of which we provide in the following section. We begin with the contributions of James Davison Hunter. Dr. Hunter is the LaBrosse-Levinson Distinguished Professor of Religion, Culture and Social Theory at the University of Virginia and Director of the Institute for Advanced Studies in Culture. In his outstanding volume, *To Change the World: The Irony, Tragedy, and Possibility of Christianity in the Late Modern World,* Hunter proposes a biblical response to the challenges of life in the secular age, formulating his wise counsel from Saint Paul:

> "For Christian believers, the call to faithfulness is a call to live in fellowship and integrity with the person and witness of Jesus Christ. There is a timeless character to this call that evokes qualities of life and spirit that are recognizable throughout history and across cultural boundaries. But this does not mean that faith faithfulness is a state of abstract piety floating above the multifaceted and compromising realities of daily life in actual situations. St. Paul, in Acts 13:36, refers to King David having "served God's purposes in *his own generation.*" This suggests, of course, that faithfulness works itself out in the context of

complex social, political, economic, and cultural forces that prevail at a particular time and place.[1]

The strategy that Hunter refers to as "Faithful Presence" can be seen not only in David but also in other biblical figures such as Daniel, Jeremiah, Isaiah, Paul, and Jesus Christ. This posture of "faithful presence" is a common thread that runs through all of those who announced the Kingdom of God in the midst of troubles.What if we took this path today?"

Faithful Presence: Daniel is a model for *faithful presence* in an antagonistic age, *a strange land.* Daniel's unwavering resolve in a foreign land (Daniel 1:8) is a beacon for us. We remember his obedience. Yet, we must also recall how Daniel worked with integrity for the good of Babylon. He became a trusted man of God in a place where such faith was unwelcome. But what Daniel offered is always in demand: honor, humility, cooperation without compromise, and support without approval. Daniel is the picture of a faithful presence by standing firm for his faith. Yet his faithful presence is exercised by supporting Nebuchadnezzar—when it didn't compromise the Lordship of God in his life—telling him the truth (unlike his courtiers) and working diligently for the good of the community. Faithful presence is an uncompromisingly dedicated servant of God who works for the good of those around him. In this attitude of serving God by serving others, even otherwise enemies, he practiced what Jeremiah instructed the Exiles:

> "And seek the peace of the city where I have caused you to be carried away captive, and pray to the LORD for it; for in its peace you will have peace" (Jeremiah 29:7 NKJV).

Amidst cultural currents that seek to sweep us off our feet, our stance must be unwavering faith and integrity. Yet, a faithful presence means even more.

Helpful Engagement: Daniel and his friends found a way to serve their captors without compromising their identity (Daniel 1:19–20). Faithful presence is not a mere afterthought in life within a challenging environment. On the contrary, it is a personal commitment and an ethos that the Christian community should strive to cultivate. Miroslav Volf argues that believers can contribute to the common good by bringing the wisdom of the Church and the hope of Christ through helpful engagement. This approach serves to announce the Gospel by means of practical action.In *A Public Faith: How Followers of Christ Should Serve the Common Good*, Volf's message embodies "cooperation without compromise."[2] Dr. Volf's guidance is succinct and unambiguous:

> "A combination of moral clarity that does not shine away from calling evil by its proper name and of deep compassion toward evil-doers that is willing to sacrifice one's own life on their behalf was one of the extraordinary features of early Christianity. It should also be the central characteristic of contemporary Christianity."[3]

What a hopeful response! It reminds me of Dietrich Bonhoeffer, a German seminary leader and pastor who, during his final days in prison, preached a sermon about suffering during persecution. Bonhoeffer stated that in such times, the believer learns "to love God for God's own sake." Perhaps we love God for His sake when we dare to speak the grace and truth of the Lord Jesus into the chaos of self-destructive unbelief.

In the secular age, approaching the world with common grace should be an obedient response to the grace of God that was offered to us through the Incarnation. Just like how Christ came to us, engaged with us, and taught us to give us comfort through the Holy Spirit, we too must find constructive ways to engage with our society. This response is another way of embracing the mature life of following the Lord Jesus, where we strive to be salt and light in the world without losing our essence or compromising our values. I can hardly think of a better way of putting it than Justin Bailey in his *Reimagining Apologetics: The Beauty of Faith in a Secular Age* :

> "By Christian faith, I mean a holistic pattern of life. This includes the embodied practices that make belief intelligible (Prayer, worship, hospitality, peacemaking, creation care, etc.), as well as the felt sense of what belief means for every day. In other words, to be a Christian is not simply to believe a list of propositions but also to experience the world

through the lens of a meaningful imaginative vision. This vision is a theodrama in which a world of meaning has been gifted to our perception, and ultimate reality is personal, revealed most fully in Jesus Christ."[4]

I would only add that propositions are necessary as a foundation is indispensable. Yet, I affirm the helpful analysis by underscoring the need to "experience the world through the lens of a meaningful imaginative vision." Such words are potent for mission effectiveness but susceptible to misunderstanding. I would add that a Christian preacher's meaningful "imaginative vision" is to trust the sufficiency of Scripture, the efficacy of the Holy Spirit, and the divine nature of Gospel proclamation in a place and to a people that rejects all of it. To imagine transformation in Babylon is a gloriously defiant act of authentic Christian vision.

Hopeful Proclamation: The transformation of Nebuchadnezzar (Daniel 4:37) is a testament to the activity of the Lord in our apparent internment. Gospel proclamation often happens in the shadow of secular towers, if not the chains of cultural or actual persecution. For the Apostle Paul, the Second Letter to the Corinthians demonstrates the faithful method of proclamation in times of trouble. Michael Knowles characterized the Apostle's preaching in the Corinthian context:

> "Paul articulates a Jesus-centered spirituality that can best be described as cruciform, a spiritual vision essentially shaped by Jesus is crucifixion and resurrection."[5]

No scholar has written more on the "cruciformity" as the central motif in Pauline homiletics than Michael J. Gorman. In his classic book on the subject, Gorman wrote,

> "Paul conceives of identification with and participation in the death of Jesus as the believer's fundamental experience of Christ. No letter stresses cruciform as the norm of experience in Christ more than 2 Corinthians."[6]

Our message can still reach the hearts of kings and commoners alike. How did Paul put it as he wrote the Philippian church?

> "But I want you to know, brethren, that the things *which happened* to me have actually turned out for the furtherance of the gospel, so that it has become evident to the whole palace guard, and to all the rest, that my chains are in Christ; and most of the brethren in the Lord, having become confident by my chains, are much more bold to speak the word without fear" (Philippians 1:12-13 NKJV).

Embracing Our Role as Church Leaders

It is as if the time we have heard about that would one day come in here. Whether we were prepared to admit that the winter came to America is now irrelevant. It is here. Our roles as pastors and other expressions of ordained ministry, along with so many other believers in leadership positions in the Church of our Lord, exist for the functioning of the Church on earth in such times. Shepherds exist because wolves exist, and lambs can fall prey to threats of their own making. Of course, shepherds are in the same situation as lambs, with one exception: you have been called to lead. And to lead is to know the burden of the Lord—a visceral reaction to sin and its tragic consequences to God's people and God's Creation—and to seek a pathway through the apocalyptic debris to find good pasture and running water. And you have the vision of souls safe in the arms of Jesus when He comes again. In other words, God called you to serve His mission, flock, and kingdom.

The road will take on new dimensions as we traverse this secular landscape. The exponential effect means that by the time these words go to press, there will have been new foreboding storms developing on the horizon, unexpected boulders blocking our way, and deadly rapids appearing to destroy our vessels and end our voyage. Thus, we assess. We diagnose. We treat. We observe, we discover, we guide. We are spiritual physicians, faithful shepherds, enduring athletes, military captains, and wise farmers. Each metaphor is placed to convey a dimension of the sacred calling God has given us. This is certain: we are not merely caretakers of traditions or sitters offering palliative care to the dying. We must be active agents in God's unfolding drama. Our ministries, in all their varied forms and contexts, are lighthouses in a stormy sea, guiding vessels adrift toward the safe harbor of truth and grace in Christ Jesus our Lord.

Should the Lord tarry, or should we meet on the other side, after enduring these times, we can expect to say, "It was a difficult journey. But where sin abounds, grace abounds more (Romans 5:20). Others will respond, "I came to understand my role as a Christian shepherd during those troubled times in a way I could never have in fairer weather." And yet another will remind us that we should have expected such Gospel success all along. I can almost hear the voice of such a one:

> "Fathers and Brothers did not God demonstrate in the Book of Daniel that in Babylon or Birmingham, Chicago or Chennai, Cape Town or Copenhagen, His Spirit attends the faithful efforts of those who announce the liberty of Christ in the captivity of the devil and the world? And such faithful discharge of duties born of love—in a secular age, in any age—always leads to a legacy of honor:
>
> "And those who are wise shall shine like the brightness of the sky above; and those who turn many to righteousness, like the stars forever and ever" (Daniel 12:3 ESV).

Notes

Introduction

1. W. H. Auden, *For the Time Being: A Christmas Oratorio* (Princeton University Press, 2013), line 1.
2. Martin Esslin, *The Theatre of the Absurd* (Knopf Doubleday Publishing Group, 2009). See, also,

Preface

1. Jean Calvin, *Commentaries*, vol. Commentary on the Epistle to the Hebrews (United Kingdom: Calvin Translation Society, 1853), 266.
2. The Westminster Shorter Catechism, question and answer 1.

1. Cry Aloud and Spare Not

1. John Donne, "A Lincoln Inn Sermon," in Carl Hulet Hamilton, "A Study of Imagery in John Donne's Sermons" (Doctor of Philosophy dissertation, Fayetteville, Arkansas, University of Arkansas, 1968), 16.
2. "And he said to them, 'Go and tell that fox, 'Behold, I cast out demons and perform cures today and tomorrow, and the third day I finish my course'" (Luke 13:32 ESV).
3. This was the first sermon I ever preached (other than some pretend oracles at age four in a rough-hewn piney pulpit at the "tabernacle" down the gravel road from our farm). I was not ordained, but I preached to fill in where pastors had no backup plan. Like the other half dozen sermons of this period, this instance was in a country church on a three-point charge (Methodists will recognize such an ecclesial arrangement). I think it must have been about 1979. The sad irony of my attempt (I was a miserable offender unsure of how to be saved, calling others in the same shape to do something) was not unlike John Wesley in Savannah before the famous divine heard Martin Luther's Preface to the Book of Romans read at St. Paul's.
4. {$NOTELABEL}. *The Holy Bible: English Standard Version* (Wheaton, IL: Crossway Bibles, 2016), Is 58:1–14.
5. Sebastian Kim, *Theology in the Public Sphere: Public Theology as a Catalyst for Open Debate* (London: SCM Press, 2013), 3.
6. Kim, *Public Theology*, 3.
7. Deidre King Hainsworth, Scott R. Paeth, and Breitenberg Jr., E. Harold, "What is Public Theology?" *Public Theology for a Global Society: Essays in Honor of Max Stackhouse* (Grand Rapids: Wm. B. Eerdmans Publishing, 2010), 4.
8. Matthew Kaemingk, *Reformed Public Theology: A Global Vision for Life in the World* (Baker Academic, 2021), 14. Kindle edition.

9. Kathryn Tanner, "Public Theology and the Character of Public Debate," *The Annual of the Society of Christian Ethics* 16 (1996): 79.
10. Gary Smith, *Isaiah 40-66*, vol. 15B, The New American Commentary (Nashville, TN: Broadman & Holman Publishers, 2009), 569.
11. Gary Smith, *Isaiah 40-66*, vol. 15B, The New American Commentary (Nashville, TN: Broadman & Holman Publishers, 2009), 569–570.
12. See Edward's journal entry in George M. Marsden, *Jonathan Edwards: A Life* (Yale University Press, 2004), 315.
13. Neil Howe, *The Fourth Turning Is Here: What the Seasons of History Tell Us about How and When This Crisis Will End* (Simon and Schuster, 2023).
14. Of course, one might argue that such cyclical periods of human history are precisely the demonstrable activity of a sovereign God. While Howe's work is helpful, the Christian theological assertion of catastrophism requires that one acknowledge that the Fall, the Flood, and the advent of our Lord Jesus Christ have upended cycles of history. Things are not as they have always been.
15. Michael A. Milton, *From Flanders Fields to the Moviegoer: Philosophical Foundations for a Transcendent Ethical Framework* (Eugene, OR: Wipf and Stock Publishers, 2019).
16. T. S. Eliot, *The Waste Land and Other Writings* (Random House Publishing Group, 2009).
17. Deirdre Bair, *Samuel Beckett: A Biography* (Simon and Schuster, 1990); Samuel Beckett, *Waiting for Godot: A Tragicomedy in Two Acts* (Grove/Atlantic, Inc., 2011); Hugh Kenner, *Samuel Beckett, a Critical Study* (University of California Press, 1968). See, also, Martin Esslin, *The Theatre of the Absurd* (Knopf Doubleday Publishing Group, 2009).
18. Charles Taylor, *A Secular Age* (Harvard University Press, 2009).
19. Jürgen Habermas, *An Awareness of What Is Missing: Faith and Reason in a Post-Secular Age* (John Wiley & Sons, 2014).
20. Referring to Barbara W. Tuchman, *The Guns of August: The Pulitzer Prize-Winning Classic About the Outbreak of World War I* (Random House Publishing Group, 2004).

2. For the Love of God

1. A. D. Sertillanges and Mary Ryan, *The Intellectual Life: Its Spirit, Conditions, Methods* (Washington, D.C.: Catholic University of America Press, 1987), 257.
2. A. D. Sertillanges and Mary Ryan, *The Intellectual Life: Its Spirit, Conditions, Methods* (Washington, D.C.: Catholic University of America Press, 1987).
3. Sertillanges, *The Intellectual Life*, 180.
4. Sertillanges, *The Intellectual Life*, 178.
5. Hans Urs von Balthasar, *Love Alone Is Credible* (San Francisco: Ignatius Press, 2004).

3. Fragments of Nature's Lore

1. Walker Percy, "Morality and Religion." *Sign Posts in a Strange Land* (New York: Farrar, Straus and Giroux, 1991), 369.
2. Sertillanges, *The Intellectual Life*, 108.

4. The Family in the Secular Age

1. Presbyterian Church (U.S.A.), *Book of Common Worship, Pastoral Edition* (Westminster John Knox Press, 1993), 340.
2. Wayne Parker, "What Research Tells Us About the Effect of Divorce on Children," *Verywell Family*, no. Online (February 20, 2022), https://www.verywellfamily.com/children-of-divorce-in-america-statistics-1270390.
3. Wayne Parker, "Key Statistics About Kids from Divorced Families," Key Statistics About Children of Divorced Parents (verywellfamily.com).
4. Parker, "Statistics."
5. Amy Morin, "How to Help a Teen Who Is Failing High School Classes," *Verywell Family*, no. Online (October 1, 2020), https://www.verywellfamily.com/what-to-do-if-your-teen-has-failing-grades-2609570.

5. What the Bible Says about Transgenderism

1. Walker Percy, "Science, Language, Literature." *Sign Posts in a Strange Land* (New York: Farrar, Straus and Giroux, 1991), 214.

6. True Oikonomia

1. John G. Panagiotou, *The Path to Oikonomia with Jesus Christ as Our Lighthouse* (OCP Publications, 2020).
2. G.F. Hawthorne, "Tithe," *The New International Dictionary of New Testament Theology* vol. 3: Pri-Z, general editor Colin Brown (Grand Rapids: Zondervan Publishing House, 1975), 851.
3. Panagiotou, 39.
4. Panagiotou, 60-62.
5. John Chrysostom, *On Wealth and Poverty* (St. Vladimir's Seminary Press, 1984).
6. Arthur R. McKay, *Servants and Stewards: The Teaching and Practice of Stewardship* (Philadelphia: Geneva, 1963), 12.
7. St. Basil the Great, *Sermon the Rich, ch. 2*. De unione ecclesarium. October 25, 2008. https://bekkos.wordpress.com/st-basils-sermon-to-the-rich/. Accessed August 7, 2021. [for original Greek text see J.P. Migne's *Patrologia Graeca*, vol 31, cols. 277C-304C].
8. Anthony N.S. Lane, *John Calvin: Student of the Church Fathers* (Grand Rapids: Baker, 1999), 15.

9. John Calvin, *Institutes of the Christian Religion*, 1559 ed. Trans. Ford Lewis Battles (Westminster John Knox Press, 2001).
10. John Calvin, *Preface to Homilies of St. John Chrysostom*, trans. Hazlet, 145-6.
11. For a study of the influence of Chrysostom as an exegetical guide to Calvin, see John R. "Jack" Walchenbach, *John Calvin as Biblical Commentator: An Investigation into Calvin's Use of John Chrysostom as an Exegetical Tutor* (Wipf and Stock Publishers, 2010).
12. Kenneth Stewart, "Evangelicalism and Patristic Christianity: 1517 to the Present." *Evangelical Quarterly* 80, no. 4: 307-321, 2008.
13. Curran D. Bishop, "Reformation Appropriations of Creedal Theology and Contemporary Methodology for Understanding the Past: Calvin's Use of Chrysostom in the *Institutes of the Christian Religion*" A Paper Presented to the Covenant Theological Seminary Theological Society's First Annual Covenant Theological Conference (January 23, 2012), 6.
14. Nathan Dorn. "The Consilia of Alessandro Nievo: On Jews and Usury in 15th Century Italy," In Custodia Legis: Law Librarians of Congress. (May 201, 2016) https://blogs.loc.gov/law/2016/05/the-consilia-of-alessandro-nievo-on- jews-and-usury-in-15th-century-italy/ Accessed August 7, 2021
15. Andre Bieler, *Calvin's Economic and Social Thought* (Geneva: World Council of Churches, 2005).
16. Thomas Purifoy, Jr. The Economics of John Calvin. Compass Classroom https://compassclassroom.com/blog/economics-of-john-calvin/ Accessed August 7, 2021.
17. John Calvin, *Treatises Against the Anabaptists and Against the Libertines*, trans. and edit. Benjamin W. Farley, 284-5.
18. Max Weber, *The Protestant Ethic and the Spirit of Capitalism*. (New York: Scribner, 1958).
19. *Treatises Against the Anabaptists and Against the Libertines*, 284-5.
20. Douglas F. Kelly, *The Emergence of Liberty in the Modern World: The Influence of Calvin on Five Governments from the 16th Through 18th Centuries*. (P&R Publishing, 1992).
21. Thomas Purifoy, "The Economics of John Calvin," *Compass Classroom* (blog), October 10, 2012, https://compassclassroom.com/blog/economics-of-john-calvin/.
22. Thomas Purifoy, "The Economics of John Calvin."
23. Peter Feurherd, "John Calvin: The Religious Reformer Who Influenced Capitalism." JSTOR.org. July 10, 2017.
24. Andre Bieler, *Calvin's Economic and Social Thought* (Geneva: World Council of Churches, 2005), 286.

7. Open Borders or Open Hearts?

1. Victor Davis Hanson, *The Dying Citizen: How Progressive Elites, Tribalism, and Globalization Are Destroying the Idea of America* (Basic Books, 2021), 96.
2. For a helpful definition of terminology related to immigration see J. D. Payne, *Strangers Next Door: Immigration, Migration and Mission*. IVP Books, Downers Grove, 2012, pp. 27-29. Payne provides statistics of global migration of people groups and summarizes the extensive biblical record of the role of migrations in salvation history.

3. https://neonnettle.com/news/16851-abc-censors-obama-s-criticism-of-biden-s-open-borders-from-interview. ABC News has censored former President Barack Obama's recent remarks criticizing Joe Biden's *"open borders"* as "unsustainable" from a televised portion of his interview. Obama told co-host, Robin Roberts: *"Immigration is tough." "It always has been because, on the one hand, I think we are naturally a people that want to help others." "We have borders." "The idea that we can just have open borders is something that ... as a practical matter, is unsustainable,"* he added.
4. For example, see Joseph Carens, "Politics, Principles, and Open Borders" in *Abolition Democracy 13/13*. blogs.law.columbia.edu/abolition1313. Carens in "The Case for open borders" in opendemocracy.net states three assumptions of open borders: 1. There is no natural social order. 2. In evaluating the moral status of alternative forms of political and social organization, we must start from the premise that all human beings are of equal moral worth. 3. Restrictions on the freedom of human beings require a moral justification. Based on these, he asserts that is a prima facie case that borders "should be open, for again three interrelated reasons. First, state control over immigration limits freedom of movement. The right to go where you want is an important human freedom in itself. ... The second reason why borders should normally be open is that freedom of movement is essential for equality of opportunity. ... A third, closely related point is that a commitment to equal moral worth entails some commitment to economic, social, and political equality, partly as a means of realizing equal freedom and equal opportunity and partly as a desirable end in itself."
5. See, for example, cis.org, "Reihan Salam's Powerful Case Against Open Borders" that engages Riehan Salam's book *Melting Pot or Civil War? A Son of Immigrants Makes the Case Against Open Borders* (Sentinel, 2018).
6. See *Global Diasporas and Mission*. Ed. Chandler H. Im and Amos Yong. Regnum Edinburgh Centenary Series, vol. 23. Wipf and Stock, 2014; R. M. Daniel Carroll, *Christians at the Border: Immigration, the Church, & the Bible*. Baker, Brazos Press, 2013. Carroll engages the Hispanic immigration into the United States' southern border and regards it as an opportunity for the Church's ministry considering the Old and New Testaments' teachings on caring for the immigrant, refugee and exile. He helpfully summarizes the Old Testament's laws for the sojourner and the New Testament's teaching on welcoming the stranger. Elliot Clark. *Evangelism As Exiles: Life on Mission as Strangers in Our Own Land*. The Gospel Coalition 2019. Clark's missional experience with Christian minorities leads him to the conclusion that such believers are essentially exiles in their own middle Asian Muslim lands and serve as models for the committed Christian in post-Christian western culture. He asserts that not only should we offer hospitality to the exiles we minister to in America, but we must recognize that as fellow exiles, hospitality is central to our evangelism. Clark writes, "... we'd be mistaken to assume that Peter [in 1 Peter 4:8-9] limited such kindness to only brothers and sisters in Christ. Our homes and our tables aren't reserved for people like us. As Jesus said, our love and greeting should also be for those different from us (Matt. 5:47). The Christian call to hospitality includes a love for outsiders—for strangers, foreigners, and the other. It implies sharing our homes with sinners. As such the ministry of hospitality is essential for our evangelistic endeavor." P. 134.
7. *Cf.* Bo H. Lim, "Exile and Migration: Toward a Biblical Theology of Immigration and Displacement", *The Covenant Quarterly* 74, n. 2, May 2016. Pp. 3-8.

8. Gloria L. Schaab. "Which of These Was Neighbour?: Spiritual Dimensions of the US Immigration Question". *International Journal of Public Theology* 2, 2008, pp. 182-202. She writes, "Thus rooted in a theological anthropology of *imago Dei*, Pope John's [XXIII] argument for the right to emigrate based on each person's membership in the human family is a radically compelling one that explicitly supersedes national interests and economic obstacles. Unfortunately, the human family of which the Pope speaks has, to many in the contemporary context, proven to be quite dysfunctional. Global acts of terrorism, rocketing oil prices, vacillating rates of monetary exchange, rising healthcare costs, increasing urban crime and a tenuous national economy provide an array of reasons why many United States politicians and citizens opt for strategies that control the borders and facilitate the deportation of immigrants, rather than for strategies that offer hospitality and welcome to the stranger in our midst. In response to this national reality the United States Catholic Bishops maintain that 'nations have the right to control their borders'. Moreover, they insist that they have no intention of 'condoning undocumented migration.', p. 195.
9. *Cf.* Jean-Pierre Ruiz, "The Bible and People on the Move: Another Look at Matthew's Parable of the Day Laborers". *New Theology Review*, August 2007, 20, 3, pp. 15-23.
10. Matthew Kaemingk, *Christian Hospitality and Muslim Immigration in an Age of Fear*. Wm. B. Eerdmans, 2018. The concerns of immigration are an integral part of Reformed public theology in Kaemingk's perspective as seen in his *Reformed Public Theology: A Global Vision for Life in the World*. Ed. by Matthew Kaemingk. Baker Academic Grand Rapids, 2021.
11. Ellis Island in New York Harbor was the United States' leading immigrant inspection point from 1892 to 1954. Almost 12 million immigrants who arrived at the Port of New York and New Jersey were processed there under federal law. *Cf.* https://en.wikipedia.org/wiki/EllisIsland.
12. For a review of the history of US immigration legislation see https://www.fairus.org/legislation/reports-and-analysis/history-of-us-immigration-laws.
13. A recent textbook states, for example, "Today I have a message....to the children, the students, the workers, the masses, and to the bloodsuckers, the parasites, the vampires who are the capitalists of the world: The schools are tools of the power structure that blind and sentence our youth to a life of confusion, and hypocrisy, one that preaches assimilation and practices institutional racism." http://thenewamerican.com/culture/education/7452-tucson-parents-challenge-ethnic-studies-cjurriculum
14. John Aman. *Hijacked: How George Soros and Friends Exploit Your Church*. D. James Kennedy Ministries, 2021, pp. 31-37.
15. *Cf.* Joan Maruskin, "The Bible: The Ultimate Migration Handbook", *Church and Society* 95, n. 6, July to August 2005, pp. 77-90. J. D. Payne, *Strangers Next Door: Immigration, Migration and Mission*. IVP Books, Downers Grove, 2012, p. 20. Payne in contrast to Maruskin writes concerning immigration with mission and evangelism in mind as political and moral dimensions of the issue are not his primary concern.
16. Karla R. Suomala. "Immigrants and Evangelicals: What Does the Bible Say?" *Crosscurrents*, 67, n. 3. September 2017, pp. 590-99. Suomala summarizes some evangelicals' biblical responses to counter Christianly motivated demands for open borders.

These arguments include the need to carefully consider the distinct contexts of ancient practices in comparison with contemporary international realities and the legitimate authority of governments according to Scripture to protect their boundaries.

17. Consider the Marxist ideology reflected in Saul Alinsky's *Rules for Radicals: A Pragmatic Primer for Realistic Radicals* (New York: Vintage Books, 1989). Alinsky argues that ethical commitments are nearly meaningless for a person or movement's ultimate interests. Alinsky explains, "Life and how you live it is the story of means and ends. The end is what you want, and the means is how you get it. Whenever we think about social change, the question of means and ends arises. The man of action views the issue of means and ends in pragmatic and strategic terms. He has no other problem; he thinks only of his actual resources and the possibilities of various choices of action. He asks of ends only whether they are achievable and worth the cost; of means, only whether they will work. To say that corrupt means corrupt the ends is to believe in the immaculate conception of ends and principles. The real arena is corrupt and bloody. Life is a corrupting process ... he who fears corruption fears life." (pp. 24-25.) "Moral rationalization is indispensable at all times of action whether to justify the selection or the use of ends or means. Machiavelli's blindness to the necessity for moral clothing to all acts and motives—he said 'politics has no relation to morals'—was his major weakness." (p. 43). Perhaps Alinsky's radicalism might be summarized as "get what you want with whatever means are at hand and make it look morally right".

18. "During Calvin's time, Geneva – a city of about 10,000 inhabitants – doubled in size as a result of Reformed Protestant refugees coming from France. As Geneva became known as a welcome asylum for Reformed Protestants fleeing persecution, refugees came from elsewhere as well. As the English exile John Bale living in Geneva wrote of that city, '[I]s it not wonderful that Spaniards, Italians, Scots, Englishmen, Frenchmen, Germans, disagreeing in manners, speech, and apparel ... being coupled only with the yoke of Christ, should live so lovingly and friendly ... like a spiritual and Christian congregation.'", https://www.cambridge.org/core/books/abs/john-calvin-in-context/refugees/FC26443A1BFB15815811E53F508CF90E.

19. Two helpful studies are Gopalswamy Jacob, *The Motif of Stranger in Calvin's Old Testament Commentaries*. Instituut voor Reformatienonderzoek. Apeldoorn 2008; and, Ruben Rosario Rodriguez, "Immigrants, Refugees, and Asylum Seekers: The Migratory Beginnings of Reformed Public Theology" in *Reformed Public Theology: A Global Vision for Life in the World*. Ed. by Matthew Kaemingk. Baker Academic Grand Rapids, 2021. Pp. 23-34. Rodriguez asserts, "Today in the United States, ironically, many self-identified Calvinists willingly support anti-immigration (and borderline racist) leaders and cruel immigration policies. These Calvinists will sometimes even attempt to use their faith as a tool by which they can calmly turn refugees away and ignore the moral horrors being perpetrated on the US southern border. Their moral and political quietism will sometimes be fostered through politically passive readings of Romans 13 and a vague emphasis on submissive acceptance of the laws and leaders whom God has placed in authority.", p. 24.

20. Jacob, *The Motif of Stranger*, p. 150.

21. Jacob demonstrates that the Hebrew concept of the *GER*, or the stranger, was a vital biblical context for Calvin given his own story and the Genevan center of his ministry. "For Calvin, the notion of *GER* is not just an abstract theological concept;

it is reality, a reality that shapes his whole ministry in Geneva. He did not become a citizen of Geneva until merely three years before his death, and was thus a stranger for the greatest part of his life. Calvin also married a woman who was not only a widow, but also a refugee. He served as minister among a congregation filled with strangers from around the world. The reality of being stranger among strangers is evident in his exegetical work on the Old Testament, particularly on passages where the idea of *GER* occurs." Jacob, *op. cit.*, p. 152.

22. "When in 1533 Calvin's appeal to the Geneva city council was overturned, and he was consequently told to leave the city; when in 1553 Ami Perrin was elected as syndic, and the atrocities committed against the strangers increased; when Calvin's other appeals were time and again turned down—he reminded the Genevans of the importance the Old Testament gives to listening to the words of strangers. For Egypt was spared because they heeded the words of the stranger Joseph, the king of Babylon was spared because he regarded the words of the foreigner Daniel, and finally the Lord also spared Nineveh because the inhabitants listened to the words of the prophet Jonah, who was *GER*, and repented." Jacob, *Op. Cit.*, p. 153.
23. Rodriguez, *op. cit.*, p. 25.
24. John Calvin, *Institutes of the Christian Religion*, trans. Ford Lewis Battles (Westminster Press), III.7.6.
25. Rodriguez, *op. cit.*, p. 27.
26. For Castellio's critique of Calvin's changing views regarding the heretic's right to life and thought, see richardmerrell.com/castellioagainstcalvin.pdf.
27. Rodriguez, *op. cit.*, pp. 27-33.
28. Rodriguez, *op. cit.*, pp. 32-33. Rodriguez writes, "Whatever Admiral Coligny's original intentions, Villegagnon's Protestant profession of faith proved insincere: he eventually imposed Roman Catholic doctrine over all of Fort Coligny, forbade Reformed worship (though it continued in secret), and eventually drove the Huguenots off the island. They were refugees yet again. The Huguenots as exiles on the Brazilian mainland began mission work with the Topinambu tribe who had welcomed them in their vulnerable state. Villegagnon charged them as heretics and had them arrested as spies and sentenced to death. One recanted, but three were executed, the first martyrs to die for sake of Protestant doctrine and mission in the New World. A fifth, John Boles, settled south of Fort Coligny and became such a successful preacher among the indigenous tribes that the Jesuits had him arrested and imprisoned for eight years before burning him at the stake in 1567, "the first Protestant auto-da-fe in America." (pp. 32-33).
29. See capitalresearch.org, "Mapping Soros's 'Philanthropy' at Home and Abroad".
30. These themes are given dramatic prominence in the survey of the biblical story as summarized by Joan Maruskin, "The Bible: The Ultimate Migration Handbook", *Church and Society* 95, n. 6, July to August 2005 pp. 77-90. J. D. Payne offers substantial statistics on g-obal migration of people groups and summarizes the extensive biblical record of the role of migrations in salvation history. Yet quoting James K. Hoffmeier, he notes the minimal comment of the Evangelist on Jesus as infant refugee: "The Gospels pass over this segment of the life of Jesus in silence. We do not know under what circumstances they entered Egypt and where the Holy Family lived." p. 80.
31. Schaab, *op. cit.*, p. 196.

32. Elliot Clark, *Evangelism As Exiles: Life on Mission as Strangers in Our Own Land* (The Gospel Coalition 2019), p. 137.

8. The Thanatos Syndrome

1. Walker Percy, *The Thanatos Syndrome*, The Signed First Edition Society, Franklin Library (New York: Farrar, Straus, Giroux New York, 1987), 361.
2. See Horace McCoy, "Chapter Thirteen," in *They Shoot Horses, Don't They?* (Serpent's Tail, 1995), 120–121.
3. Horace McCoy, "Chapter Thirteen," in *They Shoot Horses, Don't They?* (Serpent's Tail, 1995), 120–121. The film citation is *They Shoot Horses, Don't They?*, film version, psychological drama (Cinerama Releasing Corporation, 1969).
4. The noted film critic Robert Ebert wrote of the film version, "The movie begins on a note of alienation and spirals down from there. 'Horses' provides us no cheap release at the end; and the ending, precisely because it is so obvious, is all the more effective. We knew it was coming. Even the title gave it away. And when it comes, it is effective not because it is a surprise but because it is inevitable. As inevitable as death. The performances are perfectly matched to Pollack's grim vision."
5. See, e.g., Francis A. Schaeffer, *How Should We Then Live?*(L'abri 50th Anniversary Edition): *The Rise and Decline of Western Thought and Culture* (Crossway, 2005).
6. Euthanasia is some form is legal in Belgium, Luxembourg, the Netherlands, Switzerland, Oregon, Washington, and Montana. See Nicole Steck et al., "Euthanasia and Assisted Suicide in Selected European Countries and US States: Systematic Literature Review," *Medical Care* 51, no. 10 (2013): 938–944.
7. "The Greek words 'eu'", goodly or well + 'thanatos', death = the good death." From William Shiel Jr., MD, "Definition of Euthanasia," *MedicineNet*, last modified 31 2018, accessed September 15, 2019, https://www.medicinenet.com/script/main/art.asp?articlekey=7365
8. For a study of Walker Percy, see Patrick H. Samway, *Walker Percy: A Life*, First edition. (New York: Farrar, Stause & Giroux, 1997).
9. Walker Percy, *The Thanatos Syndrome* (Macmillan, 1999).
10. Percy, *Thanatos*, ix.
11. Percy, *Thanatos*, 139.
12. See "Palliative Therapy - an Overview | ScienceDirect Topics," accessed September 15, 2019, https://www.sciencedirect.com/topics/nursing-and-health-professions/palliative-therapy.
13. For a balanced view of this text in context see John Piper, "Does the Bible Prescribe Alcohol to the Depressed?," *Desiring God*, last modified April 21, 2017, accessed September 15, 2019, https://www.desiringgod.org/interviews/does-the-bible-prescribe-alcohol-to-the-depressed
14. Ludwig Edelstein, *The Hippocratic Oath, Text, Translation and Interpretation* (Baltimore: Johns Hopkins University Press, 1943).

9. The Course of Nations

1. Tom Holland, *Pax: War and Peace in Rome's Golden Age* (New York: Basic Books, 2023), 8.
2. Our lay observations can be measured against the demonstration of Prof. Costa Papaliolios, at "Relativity Train," *Harvard University Natural Sciences* department page, January 1981, https://sciencedemonstrations.fas.harvard.edu/presentations/relativity-train.
3. Madison et al., "Convention and Ratification - Creating the United States | Exhibitions - Library of Congress."
4. Acts 5, scene 5. See, e.g., Walter Gierasch, "13. Shakespbare's Macbeth, I, Iii, *The Explicator*, volume 30 (1971), 137-142."
5. Such as William Ophuls. *Immoderate Greatness: Why Civilizations Fail*. United States: CreateSpace Independent Publishing Platform, 2012.
6. John G. Wofford, "Happy Puritan | News | The Harvard Crimson," The Harvard Crimson, Faculty Profile, March 4, 1955, https://www.thecrimson.com/article/1955/3/4/happy-puritan-pfrom-the-lettuce-fields/.
7. See, e.g., George M. Marsden, "Perry Miller's Rehabilitation of the Puritans: A Critique," *Church History* 39, no. 1 (1970): 91–105; Scott Michaelsen, "John Winthrop's" Modell" *Covenant and the Company Way*," Early American Literature 27, no. 2 (1992): 85–100; Perry Miller, *The New England Mind: The Seventeenth Century*, vol. 2 (Harvard University Press, 1983); Perry Miller, *Errand into the Wilderness*, vol. 81 (Harvard University Press, 2009); Perry Miller and Perry Miller, *The New England Mind: From Colony to Province* (Harvard University Press, 2009).
8. John Winthrop, "A Modell of Christian Charity," in *Collections of The Massachusetts Historical Society*, 3rd ed., Sixth (Boston: The Society, 1838), 7:31-38.
9. See, e.g., Ronald Reagan, *A Shining City: The Legacy of Ronald Reagan* (Simon & Schuster, 1998); and Paul Kengor, *God and Ronald Reagan: A Spiritual Life* (Harper Collins, 2009).
10. Paul Johnson and Nadia May, *A History of the American People* (Weidenfeld & Nicolson New York, 1997), 13.
11. Czeslaw Milosz, "Six Lectures in Verse, Lecture V," *Selected and Last Poems 1931-2004* (Penguin Books Limited, 2017), 208-209
12. Deuteronomy 30:19-20.
13. Tom Holland, *Dominion: How the Christian Revolution Remade the World* (Basic Books, 2019).
14. See, e.g., Martyn Lloyd-Jones, *Hope in the Ruins*: Acts (6 Volumes in 3): Chapters 1-8 (Crossway, 2013).

10. Repaving the Pathway to Poverty

1. Pope John Paul II and J.P. Pham, *Centesimus Annus: Assessment and Perspectives for the Future of Catholic Social Doctrine* (Vatican: Libreria editrice vaticana, 1998), 173.
2. J. Christ et al., *Debating Critical Theory: Engagements with Axel Honneth* (Rowman & Littlefield Publishers, 2020), 173.

3. For a study on the causes of the demise of the Soviet Union, consider Celeste A Wallander, "Western policy and the demise of the Soviet Union," *Journal of Cold War Studies* 5, no. 4 (2003); Robert Strayer, *Why Did the Soviet Union Collapse?: Understanding Historical Change: Understanding Historical Change* (Routledge, 2016).
4. One is reminded of the Allied General of the Army, Dwight David Eisenhower, ordering that photographs be made of the Holocaust lest future generations disbelieve such mass murder and unprecedented inhumanity ever happened. See, e.g., Jack Hochwald, "The US Army T-Forces: Documenting the Holocaust," *American Jewish History* 70, no. 3 (1981).
5. Michael A Milton, "From Flanders Fields to the Moviegoer: Philosophical Foundations for a Transcendent Ethical Framework," (Wipf and Stock Publishers, 2019), 16.
6. Charles Taylor, *A Secular Age* (Harvard University Press, 2009).
7. George Orwell, "You and the atomic bomb," *the Tribune* 19 (1945).
8. Richard J Aldrich, "British Intelligence and the Anglo-American'Special Relationship'During the Cold War," *Review of International Studies* (1998).
9. Aldrich, "British Intelligence."
10. Friedrich August Hayek and Bruce Caldwell, *The Road to Serfdom: Text and documents: The definitive edition* (Routledge, 2014).
11. For research on centralization and the loss of self-determination see, e.g., G Ross Stephens, "State centralization and the erosion of local autonomy," *The Journal of Politics* 36, no. 1 (1974).
12. See Paul Kengor, *Dupes: How America's Adversaries Have Manipulated Progressives for a Century* (Open Road Media, 2014).
13. Paul Kengor, "The Disturbing Link Between Obama, Communism, and Abortion," *Life News* (2012 2012).
14. Joshua S. Goldstein. 2011. Think Again: War. Foreign Policy 188: 1-9.
15. John Lewis Gaddis, *The Long Peace: Inquiries into the History of the Cold War* (Oxford University Press on Demand, 1987).
16. Kengor, *Dupes*.
17. Michel Foucault, *The Foucault Reader* (Pantheon, 1984), 383-4.
18. Alexander Dunst, *Madness in Cold War America: Mad America* (Taylor & Francis, 2016).
19. Richard Wurmbrand, *Tortured for Christ* (Colorado Springs: David C Cook, 2017).
20. Robert Weller, "Rear Admiral Joseph N. Wenger, USN (RET) and the Navy Cryptological Museum," *Cryptologia* 8, no. 3 (1984/07/01 1984), https://doi.org/10.1080/0161-118491859006, https://doi.org/10.1080/0161-118491859006.
21. M.A. Milton, *Foundations of a Moral Government: Lex, Rex - A New Annotated Version in Contemporary English* (Fortress Book Service, 2019).
22. John Locke, "Property," in *2 / Of Property*, ed. C. B. MacPherson (Toronto: University of Toronto Press, 2019), 15-28. John Locke's political philosophy is grounded in his understanding of Christian doctrine. See Steven Menashi, "Cain as His Brother's Keeper: Property Rights and Christian Doctrine in Locke's Two Treatises of Government," *Seton Hall L. Rev.* 42 (2012).
23. Edmund. Burke, I. Harris, and R. Geuss, *Pre-Revolutionary Writings* (Cambridge University Press, 1993), 2.
24. Michael A. Milton, "Statism, Frankenstein's Monster, and the Road to Serfdom," in *Statism: The Shadows of Another Night*, ed. Charles Rodriguez (Clinton, MS:

Fortress Book Service, Tanglewood Publishing, 2015).

25. Steven M. Teles. 2016. 20. How the Progressives Became the Tea Party's Mortal Enemy. The Progressives' Century. New Haven: Yale University Press, pp. 453-477; see, also, C.J. Wolfe. 2011. Lessons from the Friendship of Jacques Maritain with Saul Alinsky. Catholic Social Science Review 16: 229-240.
26. Kurt Aland, "The Relation Between Church and State in Early Times: A Reinterpretation," *The Journal of Theological Studies* 19, no. 1 (1968): 115, http://www.jstor.org/stable/23959560.
27. John H. Hayes, "The Usage of Oracles against Foreign Nations in Ancient Israel," *Journal of Biblical Literature* 87, no. 1 (1968), https://doi.org/10.2307/3263424, http://www.jstor.org/stable/3263424.
28. Hayes, "The Usage of Oracles against Foreign Nations in Ancient Israel."
29. Tremper Longman III and D.G. Reid, "The Task of Biblical Theology," in *God Is a Warrior* (Grand Rapids: Zondervan Academic, 2010), 14.
30. Jesus establishes the hermeneutical code for unlocking Revelation in chapter one: "Write, therefore, what you have seen, what is now and what will take place later. [20] The mystery of the seven stars that you saw in my right hand and of the seven golden lampstands is this: The seven stars are the angels[e] of the seven churches, and the seven lampstands are the seven churches" (Revelation 1:19-20 NKJV).
31. William Hendriksen, *More than Conquerors: An Interpretation of the Book of Revelation* (Grand Rapids, MI: Baker Books, 1967), 144.
32. Robert H Mounce, *The Book of Revelation*, vol. 27 (Wm. B. Eerdmans Publishing, 1998).
33. Mounce, *The Book of Revelation*, 27, 245.
34. Mounce, *The Book of Revelation*, 27, 256.
35. G.E. Ladd, *A Commentary on the Revelation of John* (Eerdmans Publishing Company, 1972), 77.
36. James Shoopman, "The Nature of the Beast," *Review & Expositor* 106, no. 1 (2009): Abstract.
37. See, e.g., Paul Kengor. 2017. A Pope and a President: John Paul II, Ronald Reagan, and the extraordinary untold story of the 20th century. Open Road Media. See also Michael A. Milton. 2013. What Ronald Reagan's Legacy Can Teach Us Today About Religious Liberty. Matthews, NC: Faith for Living, Inc.. https://michaelmilton.org/2014/02/06/what-ronald-reagans-legacy-can-teach-us-today-about-religious-liberty/
38. See, e.g., McManus, M. (2005). "How Pope John Paul Fought Communism - by Mike McManus | VirtueOnline â The Voice for Global Orthodox Anglicanism." Retrieved April 12, 2021, from https://virtueonline.org/how-pope-john-paul-fought-communism-mike-mcmanus.
39. Lee Edwards. 2005. John Paul II: Winning the Cold War. Heritage Foundation https://www.heritage.org/commentary/john-paul-ii-winning-the-cold-war.
40. E. Mëhilli, *From Stalin to Mao: Albania and the Socialist World* (Cornell University Press, 2017).
41. Nicholas Tochka, "Voicing freedom, sounding dissent: Popular music, simulation and citizenship in democratizing Albania, 1991–1997," *European Journal of Cultural Studies* 17, no. 3 (2014), https://doi.org/10.1177/1367549413508749, https://journals.sagepub.com/doi/abs/10.1177/1367549413508749.
42. *Father John is a pseudonym.

43. I share *Father John's statement, as best I can recall, the poignant points embedded into my soul; and from my journal notes prepared for World Magazine.
44. Biden integrated American history, Augustine, the Torah, and Christianity to marshal forward support for his statement, "And together, we shall write an American story of hope, not fear. Of unity, not division." See   President Joseph R. Biden, Jr. | The White House. "Inaugural Address By President Joseph R. Biden, Jr. | The White House". 2021. The White House. https://www.whitehouse.gov/briefing-room/speeches-remarks/2021/01/20/inaugural-address-by-president-joseph-r-biden-jr/
45. See Hayek on uniformity in F.A. Hayek. "The Great Utopia." In *The Road to Serfdom*. London: Routledge, 1944, 24. Hayek is quoting Walter Lippmann, "Though they promise themselves a more abundant life, they must in practice renounce it; as the organized direction increases, the variety of ends must give way to uniformity. That is the nemesis of the planned society and the authoritarian principle in human affairs." See Atlantic Monthly, November 1936, p. 552.
46. I refer to that most pernicious peddler of postmodernity, Michel Foucault (1926-1984). A deconstructionist, Foucault examined power structures, e.g., Christianity, Western Civilization, and gender, and sought to redefine them and free them from traditional centers of power. I consider him a moral anarchist whose teachings were enormously successful in permeating Western thought.

11. Loving God, Loving Others

1. Tom Holland, *Dominion: How the Christian Revolution Remade the World* (Basic Books, 2019), 540.
2. Lindquist, Spencer. 2021. "Lecturer At Yale Fantasizes About Brutally Murdering White People". Journal Article. *The Federalist*.
3. Angelopoulou, Elli. 2001. "TitleUnderstanding the Color of Human Skin/Title". In *Human Vision and Electronic Imaging VI*, edited by Bernice E. Rogowitz and Thrasyvoulos N. Pappas. SPIE. https://doi.org/10.1117/12.429495.
4. Woodson Sr, Robert L. 2021. *Red, White, and Black: Rescuing American History from Revisionists and Race Hustlers*. Emancipation Books.
5. Spencer Lindquist, "Lecturer At Yale Fantasizes About Brutally Murdering White People," *Federalist*, June 2021.
6. Relethford, John H. 1997. "Hemispheric Difference in Human Skin Color". Journal Article. *American Journal of Physical Anthropology: The Official Publication of the American Association of Physical Anthropologists* 104 (4): 449–57.
7. Bastiaens, Maarten, Jeanette ter Huurne, Nelleke Gruis, Wilma Bergman, Rudi Westendorp, Bert-Jan Ver- meer, and Jan-Nico Bouwes Bavinck. 2001. "The Melanocortin-1-Receptor Gene Is the Major Freckle Gene". Journal Article. *Human Molecular Genetics* 10 (16): 1701–8.
8. Tom Holland, *Dominion: How the Christian Revolution Remade the World* (Basic Books, 2019).
9. I referred to David Norton. 2005. *The New Cambridge Paragraph Bible with the Apocrypha: King James Version*. Cambridge University Press.
10. Milton, Michael A. 2016. "Pastoral Assessment, Diagnosis, and Treatment of Congregational Pathologies". Erskine Theological Seminary.

11. S. Mestrovic. 2004. *The Balkanization of the West: The Confluence of Postmodernism and Postcommunism*. Book. Taylor & Francis.
12. Noel Ignatiev, and John Garvey. 2007. "Abolish the White Race by Any Means Necessary". *Race, Ethnicity, and Gender: Selected Readings*, 448–51.
13. John Donne. 1624. *Meditation XVII: Devotion upon Emergent Occasions*.
14. C. H. Woolston (1856-1927). Public domain.

12. The Final Hope

1. Martyn Lloyd-Jones, *Revival* (Wheaton: Crossway, 1987), 20.
2. David Martyn Lloyd-Jones and J. I. Packer, *Revival* (Crossway Books, 1987), 100.
3. Christine Leigh Heyrman, "The First Great Awakening, Divining America, TeacherServe®, National Humanities Center," *TeachServe*® (n.d.), accessed October 8, 2021, http://nationalhumanitiescenter.org/tserve/eighteen/ekeyinfo/grawaken.htm.
4. Jessica Sophie Corneille and David Luke, "Spontaneous Spiritual Awakenings: Phenomenology, Altered States, Individual Differences, and Wellbeing," *Cornell University: PsyArXiv Preprints* (2021), 2
5. See, e.g., Troy Duncan, "Methodism and Empire," in *Methodism in Australia* (Routledge, 2015), abstract.
6. See Walker Percy, *Sign Posts in a Strange Land* (New York: Farrar, Straus and Giroux, 1991), 215.
7. Catherine L. Albanese, "Savage, Sinner, and Saved: Davy Crockett, Camp Meetings, and the Wild Frontier," *American Quarterly* 33, no. 5 (1981): 482–501.
8. Joanna Ruth Wirtz, "Samaritans and John 4" (2009).
9. Wayne Brindle, "The Origin and History of the Samaritans," *Faculty Publications and Presentations* (1984): 72.

13. Between Bethel and Ai

1.

14. Enslavement by Category

1. Dorothy L. (Dorothy Leigh) Sayers, "Are Women Human?: Address Given to a Women's Society, 1938," *Logos: A Journal of Catholic Thought and Culture* 8, no. 4 (2005): 165–78, https://muse.jhu.edu/pub/9/article/187827.
2. Dorothy Leigh Sayers, *Are Women Human?* (Alban Books Limited, 1971), 36.

15. Field Notes from Babylon

1. James Davison Hunter, *To Change the World: The Irony, Tragedy, and Possibility of Christianity in the Late Modern World* (Oxford University Press, 2010), 197.
2. Michael A. Milton, *Cooperation Without Compromise (Stapled Booklet): Faithful Gospel Witness in a Pluralistic Setting* (Wipf and Stock Publishers, 2007); Miroslav

Volf, *A Public Faith: How Followers of Christ Should Serve the Common Good* (Brazos Press, 2011).
3. Miroslav Volf, *A Public Faith: How Followers of Christ Should Serve the Common Good* (Brazos Press, 2011), 132.
4. Justin Ariel Bailey, *Reimagining Apologetics: The Beauty of Faith in a Secular Age* (InterVarsity Press, 2020), 4-5.
5. Michael P. Knowles, *We Preach Not Ourselves: Paul on Proclamation* (Grand Rapids: Brazos Press, 2008), 15.
6. Michael J. Gorman, *Cruciformity: Paul's Narrative Spirituality of the Cross, 20th Anniversary Edition* (Grand Rapids: Wm. B. Eerdmans Publishing, 2021).

VISION AND MISSION

1. Michael A. Milton, Finding a Vision for Your Church: Assembly Required (Phillipsburg, NJ: P & R Publishing, 2012).

Bibliography

Allen, Diogenes, and Frederic B. Burnham. "Postmodern Theology: Christian Faith in a Pluralist World," October 1, 2006.

Allen, Lois, and Darrow Miller. *The Worldview of the Kingdom*. YWAM Publishing, 2005.

Amosa, Faala Faamatuainu. "Courting a Public Theology of Fa'a-Vae for The Church and Contemporary Samoa," May 12, 2021.

Auden, W. H. *For the Time Being: A Christmas Oratorio*. Princeton University Press, 2013.

Audi, Robert, and Nicholas Wolterstorff. "Religion in the Public Square: The Place of Religious Convictions in Political Debate," January 1, 2000.

Bailey, Justin Ariel. *Reimagining Apologetics: The Beauty of Faith in a Secular Age*. InterVarsity Press, 2020.

Bair, Deirdre. *Samuel Beckett: A Biography*. Simon and Schuster, 1990.

Balthasar, Hans Urs von. *Love Alone Is Credible*. San Francisco: Ignatius Press, 2004.

Barnes, S J Michael. "Interreligious Learning: Dialogue, Spirituality and the Christian Imagination," December 15, 2011.

Barnes, S. J. Michael. "Theology And The Dialogue Of Religions," March 14, 2002.

Barnett, Victoria J. *The Collected Sermons of Dietrich Bonhoeffer: Volume 2*. Fortress Press, 2017.

Beckett, Samuel. *Waiting for Godot: A Tragicomedy in Two Acts*. Grove/Atlantic, Inc., 2011.

Beilby, James K. "Thinking About Christian Apologetics: What It Is and Why We Do It," September 28, 2011.

Bevans, Stephen. "Models of Contextual Theology," October 1, 1992.

Biéler, André. *Calvin's Economic and Social Thought*. World Alliance of Reformed Churches, World Council of Churches, 2006.

Bosch, David J. "Transforming Mission: Paradigm Shifts in Theology of Mission," March 20, 1991.

———. "Witness to the World: The Christian Mission in Theological Perspective," March 1, 1979.

Breitenberg, E. Harold. "To Tell the Truth: Will the Real Public Theology Please Stand Up?" *Journal of the Society of Christian Ethics* 23, no. 2 (2003): 55–96. https://www.jstor.org/stable/23561835.

———. "To Tell the Truth: Will the Real Public Theology Please Stand Up?" *Journal of The Society of Christian Ethics* 23, no. 2 (January 1, 2003): 55–96. https://doi.org/10.5840/jsce20032325.

Broome, Deborah Louise. "Living in Two Cities: Lessons for the Church Today from Augustine's City of God," January 1, 2015.

Brown, Malcolm, Stephen Pattison, and Graeme Smith. "The Possibility of Citizen Theology: Public Theology after Christendom and the Enlightenment." *International*

Journal of Public Theology 6, no. 2 (January 1, 2012): 183–204. https://doi.org/10.1163/156973212x634948.

Calvin, Jean. *Calvin's Institutes*. Westminster John Knox Press, 2001.

———. *Commentaries*. Vol. Commentary on the Epistle to the Hebrews. United Kingdom: Calvin Translation Society, 1853.

Carl Hulet Hamilton. "A Study of Imagery in John Donne's Sermons." Doctor of Philosophy dissertation, University of Arkansas, 1968. https://www.proquest.com/openview/c0a60b8c67fe6ef0b0299f3ffa3a4c81/1?pq-origsite=gscholar&cbl=18750&diss=y.

Cartledge, Mark J. "A Companion to Public Theology." *The Journal of the European Pentecostal Theological Association* 37, no. 2 (June 12, 2017): 156–57. https://doi.org/10.1080/18124461.2017.1339546.

———. "C.S. Lewis as a Public Theologian: Pentecostal Appreciation, Evaluation, and Challenge." *Pneuma* 38, no. 4 (January 1, 2016): 436–55. https://doi.org/10.1163/15700747-03804001.

———. "Public Theology and Empirical Research: Developing an Agenda." *International Journal of Public Theology* 10, no. 2 (June 4, 2016): 145–66. https://doi.org/10.1163/15697320-12341440.

Casey, Shaun. "Teaching the Arts of Public Theology." *Christian Higher Education* 5, no. 1 (August 19, 2006): 37–54. https://doi.org/10.1080/15363750500382626.

Cavanaugh, William T. *Being Consumed: Economics and Christian Desire*. Wm. B. Eerdmans Publishing, 2008.

Chambers, Oswald. *My Utmost for His Highest*. Christian Classics Reproductions, 2022.

———. *My UtmostforHisHighest*. NewDelihi: GrapevineIndiaPublications, 2022. https://read.amazon.com/?asin=B0BSFJ5XB2&ref_=dbs_t_r_kcr.

Church (U.S.A.), Presbyterian. *Book of Common Worship, Pastoral Edition*. Westminster John Knox Press, 1993.

Clive Pearson, Clive Pearson, and Clive Pearson. "Being Responsible in the Public Domain," June 26, 2020, 173–88. https://doi.org/10.1007/978-981-15-5081-2_12.

Connolly, William E. "Why I Am Not a Secularist," January 1, 1999.

Cowdell, Scott. "What Is Public Theology." *St. Mark's Review* 3, no. 209 (September 1, 2009): 59–68.

Daniel L. Migliore, Daniel L. Migliore, and Daniel L. Migliore. "Faith Seeking Understanding: An Introduction to Christian Theology," January 1, 2004.

David W. Miller, and David W. Miller. "God at Work," January 1, 2007. https://doi.org/10.1093/acprof:oso/9780195314809.001.0001.

Dirkie Smit. "Notions of the Public and Doing Theology in: International Journal of Public Theology Volume 1 Issue 3 (2007)." *International Journal of Public Theology Through* I, no. 3 (January 1, 2007): 431–54. https://doi.org/10.1163/156973207X231716.

Doak, Mary. "Reclaiming Narrative for Public Theology," October 14, 2004.

Don S. Browning, Don S Browning, Don S. Browning, and Francis Schüssler Fiorenza. "Habermas, Modernity, and Public Theology," January 1, 1992.

Duncan B. Forrester, and Duncan B. Forrester. "Theology and Politics," January 1, 1988.

Eliot, T. S. *The Waste Land and Other Writings*. Random House Publishing Group, 2009.

Eliot, Thomas Stearns. *Poems*. A.A. Knopf, 1920.
Elliott, Alison. "Theology in the Public Sphere." *Practical Theology* 5, no. 3 (January 1, 2012): 351–52. https://doi.org/10.1558/prth.v5i3.351.
Elshtain, Jean Bethke. "Augustine and the Limits of Politics," February 15, 1996.
Esslin, Martin. *The Theatre of the Absurd*. Knopf Doubleday Publishing Group, 2009.
Filho, Carlos Ribeiro Caldas, and Carlos Caldas. "Dietrich Bonhoeffer e a Teologia Pública No Brasil." *Theologica Xaveriana* 66, no. 182 (November 28, 2016): 289–312. https://doi.org/10.11144/javeriana.tx66-182.dbtpb.
Forrester, Duncan B., and Duncan B. Forrester. "The Scope of Public Theology." *Studies in Christian Ethics* 17, no. 2 (August 1, 2004): 5–19. https://doi.org/10.1177/095394680401700209.
Forster, Dion Angus, and Johann W. Oosterbrink. "Where Is the Church on Monday?: Awakening the Church to the Theology and Practice of Ministry and Mission in the Marketplace" 49, no. 3 (August 21, 2015): 1–8. https://doi.org/10.4102/ids.v49i3.1944.
Garner, Stephen. "Contextual and Public Theology: Passing Fads or Theological Imperatives?," January 1, 2015.
———. "Eschatological Companions: Christian Hope in Virtual Worlds." *Theology and Sexuality* 26 (August 20, 2020): 140–57. https://doi.org/10.1080/13558358.2020.1803721.
Gorman, Michael J. *Cruciformity: Paul's Narrative Spirituality of the Cross, 20th Anniversary Edition*. Wm. B. Eerdmans Publishing, 2021.
Graham, Elaine. "Between a Rock and a Hard Place: Public Theology in a Post-Secular Age," July 31, 2013.
———. "Pastoral Care and Communitarianism" 125, no. 1 (January 1, 1998): 2–9. https://doi.org/10.1080/13520806.1998.11758825.
———. "Pastoral Theology in an Age of Uncertainty." *Hts Teologiese Studies-Theological Studies* 62, no. 3 (September 28, 2006): 845–65. https://doi.org/10.4102/hts.v62i3.392.
———. "Showing and Telling: The Practice of Public Theology Today." *Practical Theology* 9, no. 2 (July 4, 2016): 145–56. https://doi.org/10.1080/1756073x.2016.1157663.
———. "The Archbishop Speaks, But Who Is Listening? The Dilemmas of Public Theology Today." *Ecclesiology* 8, no. 2 (January 1, 2012): 200–222. https://doi.org/10.1163/174553112x630462.
———. "The Pastoral Significance of Community Work." *The Modern Churchman* 30, no. 2 (January 1, 1988): 15–23. https://doi.org/10.3828/mc.30.2.15.
———. "The Real Questions Are Theological." *Religious Studies Review* 8, no. 3 (June 1, 2001): 256–62. https://doi.org/10.1111/1467-9418.00100.
———. "The Unquiet Frontier." *Political Theology* 16, no. 1 (April 21, 2015): 33–46. https://doi.org/10.1179/1462317x14z.000000000128.
———. "THEOLOGY AND THE PUBLIC SQUARE: MAPPING THE FIELD." *Modern Believing* 61, no. 1 (January 8, 2020): 7–21. https://doi.org/10.3828/mb.2020.3.
———. "Why Practical Theology Must Go Public." *Practical Theology* 1, no. 1 (February 22, 2008): 11–17. https://doi.org/10.1558/prth.v1i1.11.

Graham, Elaine, Heather Walton, Frances Ward, and Katja Stuerzenhofecker. "Theological Reflection: Methods," January 1, 2005.
Greenawalt, Kent, Robert Audi, and Nicholas Wolterstorff. "Religion in the Public Square: The Place of Religious Convictions in Political Debate." *The Philosophical Review* 108, no. 2 (April 1, 1999): 293. https://doi.org/10.2307/2998308.
Gruchy, John W. de, John W. de Gruchy, and John W. de Gruchy. "Public Theology as Christian Witness: Exploring the Genre." *International Journal of Public Theology* 1, no. 1 (January 1, 2007): 26–41. https://doi.org/10.1163/156973207x194466.
Habermas, Jürgen. "An Awareness of What Is Missing." *Esprit*, no. 5 (January 1, 2007): 5–13.
———. *An Awareness of What Is Missing: Faith and Reason in a Post-Secular Age*. John Wiley & Sons, 2014.
———. "Notes on Post-Secular Society." *New Perspectives Quarterly* 25, no. 4 (September 1, 2008): 17–29. https://doi.org/10.1111/j.1540-5842.2008.01017.x.
Habermas, Jürgen, Thomas Burgerm, and Thomas Burger. "The Structural Transformation of the Public Sphere: An Inquiry into a Category of Bourgeois Society" 27, no. 1 (January 1, 1989).
Hainsworth, Deidre King, Scott R. Paeth, and Breitenberg Jr., E. Harold. *Public Theology for a Global Society: Essays in Honor of Max Stackhouse*. Grand Rapids: Wm. B. Eerdmans Publishing, 2010.
Hak Joon Lee. "Public Theology," n.d. https://doi.org/10.1017/cco9781107280823.004.
Hamlyn, D. W., Charles Taylor, and Charles Taylor. "Sources of the Self: The Making of the Modern Identity." *British Journal of Educational Studies* 39, no. 1 (February 1, 1991): 101. https://doi.org/10.2307/3120882.
Hanson, Victor Davis. *The Dying Citizen: How Progressive Elites, Tribalism, and Globalization Are Destroying the Idea of America*. Basic Books, 2021.
Harrison, Carol and Carol Harrison. "Augustine: Christian Truth and Fractured Humanity," July 27, 2000.
Hauerwas, Stanley, William H. Willimon, and William H. Willimon. "Resident Aliens: Life in the Christian Colony," January 1, 1989.
Hedman, Terese Norstedt. "Catholic Public Theology on YouTube: The Articulation of Public Theology on Social Media," January 28, 2021.
Himes, Brant Micah. "For a Better Worldliness: The Theological Discipleship of Abraham Kuyper and Dietrich Bonhoeffer," November 30, 2015.
Hodge, A. A., and J. Aspinwall Hodge. *The System of Theology Contained in the Westminster Shorter Catechism: Opened and Explained*. Wipf and Stock Publishers, 2004.
Hogue, Michael S. "After the Secular: Toward a Pragmatic Public Theology." *Journal of the American Academy of Religion* 78, no. 2 (June 1, 2010): 346–74. https://doi.org/10.1093/jaarel/lfp081.
Holland, Tom. *Dominion: How the Christian Revolution Remade the World*. Basic Books, 2019.
———. *Pax: War and Peace in Rome's Golden Age*. New York: Basic Books, 2023.
Hollis, Daniel W. "Religious Liberty and the Founding Fathers: The Commonwealthman's Influence." *Journal of Interdisciplinary Studies* 2, no. 1/2 (July 1, 1990): 87–102. https://doi.org/10.5840/jis199021/26.
Horne, Brian. "Imaginative Apologetics. Theology, Philosophy and the Catholic Tradi-

tion." *International Journal for The Study of The Christian Church* 12, no. 1 (July 27, 2012): 86–87. https://doi.org/10.1080/1474225x.2012.656490.
Howe, Neil. *The Fourth Turning Is Here: What the Seasons of History Tell Us about How and When This Crisis Will End*. Simon and Schuster, 2023.
Hunter, James Davison. *To Change the World: The Irony, Tragedy, and Possibility of Christianity in the Late Modern World*. Oxford University Press, 2010.
Ian S. Markham, and Ian Markham. "Plurality and Christian Ethics," January 1, 1994.
Jacobsen, Eneida. "Models of Public Theology*." *International Journal of Public Theology* 6, no. 1 (January 1, 2012): 7–22. https://doi.org/10.1163/156973212X617154.
Jenkins, Philip. "The Next Christendom," May 30, 2002. https://doi.org/10.1093/0195146166.001.0001.
Johannes Willem Bertens, and Hans Bertens. "The Idea of the Postmodern: A History" 69, no. 4 (January 1, 1995): 883.
Johnson, Kristen Deede. "Theology, Political Theory, and Pluralism: Beyond Tolerance and Difference," February 5, 2007.
Juergen Moltmann, and Jürgen Moltmann. "God for a Secular Society: The Public Relevance of Theology," January 1, 1999.
Kaemingk, Matthew. *Reformed Public Theology: A Global Vision for Life in the World*. Baker Academic, 2021.
Kenner, Hugh. *Samuel Beckett, a Critical Study*. University of California Press, 1968.
Kim, Sabastian. *A Companion to Public Theology*. BRILL, 2017.
Kim, Sebastian. "Public Theology in the History of Christianity." In *A Companion to Public Theology*, 40–66. Brill, 2017. https://doi.org/10.1163/9789004336063_004.
———. "Theology in the Public Sphere," 2011.
———. *Theology in the Public Sphere: Public Theology as a Catalyst for Open Debate*. London: SCM Press, 2013.
Knowles, Michael P. *We Preach Not Ourselves: Paul on Proclamation*. Brazos Press, 2008.
Langmead, Ross. "The Word Made Flesh: Towards an Incarnational Missiology," July 29, 2004.
Lindquist, Spencer. "Lecturer At Yale Fantasizes About Brutally Murdering White People." *Federalist*, June 2021. https://thefederalist.com/2021/06/04/lecturer-at-official-yale-event-fantasizes-about-brutally-murdering-white-people-claims-all-white-people-are-rotten/.
Lloyd-Jones, Martyn. *Revival*. Wheaton: Crossway, 1987.
Lyotard, Jean-François, Geoffrey Bennington, Brian Massumi, and Fredric Jameson. "The Postmodern Condition: A Report on Knowledge," January 1, 1984.
MacMillan, Margaret. *The War That Ended Peace: The Road to 1914*. Random House Publishing Group, 2013.
Maddox, Marion. "Religion, Secularism and the Promise of Public Theology." *International Journal of Public Theology* 1, no. 1 (January 1, 2007): 82–100. https://doi.org/10.1163/156973207x194501.
Mannion, Gerand. "Church in the World: Theology Goes Public." *Sociologia: Rivista Quadrimestrale Di Scienze Storiche e Sociali: XLV, 2, 2011*, 2011, 7–10. https://doi.org/10.36165/1685.
Markus, R. A. "Saeculum: History and Society in the Theology of St Augustine," April 1, 1970.

Marsden, George M. *Jonathan Edwards: A Life.* Yale University Press, 2004.
Marty, Martin E. "1988 Presidential Address: Committing the Study of Religion in Public." *Journal of the American Academy of Religion* 57, no. 1 (1989): 1–22. https://www.jstor.org/stable/1464967.
———. "Reinhold Niebuhr: Public Theology and the American Experience." *The Journal of Religion* 54, no. 4 (October 1974): 332–59. https://doi.org/10.1086/486401.
———. "Religion, Theology, Church, and Bioethics." *The Journal of Medicine and Philosophy: A Forum for Bioethics and Philosophy of Medicine* 17, no. 3 (June 1, 1992): 273–89. https://doi.org/10.1093/jmp/17.3.273.
———. "The Public Church: Mainline - Evangelical - Catholic," January 1, 1981.
———. *The Public Church: Mainline - Evangelical - Catholic.* Wipf and Stock Publishers, 2012.
Mathewes, Charles T. "A Theology of Public Life," January 1, 2007.
Max L. Stackhouse, and Max L. Stackhouse. "Civil Religion, Political Theology and Public Theology: What's the Difference?" *Political Theology* 5, no. 3 (February 10, 2004): 275–93. https://doi.org/10.1558/poth.5.3.275.36715.
McCoy, Horace. *They Shoot Horses Don't They?* Barker, 1935.
———. *They Shoot Horses, Don't They?* Profile Books, 2011.
Milbank, John. "Theology and Social Theory: Beyond Secular Reason" 44, no. 2 (June 1, 1993): 360.
Milton, Michael A. *Cooperation Without Compromise (Stapled Booklet): Faithful Gospel Witness in a Pluralistic Setting.* Wipf and Stock Publishers, 2007.
———. *Finding a Vision for Your Church: Assembly Required.* Philipsburg, NJ: P & R Publishing, 2012.
———. *From Flanders Fields to the Moviegoer: Philosophical Foundations for a Transcendent Ethical Framework.* Eugene, OR: Wipf and Stock Publishers, 2019.
———. *Involved with Mankind: A Theology of Chaplain Ministry.* Bethesda Publishing Group, 2023.
Morin, Amy. "How to Help a Teen Who Is Failing High School Classes." *Verywell Family*, no. Online (October 1, 2020). https://www.verywellfamily.com/what-to-do-if-your-teen-has-failing-grades-2609570.
Murphy, Andrew R., Andrew R. Murphy, and Andrew W. Murphy. "Conscience and Community: Revisiting Toleration and Religious Dissent in Early Modern England and America," June 1, 2001.
Napier, B. Davie, John Bright, and John Bright. "The Kingdom of God," January 1, 1953.
Nelson, Robert Henry. *Reaching for Heaven on Earth: The Theological Meaning of Economics.* Rowman & Littlefield Publishers, 1991.
Newberg, Andrew B. and Andrew B. Newberg. "Principles of Neurotheology," September 28, 2010.
Nicholas Wolterstorff, and Nicholas Wolterstorff. "Religion in the University," April 2, 2019.
———. "The Way of Ideas: Structure and Motivation," November 1, 2000, 23–44. https://doi.org/10.1017/cbo9780511613845.003.
Niebuhr, H. Richard. "Christ and Culture," January 1, 1975.
Nn, Koopman. "Some Comments on Public Theology Today," January 1, 2004.

O'Daly, Gerard. "Augustine's City of God: A Reader's Guide," 1999.
Parker, Wayne. "What Research Tells Us About the Effect of Divorce on Children." *Verywell Family*, no. Online (February 20, 2022). https://www.verywellfamily.com/children-of-divorce-in-america-statistics-1270390.
Pearson, Clive. "The Quest for a Glocal Public Theology." *International Journal of Public Theology* 1, no. 2 (January 1, 2007): 151–72. https://doi.org/10.1163/156973207x207317.
———. "Twittering the Gospel." *International Journal of Public Theology* 9, no. 2 (June 2, 2015): 176–92. https://doi.org/10.1163/15697320-12341391.
Percy, Walker. *Sign Posts in a Strange Land*. New York: Farrar, Straus and Giroux, 1991.
———. *The Thanatos Syndrome*. The Signed First Edition Society, Franklin Library. New York: Farrar, Straus, Giroux New York, 1987.
Plantinga, Alvin. "Divine Action in the World" 19, no. 4 (January 29, 2010): 317–23. https://doi.org/10.1002/9781444317350.ch23.
———. "Divine Action in the World: The Old Picture," December 9, 2011, 64–90. https://doi.org/10.1093/acprof:oso/9780199812097.003.0003.
———. "The Reformed Objection to Natural Theology" 54 (July 1, 1980): 49–62. https://doi.org/10.5840/acpaproc1980547.
———. "Warranted Christian Belief: The Aquinas/Calvin Model," January 1, 1999, 125–43. https://doi.org/10.1007/978-94-015-9289-5_7.
———. "Which Worlds Could God Have Created." *The Journal of Philosophy* 70, no. 17 (October 11, 1973): 539–52. https://doi.org/10.2307/2025307.
Plantinga, Alvin, and Charles Hartshorne. "Anselm's Discovery: A Re-Examination of the OntoLogical Proof for God's Existence." *The Philosophical Review* 78, no. 3 (July 1, 1969): 405. https://doi.org/10.2307/2183841.
Plantinga, Alvin, and Nicholas Wolterstorff. "Faith and Rationality: Reason and Belief in God" 16, no. 2 (January 1, 1983).
Purifoy, Thomas. "The Economics of John Calvin." *Compass Classroom* (blog), October 10, 2012. https://compassclassroom.com/blog/economics-of-john-calvin/.
Putnam, Robert D. "Bowling Alone: The Collapse and Revival of American Community," January 1, 2000.
Robert C. Fuller. "Spiritual, but Not Religious," November 15, 2001. https://doi.org/10.1093/0195146808.001.0001.
Roux, Le, and Arthur Malcolm. "Tamar's Cry as a Metaphor for Public Awareness against Women Abuse: A Practical Theological Engagement," January 1, 2014.
Saint Augustine, Chara Lewis, Alvin Plantinga, Peter Kreeft, Blaise Pascal, Khaldoun A. Sweis, and Chad Meister. "Christian Apologetics: An Anthology of Primary Sources," January 1, 2012.
Sayers, Dorothy L. (Dorothy Leigh). "Are Women Human?: Address Given to a Women's Society, 1938." *Logos: A Journal of Catholic Thought and Culture* 8, no. 4 (2005): 165–78. https://muse.jhu.edu/pub/9/article/187827.
Sayers, Dorothy Leigh. *Are Women Human?* London: Alban Books Limited, 1971.
Scruton, Roger. *The Soul of the World*. Princeton University Press, 2016.
Seligman, Adam B. "The Idea of Civil Society," January 1, 1992.
Sertillanges, A. D., and Mary Ryan. *The Intellectual Life: Its Spirit, Conditions, Methods*. Washington, D.C.: Catholic University of America Press, 1987.

Sire, James W. *Discipleship of the Mind*. InterVarsity Press, 1990.
———. *Habits of the Mind: Intellectual Life as a Christian Calling*. InterVarsity Press, 2022.
———. *Naming the Elephant: Worldview as a Concept*. InterVarsity Press, 2004.
———. *Naming the Elephant: Worldview as a Concept*. InterVarsity Press, 2004.
———. *The Universe Next Door: A Basic Worldview Catalog*. ReadHowYouWant.com, 2001.
Skinner, Quentin. "The Foundations of Modern Political Thought," January 1, 1978.
Smit, Dirkie. "Notions of the Public and Doing Theology." *International Journal of Public Theology* 1, no. 3 (January 1, 2007): 431–54. https://doi.org/10.1163/156973207x231716.
Stoddart, Eric. "(In)Visibility and the Process of Public Theology." *International Journal of Public Theology* 7, no. 1 (January 1, 2013): 45–64. https://doi.org/10.1163/15697320-12341269.
Strenski, Ivan. "Why Politics Can't Be Freed From Religion," March 8, 2010.
Tanner, Kathryn. "Public Theology and the Character of Public Debate." *The Annual of the Society of Christian Ethics* 16 (1996): 79–101. https://www.jstor.org/stable/23559710.
———. "Public Theology and the Character of Public Debate" 16 (January 1, 1996): 79–101. https://doi.org/10.5840/asce1996166.
———. "Theories of Culture: A New Agenda for Theology," January 1, 1997.
Taylor, Charles. *A Secular Age*. Harvard University Press, 2009.
TeSelle, Eugene. "Augustine, the Theologian," January 1, 1970.
"The New Spirituality," n.d. https://doi.org/10.5040/9780755626335.
They Shoot Horses, Don't They? Film, Psychological drama. Cinerama Releasing Corporation, 1969.
Thiemann, Ronald F. "Constructing a Public Theology: The Church in a Pluralistic Culture," November 1, 1991.
———. *Religion in Public Life: A Dilemma for Democracy*. Georgetown University Press, 1996.
Thomas, Owen C. "Public Theology and Counter-Public Spheres." *Harvard Theological Review* 85, no. 4 (October 1, 1992): 453–66. https://doi.org/10.1017/s0017816000008233.
Townsend, Bernie. "Thinking Biblically, Speaking Secularly: Thoughts on Chris Marshall's Article 'What Language Shall I Borrow?: The Bilingual Dilemma of Public Theology.'" *Stimulus: The New Zealand Journal of Christian Thought and Practice* 18, no. 1 (February 1, 2010).
Tracy, David. *The Analogical Imagination: Christian Theology and the Culture of Pluralism*, 1981.
———. "THE ANALOGICAL IMAGINATION:CHRISTIAN THEOLOGY AND THE CULTURE OF PLURALISM" 7, no. 4 (October 1, 1981): 281–332.
Tracy, David and David Tracy. "The Analogical Imagination." *Religious Studies*, 1981.
Tuchman, Barbara W. *The Guns of August: The Outbreak of World War I; Barbara W. Tuchman's Great War Series*. Random House Publishing Group, 1994.
Veling, Terry A. "Practical Theology: On Earth as It Is in Heaven," November 30, 2005.

Volf, Miroslav. *A Public Faith: How Followers of Christ Should Serve the Common Good*. Brazos Press, 2011.

Walchenbach, John R. "Jack." *John Calvin as Biblical Commentator: An Investigation into Calvin's Use of John Chrysostom as an Exegetical Tutor*. Wipf and Stock Publishers, 2010.

Williams, Rhys H., and Peter L. Berger. "The Desecularization of the World: Resurgent Religion and World Politics." *Sociology of Religion*, July 16, 1999. https://doi.org/10.2307/3712234.

Williams, Rowan. "On Christian Theology," December 27, 1999.

Wolterstorff, Nicholas. "Art in Action: Toward a Christian Aesthetic." *The Journal of Aesthetic Education* 39, no. 2 (January 1, 1980): 209–10. https://doi.org/10.2307/3332397.

———. "Civil Disagreement: Personal Integrity in a Pluralistic Society, by Edward Langerak." *Faith and Philosophy* 32, no. 3 (August 1, 2015): 338–41. https://doi.org/10.5840/faithphil201532345.

———. "Divine Discourse by Nicholas Wolterstorff," 1995. https://doi.org/10.1017/cbo9780511598074.

———. "Divine Discourse: Philosophical Reflections on the Claim That God Speaks," January 1, 1995.

———. "Educating for Responsible Action," January 1, 1980.

———. "John Locke and the Ethics of Belief," January 1, 1996.

———. "John Locke, Vindications of the Reasonableness of Christianity, Edited with an Introduction and Notes by Victor Nuevo (Oxford and New York: Oxford University Press, 2012), Pp. Cxi+400. £65.00/ $125.00." *Scottish Journal of Theology* 68, no. 1 (February 1, 2015): 120–22. https://doi.org/10.1017/s0036930614000349.

———. "Knowing God Liturgically." *The Journal of Analytic Theology* 4, no. 1 (May 6, 2016): 1–16. https://doi.org/10.12978/jat.2016-4.130818221405b.

———. "Meaning of Works of the Arts and of Artworks," September 1, 2015, 107–21. https://doi.org/10.1093/acprof:oso/9780198747758.003.0010.

———. "Miroslav Volf on Living One's Faith." *Political Theology* 14, no. 6 (January 1, 2013): 721–26. https://doi.org/10.1179/1462317x13z.00000000045.

———. "On Universals: An Essay in Ontology," January 1, 1970.

———. "Reason Within the Bounds of Religion," January 1, 1976.

———. "Religion in Public Life: Must Faith Be Privatized?" *Faith and Philosophy* 27, no. 2 (May 1, 2010): 223–25. https://doi.org/10.5840/faithphil201027222.

———. "The Reformed Tradition," February 8, 2010, 204–9. https://doi.org/10.1002/9781444320152.ch22.

———. "The Silence of the God Who Speaks." *Philosophia* 30, no. 1 (March 1, 2003): 13–32. https://doi.org/10.1007/bf02383298.

———. "What Happened to Beauty," September 1, 2015, 304–21. https://doi.org/10.1093/acprof:oso/9780198747758.003.0020.

Wolterstorff, Nicholas, and Robert Audi. "Religion in the Public Square," December 1, 1996.

Wolterstorff, Nicholas, and Terence Cuneo. "Freedom for Religion," September 27, 2012, 298–304. https://doi.org/10.1093/acprof:oso/9780199558957.003.0013.

———. "Inquiring about God: Alston on Aquinas on Theological Predication," January 1, 2010. https://doi.org/10.1017/cbo9780511676239.008.
Wolterstorff, Nicholas, and Nicholas Wolterstorff. "God and Time" 2, no. 1 (January 1, 2000): 5–10. https://doi.org/10.5840/pc2000212.
Wyngaard, Van, and George Jacobus. "The Public Theology of David J. Bosch: The Public Role of the Christian Community," August 3, 2010.
Yancey, Andrew Paul. "The Theme of Transformation in Contemporary American Evangelical Theological Perceptions of Enterprise: A Postsecular Critique in Practical Theology," July 1, 2019.
Youn, Chul Ho. "The Points and Tasks of Public Theology," no. 46 (December 1, 2016): 175–214. https://doi.org/10.21650/ksst..46.201612.175.
김동건. "Models of Public Theology: With Special Reference to the Studies of 2010-2017," no. 180 (March 1, 2018): 109–39. https://doi.org/10.35858/sinhak.2018..180.004.

Acknowledgments

I give all thanks and glory to God for His faithfulness to His saints in all things. I dedicate this to our Lord Jesus Christ, who lives forever and is returning soon. I also pray that the Holy Spirit will perfect my imperfections and lead others to Christ Jesus.

I want to thank our contributors for their outstanding chapters. This process took longer than I had initially planned, and I am so grateful for your patience.

Thanks to Jim Tedrick and the team at Wipf and Stock. Many thanks also go to my assistants during this process, Mrs. Christine Hartung and Dr. Rebecca Rine.

I am grateful to my wife, Mae, for her unwavering and constant support. She has been an invaluable help to me amid my ongoing health concerns while I wrote and edited this. I am also proud of my son, John Michael, for being a great young man and a son any father would be proud of. Thank you, son, for your assistance in so many ways. I thank the respective institutions represented by our contributors, including Erskine Theological Seminary, Westminster Theological Seminary, and Parish Presbyterian Church.

Thank you for supporting this work. May it be of help during these difficult times.

About the D. James Kennedy Institute

The D. James Kennedy Institute of Reformed Leadership (DJK Institute) is a Christian think tank focused on research, writing, and providing resources for individuals, institutions, and organizations dedicated to fulfilling the Great Commission of Jesus Christ.

The DJK Institute is a ministry group Faith for Living, Inc., a North Carolina 501(c)(3) Nonprofit Corporation. The ministry exists and advances by faith through enterprises and donations.

As a 501(c)(3) nonprofit corporation your gifts are fully tax-deductible. Gifts may be given with confidence at https://www.paypal.com/us/fundraiser/charity/1644218.

Mailing address:
The D. James Kennedy Institute of Reformed Leadership
1167 Carolina Drive
Tryon, NC 28782
info@djkinstitute.org

―――

Learn more: djkinstitute.org

Follow Michael A. Milton at michaelamilton.com

Visit the official page of the nonprofit Faith for Living: faithforliving.org

Vision and Mission
The D. James Kennedy Institute of Reformed Leadership

The D. James Kennedy Institute of Reformed Leadership is a ministry group of Faith for Living, Inc., a North Carolina 501(c)(3) Christian Education Nonprofit Corporation.

First Things

Our Motto: *Excellence in all things and all things for Christ*
    Our Anchor Verse: "And you shall know the truth, and the truth shall make you free" (John 8:32).
    Our Vision of Teaching:
"The end then of Learning is to repair the ruins of our first Parents by regaining to know God aright, and out of that knowledge to love Him, to imitate Him, to be like Him, as we may the nearest by possessing our souls of true virtue, which being united to the heavenly grace of faith makes up the highest perfection." *On Education* (1644) by John Milton (1608–1674)

Thus, we affirm that a vision and mission statement expresses the identity and work of ministry that progresses from understanding and being captivated by God's Burden, God's Values, God's Vision, God's Mission, and a God-honoring, Christ-centered Philosophy of Ministry.[1]

Burden: why we exist

The DJK Institute is driven by a burden for the biblical revelation of universal spiritual darkness and its resulting cultural captivity, ensnaring humanity in the devil's domain.

Ephesians 6:12 ESV: "For we do not wrestle against flesh and blood, but against the rulers, against the authorities, against the cosmic powers over this present darkness, against the spiritual forces of evil in the heavenly places."

Values: non-negotiable essentials that guide us

Grounded in the Holy Scriptures and the Great Commission, the DJK Institute is guided by the principles of the Reformed faith.

Hebrews 4:14 ESV: "Since then we have a great high priest who has passed through the heavens, Jesus, the Son of God, let us hold fast our confession."

Vision: how we lift the burden

Ministering from the transformative light of the Gospel as revealed in the Scriptures, the D. James Kennedy Institute of Reformed Leadership imparts truths that transform, cultivating a faith for living under the sovereign Lordship of Christ.

John 8:31-32 ESV: "So Jesus said to the Jews who had believed him, 'If you abide in my word, you are truly my disciples, and you will know the truth, and the truth will set you free.'"

Mission: how we move toward the vision

Our mission is realized through dedicated Research, Writing, and Resource Development in service to the Church.

At the DJK Institute, we:

- Teach transformative truths grounded in John 8:32 and the Reformed and Evangelical faith through engaging biblical truths in public theology.
- Equip and nurture pastoral leaders to shepherd Christ's flock, fostering the development and guidance of fellow shepherds.

Ephesians 6:13 NKJV: "Therefore take up the whole armor of God, that you may be able to withstand in the evil day, and having done all, to stand."

Philosophy of Ministry: how we do our work

In our ministry, we uphold 'Excellence in all things and all things for Christ'—a commitment to God-glorifying excellence. Our teachings, deeply rooted in Scripture and the Reformed faith, aim to foster a 'faith for living' under Christ's Lordship.

Through dedicated research, insightful writing, and comprehensive resources, we support the Cultural Mandate (asserting Christ's Lordship over all life, as per Genesis 1:26-28, 2:15, 9:1), the Great Commandment (loving God and others, as in Matthew 22:35–40, Mark 12:28–34, Luke 10:27a), and the Great Commission (discipling nations, as per Matthew 28:19–20, Acts 1:8).

Matthew 5:16 ESV: "In the same way, let your light shine before others, so that they may see your good works and give glory to your Father who is in heaven."

www.ingramcontent.com/pod-product-compliance
Lightning Source LLC
Chambersburg PA
CBHW062020220426

43662CB00010B/1414

MGA/MGB OWNERS HANDBOOK of Maintenance & Repair

WITH EMISSION CONTROL AND DRIVER'S HANDBOOK

Published by

CLYMER PUBLICATIONS

World's largest publisher of books devoted exclusively to automobiles and motorcycles.

222 NORTH VIRGIL AVENUE, LOS ANGELES, CALIFORNIA 90004

INTRODUCTION

Welcome to the world of digital publishing ~ the book you now hold in your hand, while unchanged from the original edition, was printed using the latest state of the art digital technology. The advent of print-on-demand has forever changed the publishing process, never has information been so accessible and it is our hope that this book serves your informational needs for years to come. If this is your first exposure to digital publishing, we hope that you are pleased with the results. Many more titles of interest to the classic automobile and motorcycle enthusiast, collector and restorer are available via our website at www.VelocePress.com. We hope that you find this title as interesting as we do.

NOTE FROM THE PUBLISHER

The information presented is true and complete to the best of our knowledge. All recommendations are made without any guarantees on the part of the author or the publisher, who also disclaim all liability incurred with the use of this information.

TRADEMARKS

We recognize that some words, model names and designations, for example, mentioned herein are the property of the trademark holder. We use them for identification purposes only. This is not an official publication.

INFORMATION ON THE USE OF THIS PUBLICATION

This manual is an invaluable resource for the classic **MG** enthusiast and a "must have" for owners interested in performing their own maintenance. However, in today's information age we are constantly subject to changes in common practice, new technology, availability of improved materials and increased awareness of chemical toxicity. As such, it is advised that the user consult with an experienced professional prior to undertaking any procedure described herein. While every care has been taken to ensure correctness of information, it is obviously not possible to guarantee complete freedom from errors or omissions or to accept liability arising from such errors or omissions. Therefore, any individual that uses the information contained within, or elects to perform or participate in do-it-yourself repairs or modifications acknowledges that there is a risk factor involved and that the publisher or its associates cannot be held responsible for personal injury or property damage resulting from the use of the information or the outcome of such procedures.

It is important that the reader recognizes that any instructions may refer to either the right-hand or left-hand sides of the vehicle or the components and that the directions are followed carefully. One final word of advice, this publication is intended to be used as a reference guide, and when in doubt the reader should consult with a qualified technician.